INKY Meditations

learn to create
mindful mesmerizing paintings
with water and ink

by inky

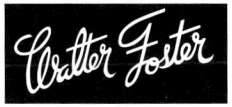

Quarto.com | WalterFoster.com

© 2024 Quarto Publishing Group USA Inc.
Artwork and text © 2024 Alisa Tanaka-King

First Published in 2024 by Walter Foster Publishing, an imprint of The Quarto Group,
100 Cummings Center, Suite 265-D, Beverly, MA 01915, USA.
T (978) 282-9590 F (978) 283-2742

Walter Foster Publishing titles are also available at discount for retail, wholesale,
promotional, and bulk purchase. For details, contact the Special Sales Manager by
email at specialsales@quarto.com or by mail at The Quarto Group, Attn: Special Sales
Manager, 100 Cummings Center, Suite 265-D, Beverly, MA 01915, USA.

28 27 26 25 24   1 2 3 4 5

ISBN: 978-0-7603-8875-4

Digital edition published in 2024
eISBN: 978-0-7603-8876-1

Library of Congress Cataloging-in-Publication Data is available.

Design and page layout: Cindy Samargia Laun
Photography: Alisa Tanaka-King except
  MDP Photography and Video on pages 5 and 128

Printed in China

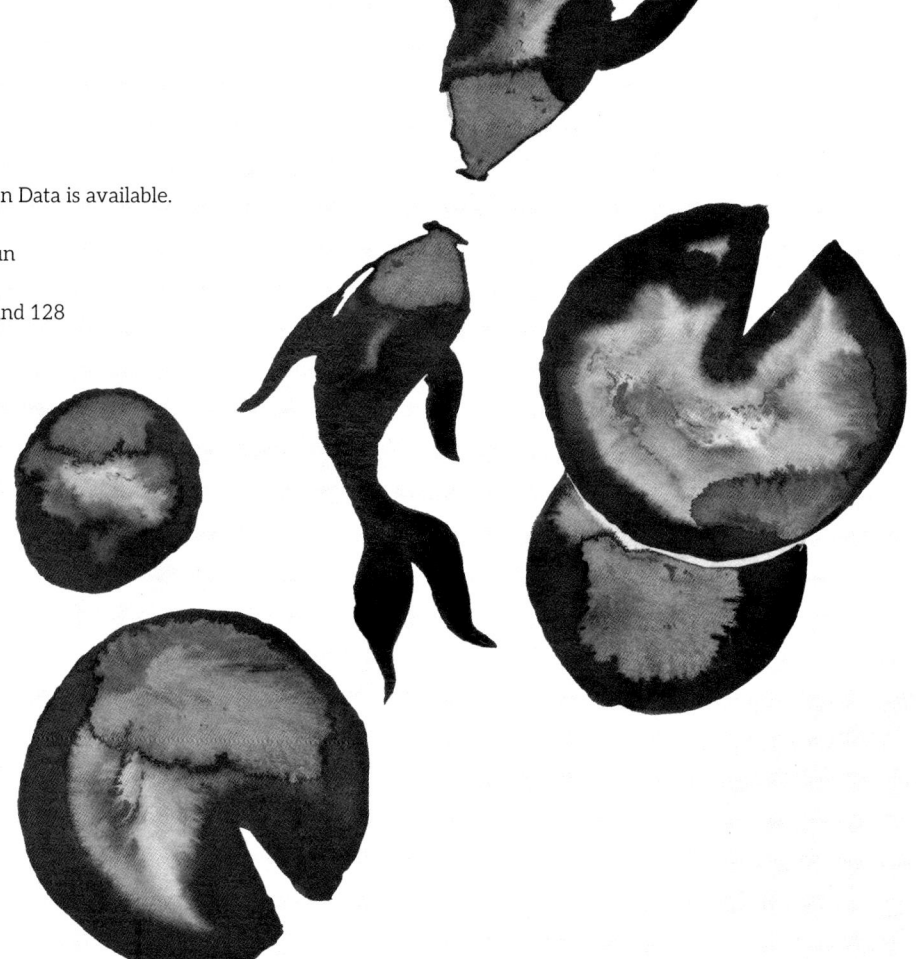

Contents

INTRODUCTION

Sumi ink is one of the most magical, alluring, timeless art mediums.
It is versatile and celebrates the simplicity of brushstrokes
and masterful line work.

I have played with ink for many years but returned to it during the COVID-19 pandemic when I was unable to access my studio, where I am spoiled with space and choice of art materials. Instead, I was confined to a small table, a paintbrush, limited paper, and a handful of art supplies that could be packed away easily. The world was very overwhelming, and many artists (including myself) lost work and had to rethink their practice. Whenever I am struggling to make art, I try to return to basic techniques and find a playful state of creative flow. This time, I turned to sumi ink. I didn't need to think about colors; I found the bold black satisfying and grounding. I could paint quickly on small pieces of paper and clear everything from the dining table in time for dinner. The watery brushstrokes felt freeing and natural—a welcomed break from excessive screen time and feeling confined inside. The experience became meditative for me. I would paint for hours without any plan or purpose, finding pleasure in playing and discovering new things about the medium. You are never too old or experienced to discover new things about art, and this was a timely and grounding reminder of that.

At one point, a friend of mine suggested that I post videos of myself making art on TikTok because many artists were reaching new audiences during the pandemic by doing this. I laughed at the idea because my arts practice is so deeply entrenched in traditional practice, and a digital platform audience seemed unthinkable. But I remembered my art school days when a friend of mine said, "I just love watching you draw. It's so relaxing." So I fumbled into starting a TikTok account and shared these little inky

meditations I was creating. I really enjoy the process of putting the videos to music and being able to share the process of placing the ink on the page, not just the finished artwork. For me, these works aren't really about the finished pieces at all. They are about the experience of combining water and ink on the page and watching the magic take place.

This book is an introduction to sumi ink, particularly the wet-on-wet technique that blends ink and water on the page. It doesn't matter if you are picking up a paintbrush for the first time or if you are an experienced artist looking to explore a new technique. The premise of this book is exploring a playful, experimental, meditative creative process. The activities are designed to introduce you to some initial techniques and warm-up activities, followed by projects that increase in complexity as the book continues. I would recommend following the chronological order, but if you feel the urge to jump ahead or come back and revisit projects in the book, please do so. So much of this is about figuring out your own creative process and what works for you. This book is here to make suggestions. Use it as a platform to bounce off and discover how you can best use sumi ink.

I feel so honored to have people interested in sharing this practice with me and wanting to explore it themselves. Writing this book and sharing my thoughts around creative process, mindfulness, and playful exploration of sumi ink has been incredibly rewarding. I never imagined that so many people would share the love of the sumi ink painting process with me. Thank you so much for coming along this inky journey—it's truly magical.

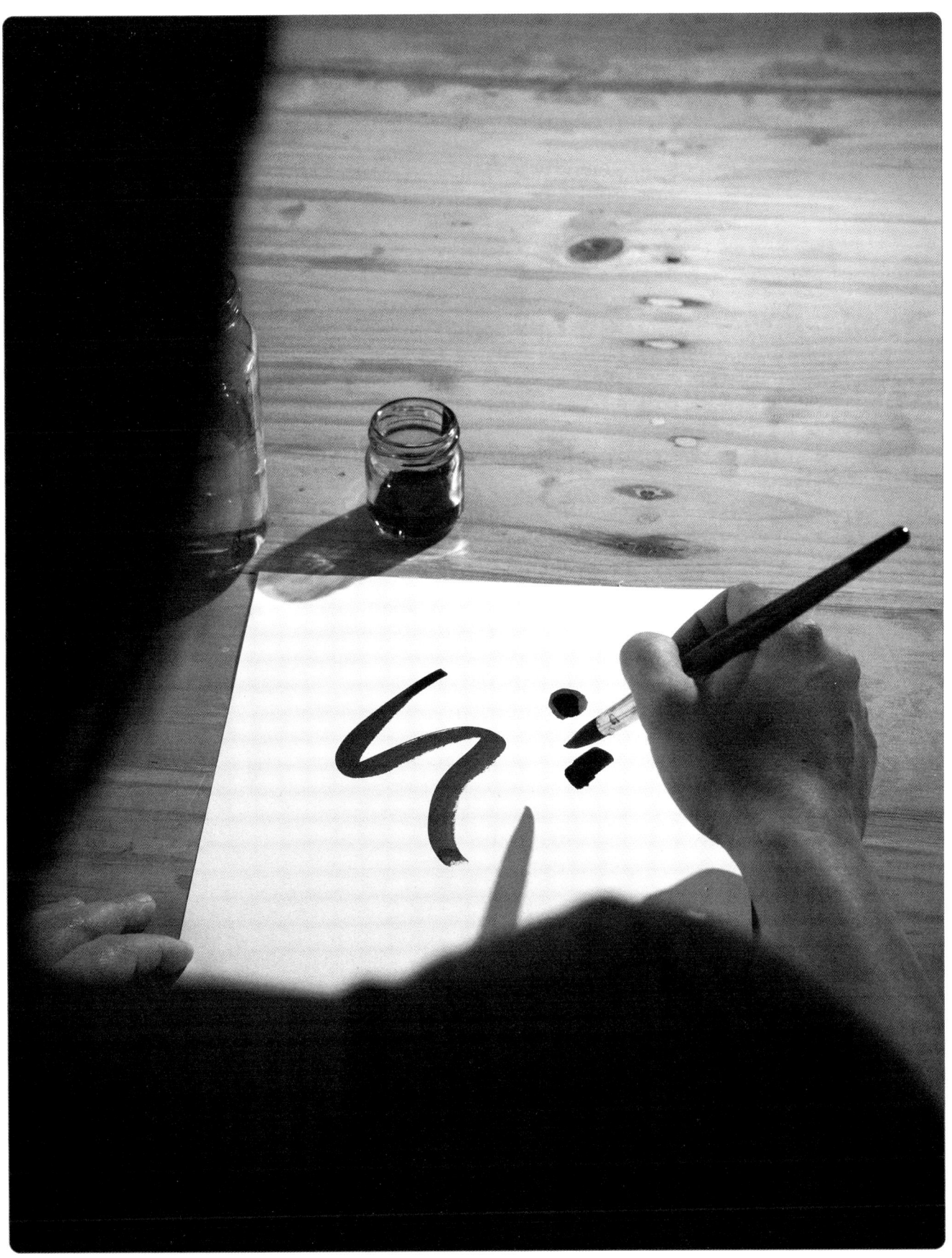

TOOLS
& Materials

When I began creating these water-and-ink paintings, I didn't have access to my studio with my copious art supplies, yet I found that I needed a daily creative outlet. Enter this brilliant art form where you only really need four tools: sumi ink, water, watercolor paper, and paintbrushes. Painting these mindful pieces gave me the outlet I needed to stay present and centered. Below, I've suggested the tools and materials that I find the most useful, but feel free to play around with what you have at home.

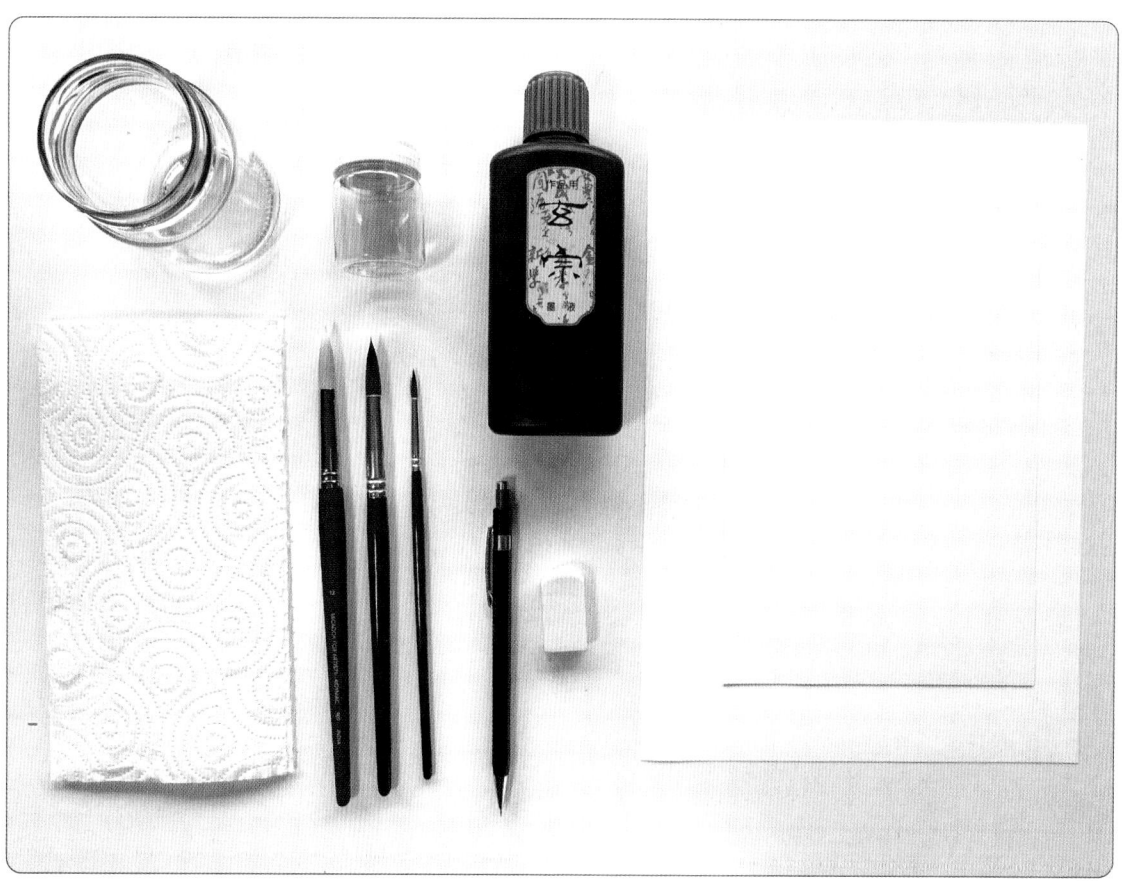

Left to right, top to bottom: water jar, ink jar, sumi ink, watercolor paper, paper towel, water brush, number 12 ink brush, number 6 ink brush, pencil, eraser

SUMI INK

Sumi ink is traditional Japanese ink that is used for calligraphy and painting. The main ingredient in sumi ink is soot, which is treated and dried through a complex and time-consuming traditional process to make a sumi ink stick. While sumi sticks are still often used for calligraphy and by some artists, the liquid form of sumi ink is readily available and quite popular in contemporary arts practice. Liquid sumi ink is interchangeable with India ink or calligraphy ink, which are usually made from a soot (carbon) base. I use Japanese liquid sumi ink when I paint, but the projects in this book can be done with other types of ink, including acrylic ink and artist drawing ink. I find that black sumi ink has the best movement and reaction with water, but I encourage you to experiment and play with whatever colors make you happy.

I love how sumi ink can produce a bold, strong line when it is painted onto dry paper, but when it is added to water on the page, or diluted, it has so many different hues. It flows beautifully and smoothly across the page and produces the most satisfying and high-quality black.

Many people ask if sumi ink is interchangeable with watercolor paint, and the simple answer is no. While you can paint watercolor onto wet-on-wet, as we do in this book, it does not give the same effect as sumi ink. Sumi ink is very fluid when mixed with water, but it dries waterproof, whereas watercolor paint has a bit more flexibility. This also means that watercolor has less contrast and creates less movement than sumi ink; it is far more subtle.

A little bit of ink goes a long way! Sumi ink is very strong, and you don't need much to cover a lot of paper. I would suggest that three to five drops of ink are enough to complete any of the projects in this book, so it's a very economical medium!

Sumi ink is nontoxic and relatively environmentally friendly (compared to paints that contain plastics or harsh chemicals), but please note that it does stain! It will wash off your hands with warm soapy water, but it is difficult to remove from clothing. It dries to a very fixed state (remember that it's waterproof), so it is also important to wash out your inky brushes straight away.

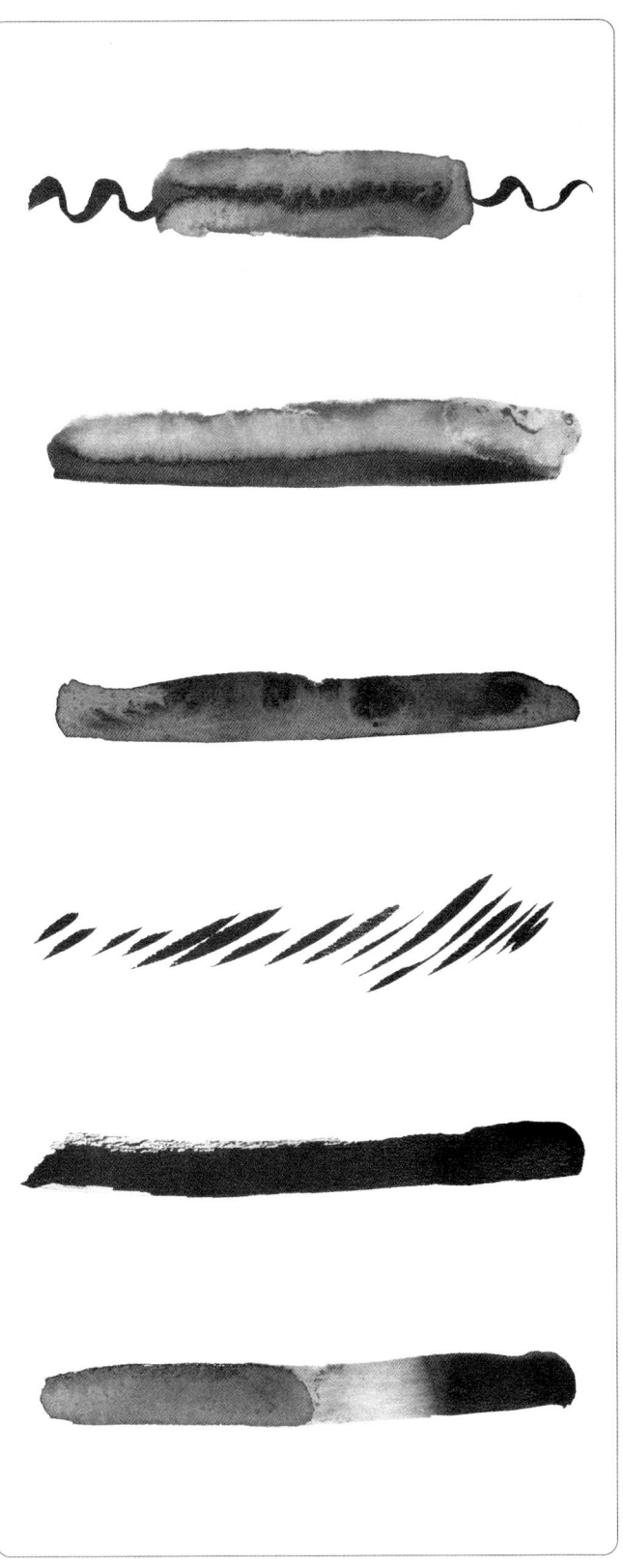

Sumi ink brushstrokes with various amounts of water

WATERCOLOR PAPER

This book shows techniques and projects that play with the combination of ink and water. This means we are adding quite a lot of water to the page, so we need paper that can cope with being wet. To ensure the paper doesn't wrinkle too much or dissolve, I recommend using watercolor paper. Watercolor paper is made with a binder that stops it from stretching and warping when it comes in contact with water. Most watercolor papers have a minimum weight of 200 gsm, and I use a minimum of 210 gsm. I would recommend a smooth, nontextured watercolor paper, called hot pressed, for these activities, as it will enhance the textures and contrast of the ink on the page.

RECOMMENDED WATERCOLOR PAPER

Unfortunately, with fine art paper, you get what you pay for, and good paper can be very expensive. If you are just starting out, I would recommend getting an entry-level paper to play with. It won't give you the same results as the good-quality papers, but you also don't want to be afraid of wasting expensive materials. Once you feel more confident, there are many brands you can purchase, all of which are available online and likely sold by your local art supply store. I recommend the hot pressed watercolor paper from the following brands, listed from least expensive to most expensive: Hanhemüle, Bockingford, Fabriano, and Arches. Most fine art stores will sell the full sheets of these (22 × 30 inches [56 × 76 cm]) as well as paper pads. I find the full sheets are great, as you can cut them down to whatever size you like, and they are often much cheaper than buying the same paper in a pad. If you prefer to purchase a pad of paper, there are two types you can buy. One is a paper block, where the pages are glued together so they don't warp; you need to cut these apart once you've finished painting. The other option is a normal pad of paper that you can tear out easily. If you purchase this type of paper pad, be sure to remove the page from the pad before you start painting, or the water will seep through to the pages below and ruin them.

PAINTBRUSHES

Synthetic watercolor brushes are the best paintbrushes to use when doing the activities in this book. It's important to note that there are a lot of different types of brushes out there. I suggest using a round-ended brush because they are very versatile and relatively easy to use, but I encourage you to explore all sorts of brush shapes and sizes so you can work out what feels best in your hand. I only use my ink brushes for ink painting. It's quite difficult to wash all the ink out of a brush (even if you do a really good job), so I prefer to keep my ink brushes separate. I have three different round brushes that I use:

WATER BRUSH (NUMBER 8 OR 12)

This is a brush I only use for painting with water, which ensures that it stays nice and clean. The water brush I use is a number 12 watercolor brush, but you can use whatever size you feel most comfortable with.

NUMBER 12 INK BRUSH

I use a number 12 watercolor brush as my larger ink brush. It has good coverage and a nice fine point, so it's very versatile.

NUMBER 6 INK BRUSH

It is useful to have a smaller, fine-detail watercolor brush to use for ink as well. I use a number 6, but you can get much finer brushes than this if you prefer.

WATER

Water is an essential medium in these inky, meditative paintings. The water does so much of the magical work that I often just sit back and don't have to do anything! I have a small jar of clean water with me when I paint. I use a separate water brush so I don't have to change my water regularly. It can be helpful to have two jars of water: one jar of clean water and one jar of water that you put your inky brushes in. Just be sure not to get them mixed up!

ADDITIONAL TOOLS & MATERIALS

While there are only four main supplies, I do find these additional items helpful in my practice.

PAPER TOWEL

I keep a sheet of paper towel beside me whenever I'm painting. It's great for wiping excess water or ink off my brush, resting my brushes on, or cleaning up any unexpected spills and splashes.

PENCILS

You may want to draw an outline of each project on your page before you start to give you some guidelines of where to paint your water and ink. I would recommend drawing these outlines in an HB (or number 2) pencil or a 0.5 mechanical pencil so it is light and easy to erase. As you gain confidence in painting with water and ink, you may find you don't need an outline and can just visualize the design and paint it with water. Do what works for you!

ERASER

I find a school eraser is useful if you need to rub out any of your outlines.

TRACING PAPER OR CARBON PAPER

This thin paper can help you copy an outline from the template onto the paper.

JARS

I would recommend one or two small (10 ounce [300 ml]) jars for your water and one tiny (1 ounce [30 ml]) jar for your ink. It's useful to have a lid for your tiny ink jar so if you don't use all the ink in one sitting, you can put the lid on and have it ready for next time.

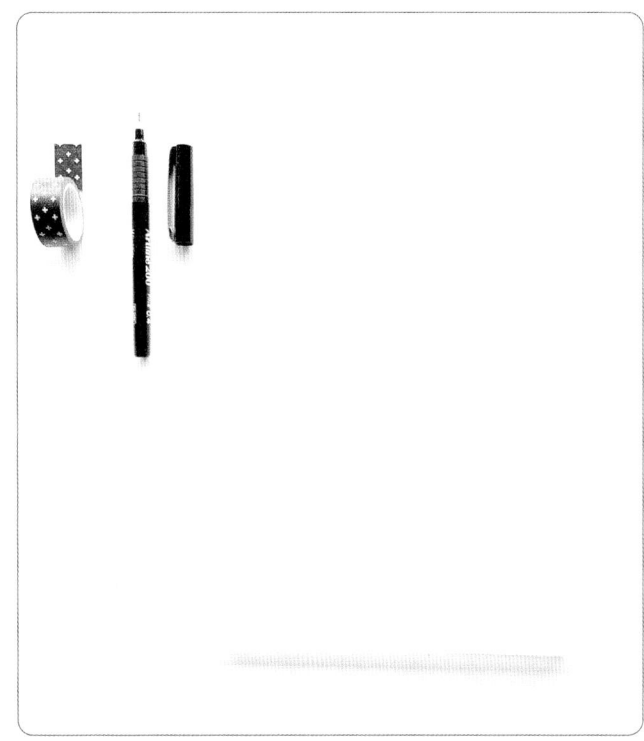

Washi tape, fineliner pen, tracing paper

WASHI TAPE

Some artists like to tape their paper to the table or a board when they paint. It can help with paper stretch and wrinkling, and some people like to have the page firmly fixed. I prefer not to tape my page, as I like to move the paper around so I can change my hand position. This is all about personal preference, so try it both ways and decide what is best for you.

FINELINER PEN

To add very thin lines to a painting, such as the legs on the Tiny Dragon, I suggest using a black fineliner pen.

PAINTING TIPS
& Techniques

Mastering anything takes practice. I find it's often easier to break things down into smaller parts and then put them all together. Before you begin the projects, I would recommend working through these techniques as a way of getting to know the ink, how it behaves, and the combination of ink and water on the page. It may be helpful to watch me as I practice each of these techniques, so I've included a QR code that links to a helpful video. Remember that repetition is everything—keep practicing, keep playing, and keep experimenting with different techniques purely for the purpose of discovering more about the ink. Repetitive, playful practice is how I learn the most about ink, and where the bulk of my ideas begin.

LOADING THE INK BRUSH

Put a small amount of ink in a little jar. A few drops go a long way. Dip your brush about halfway up the bristles into the ink, and let the ink soak in for a moment. You don't need to put the full length of the brush bristles into the ink. Before painting, wipe the brush on the rim of the jar to remove any excess ink.

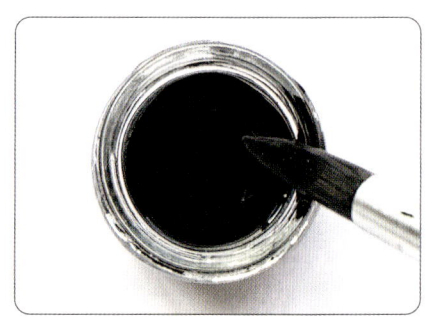

PAINTING WITH WATER

Dip your water brush into a clean jar of water, and allow it to soak the water up until it is very wet. Wipe the brush on the rim of the jar to get rid of any extra drips. Paint your water onto the surface of the paper. You want enough water so that it sits in a layer above the surface of the paper. Water tends to hold and stay in the area you paint it when you are using watercolor paper. If the water absorbs into the paper straightaway, the paper you are using isn't watercolor paper. Getting the perfect amount of water on the page takes practice. Try using different amounts of water and see how that changes when you add in the ink. In this image, I have used slightly tinted water so you can see it easily.

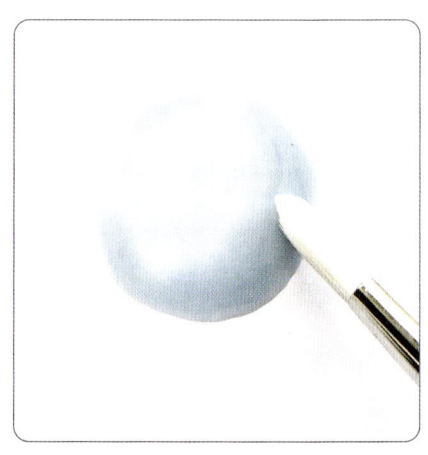

PAINTING THIN AND THICK LINES

Load your brush with ink as previously instructed. Place the brush on the paper tip first and then lower the whole brush to the page as you pull the brush across the surface of the page. Try doing this line in reverse, starting with a thick line and then gently lift your hand and release the pressure on the brush. This will naturally cause the line to go thinner as you paint it.

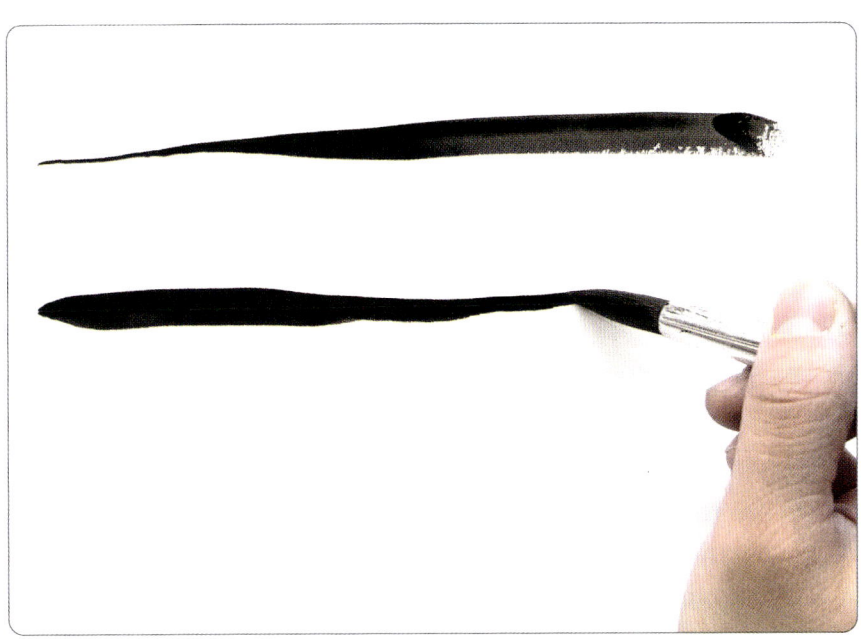

FLICKING

Load your brush with ink, and remove the excess on the rim of the jar. Place the brush on the page as if you are painting a solid line. Pass the brush along the page, applying gentle pressure to paint a solid line, but finish the line by lifting your hand off the page with a light, swift flick motion.

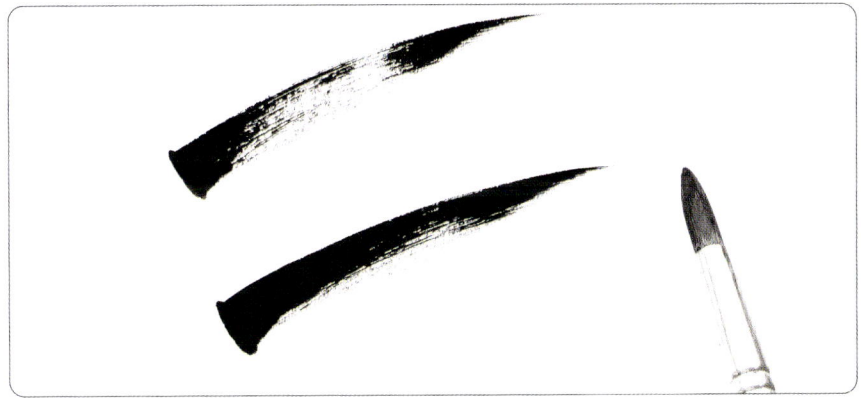

DROPPING IN INK

With water, paint a circle shape on the page. You can paint this straight on or draw a pencil outline first if that feels easier. Load your brush with ink, and remove any excess on the rim of the jar. Touch the tip of the brush to the water circle, and see how the ink moves into the water. Touch the tip of the brush to several different spots in the circle, and watch how the ink moves and flows.

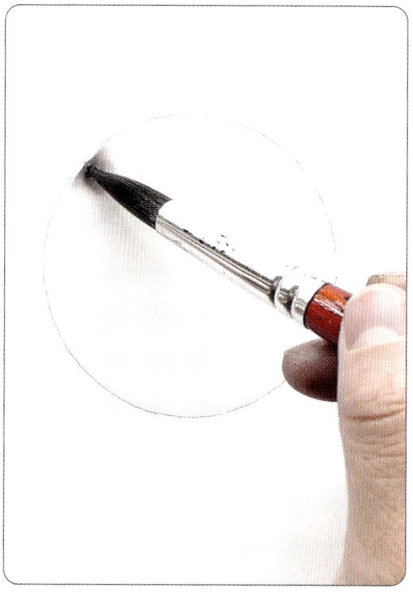 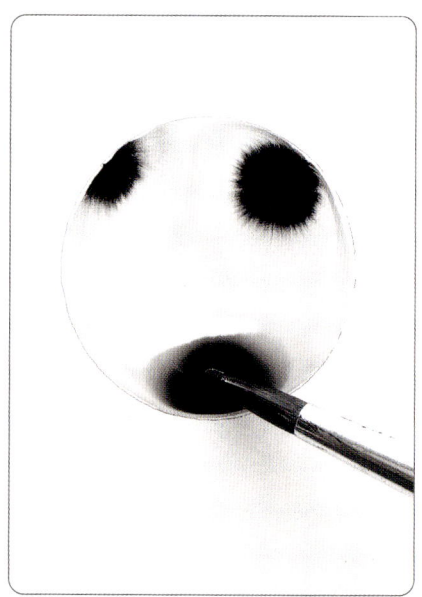

EDGING WITH INK

With water, paint a circle shape on the page. Load your brush with ink, and remove any excess on the rim of the jar. Paint a fine line using the tip of the brush along the edge of the water circle. Part of the brush will be touching the dry paper, and part of the brush will be passing through the water.

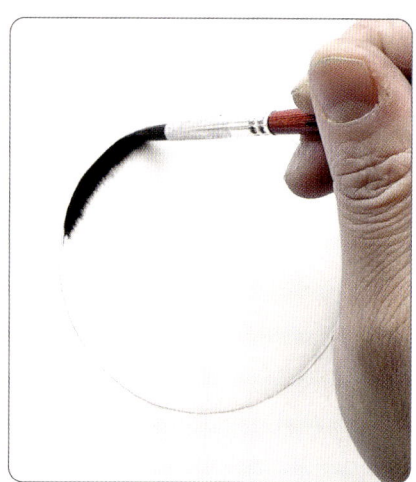 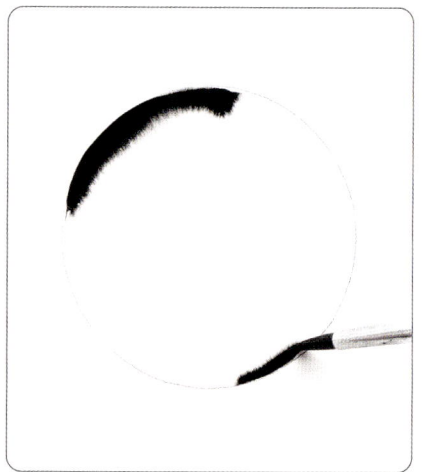

BLOTTING AWAY INK

With water, paint a circle shape. Using the tip of your ink-loaded brush, put a few spots of ink into the circle. Take a small piece of paper towel, and dab it gently on the wet, inky circle so the water and ink is absorbed. Keep dabbing until the desired amount of ink and water is removed. It will give a soft, fluffy texture when it dries completely.

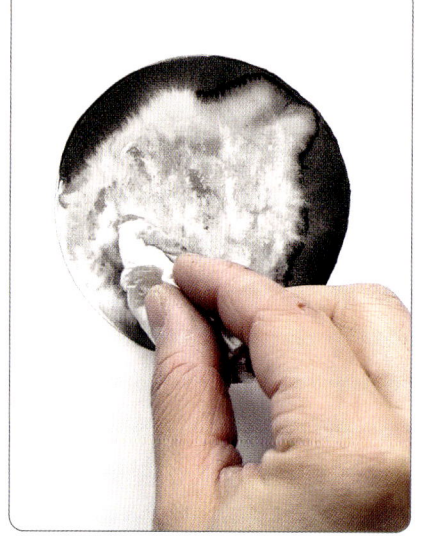

TRACING THE PROJECT TEMPLATES

When you get started on the projects, you may want to print out and trace the project templates onto your watercolor paper to guide your painting. Scan the QR code or visit quarto.com/files/InkyMeditations to download all the project templates. Here's some information on how to trace the designs using tracing paper and carbon paper.

TRACING PAPER

1 Print out the project template. Lay the tracing paper over the top of the template, and trace around the outline of the picture using your pencil.

2 Flip your tracing paper over, and scribble your pencil so it solidly covers the back of any pencil areas that you drew on the other side.

3 Flip your paper back over, and place it over the watercolor paper you are going to paint on. You can tape it lightly to the watercolor paper if you're worried it might shift around.

4 Use your pencil to re-draw firmly over the outlines of the picture you traced. This will transfer the outlines to your watercolor page, and you're ready to paint.

CARBON PAPER

1 Lay the carbon paper over the top of the watercolor paper you will be using to paint on. Lay the template over the carbon paper.

2 Using your pencil, draw firmly over the template outlines. The carbon paper will transfer the image to your watercolor page.

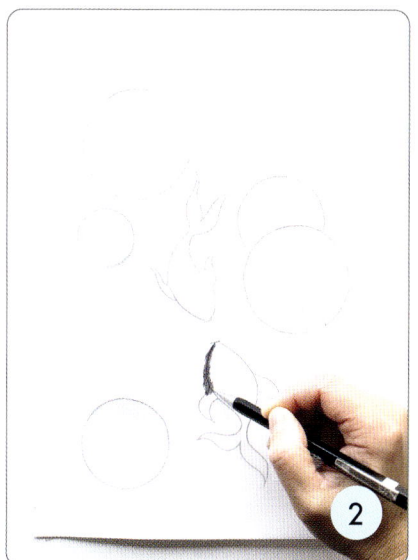

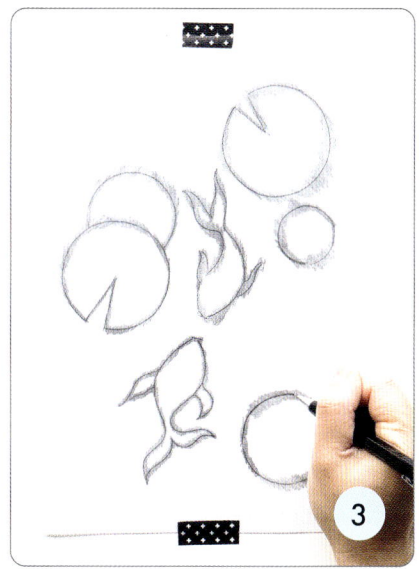

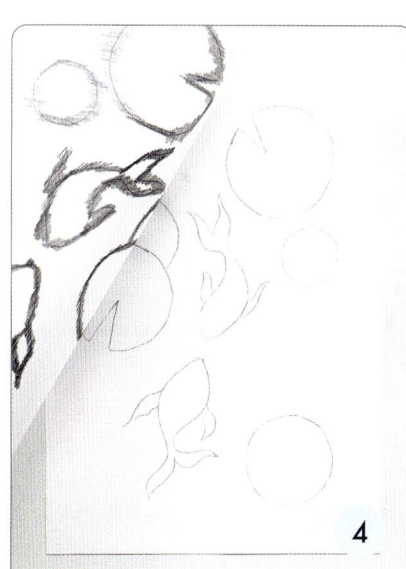

GO WITH THE INK FLOW: Warm Up

Never underestimate the importance of a warm-up!
Just as you would do a warm-up activity at the gym or before playing sport, warm-ups before painting are invaluable. The warm-ups in this book are designed to help you practice techniques you will use in the projects while getting into the rhythm of your creative space. They are just suggestions, and over time you may find certain warm-ups that are really right for you. A warm-up can be anything that gets you into the creative headspace. Sometimes my warm-up is simply cleaning my desk, preparing a stack of paper to paint with, and taking some time to look over past inky meditations I've painted.

SETTING UP YOUR PLAY AREA

Setting up a dedicated area to make artwork is a dream, but it's not always a realistic option for everyone. The beauty of these inky meditations is that they can be done almost anywhere, take up very little space, and can be packed away quite easily. The ink doesn't have fumes that require ventilation, all the materials can be washed in a regular sink, and you can work as small-scale as you like. There are a few things worth considering when setting up your space. Having the right light and positioning of light will help you see how much water you have on your page. You will also need somewhere to dry your artwork flat. I often find that every flat surface around me is covered in drying inky mediations. I would also recommend having a clean and clear space, even if it is just the end of your bench or dining table; try to move any clutter or items unrelated to your painting out of the way. I truly believe that clear physical space assists clear mental space, which allows for your creative brain to thrive.

WARM-UP 1:
WET VERSUS DRY

Dip your water brush into clean water, and remove any excess on the rim of the jar. Paint a water circle onto the page.

Dip your number 12 ink brush into the ink, and remove the excess ink by wiping it on the rim of the jar.

Place your brush a few centimeters to the right of the wet circle on the dry paper. Pull the brush toward and then through the circle so it continues on to the other side. Watch how the ink behaves differently on the dry paper versus the wet circle.

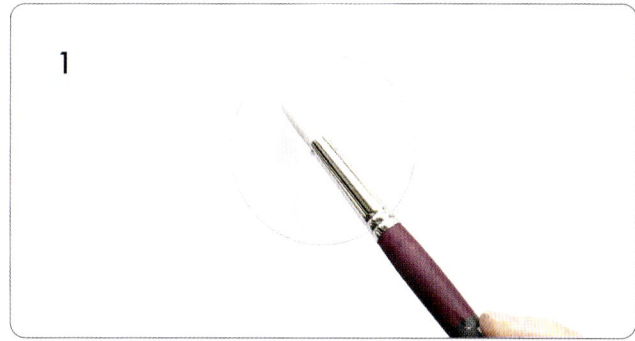

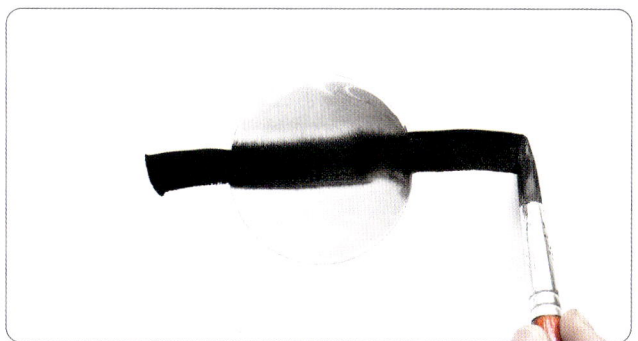

WARM-UP 2:
WATERY BUBBLES

Dip your water brush into clean water, and remove any excess on the rim of the jar. Paint several water circles on your page.

Dip your number 6 ink brush into the ink, and remove the excess by wiping it on the rim of the jar.

Using the tip of the brush, drop ink into a few of the water circles. Use the tip of the brush to run ink around the edge of the remaining water bubbles. Watch how the ink and water react differently in each of these bubbles.

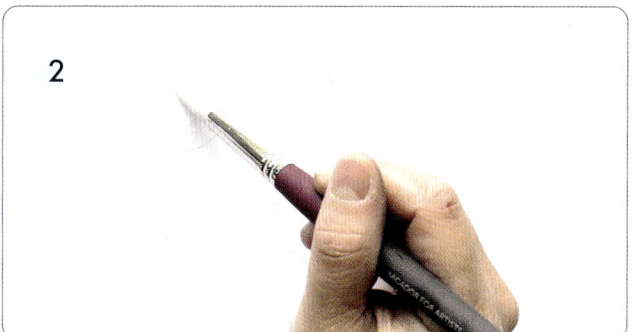

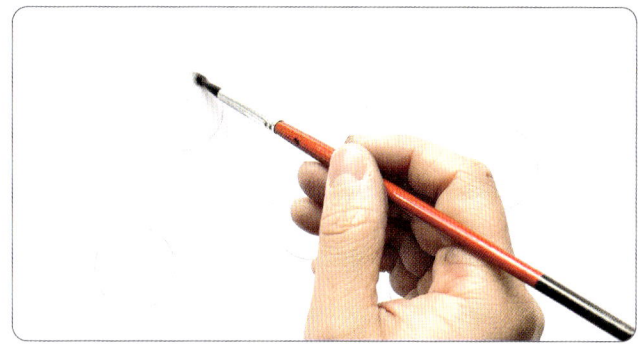

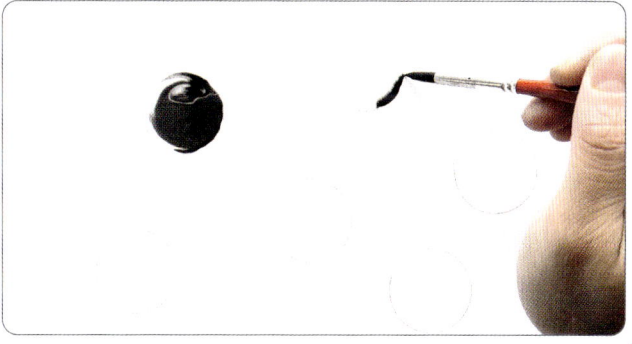

WARM-UP 3:
PLAYFUL LINES

Dip your water brush into clean water, and remove any excess on the rim of the jar. Paint four water lines on your page.

Dip your number 6 or number 12 ink brush (you may want to try this warm-up with both) into the ink, and remove the excess by wiping the brush on the rim of the jar.

On the first water line, use the tip of the brush to paint the top edge of the water line. Watch how ink moves into the rest of the water.

On the second water line, touch the tip of the brush to the very left end of the line and then the very right end of the line. See how the ink moves and reacts with the water and itself.

On the third water line, use the tip of the brush to paint the bottom edge of the water line. Watch how the ink moves into the rest of the water.

On the fourth water line, touch the tip of the brush to the surface of the water in four different spots. Watch how the ink moves within the water.

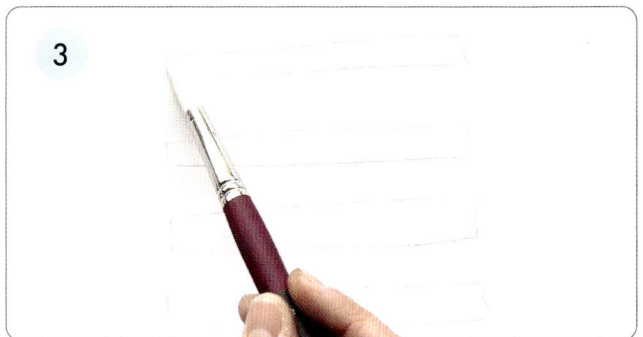

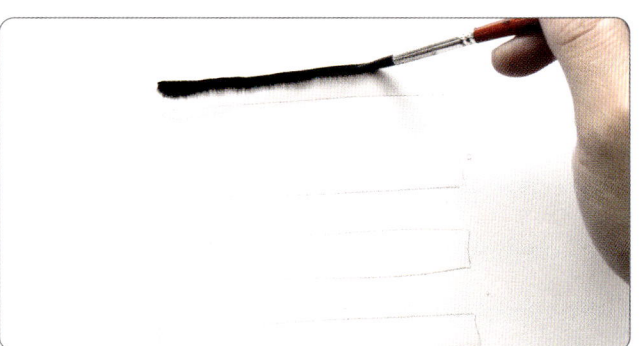

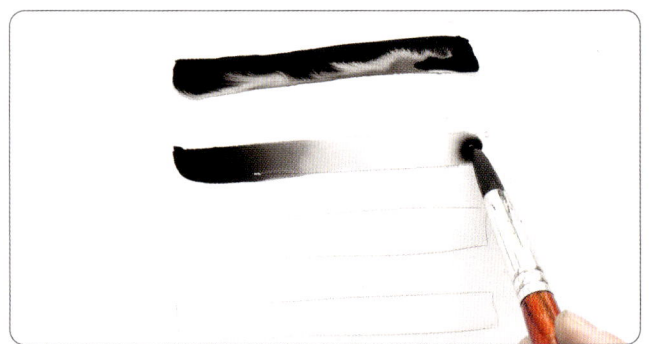

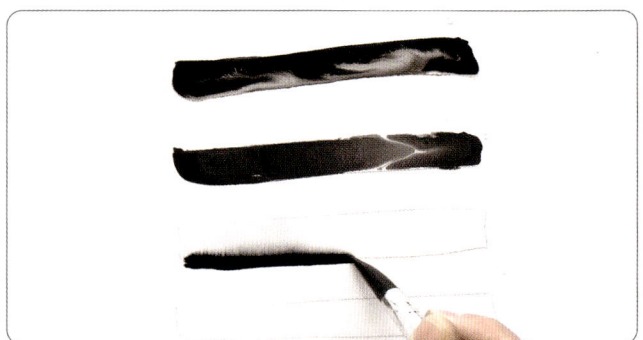

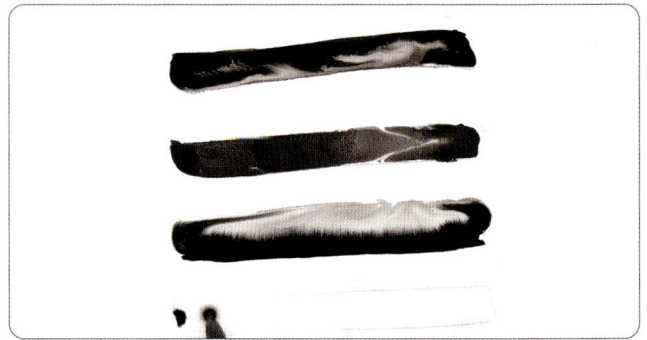

WARM-UP 4:
BREATH LINES

Dip your number 6 or number 12 ink brush (you may want to try this warm-up with both) into the ink, and remove the excess by wiping it on the rim of the jar.

Inhale through your nose, and place the brush at the top of the page. Pause with the brush, and hold your breath for a moment. Exhale, and pull the brush down the length of the page, matching painting the line with the length of your exhalation.

Repeat this across the whole page. By the end, you will have a page illustrating your breathing pattern.

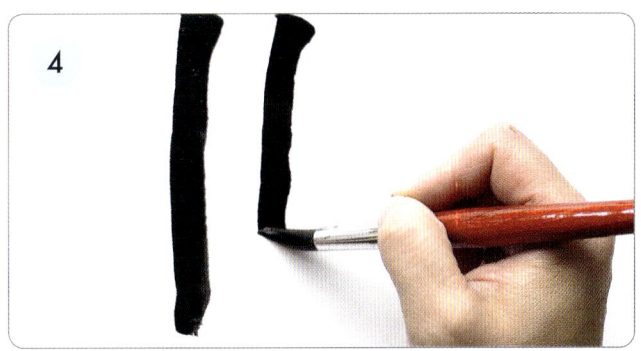

WARM-UP 5:
BREATH CIRCLES

Dip your water brush into clean water, and remove any excess on the rim of the jar. Paint several water circles on your page.

Dip your number 6 ink brush into the ink, and remove the excess by wiping it on the rim of the jar.

Place the tip of the brush on one of the water circles, and hold it there for three counts. I like to match my breath with these counts. Watch how the ink reacts with the water while you hold the brush there for an extended period of time.

Repeat this with all the water circles.

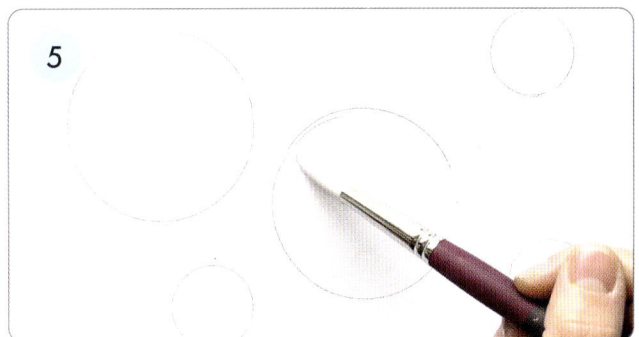

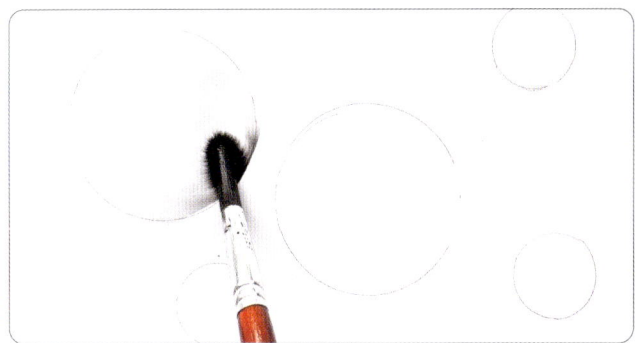

WARM-UP 6:
PLAYFUL SWIRLS

Dip your water brush into clean water, and remove any excess on the rim of the jar. Paint random water shapes on the page; these can be geometric or abstract.

Dip your number 6 ink brush into the ink, and remove the excess by wiping the brush on the rim of the jar.

Keeping your hand light and high above the page, paint squiggly, swirly lines across the page, painting over the wet and dry areas of the paper. Keep painting lines until all your water shapes have ink running through them.

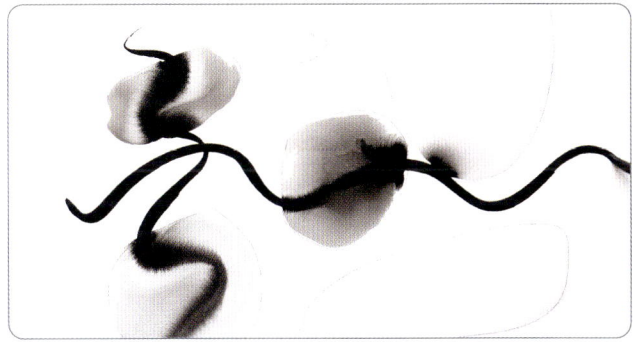

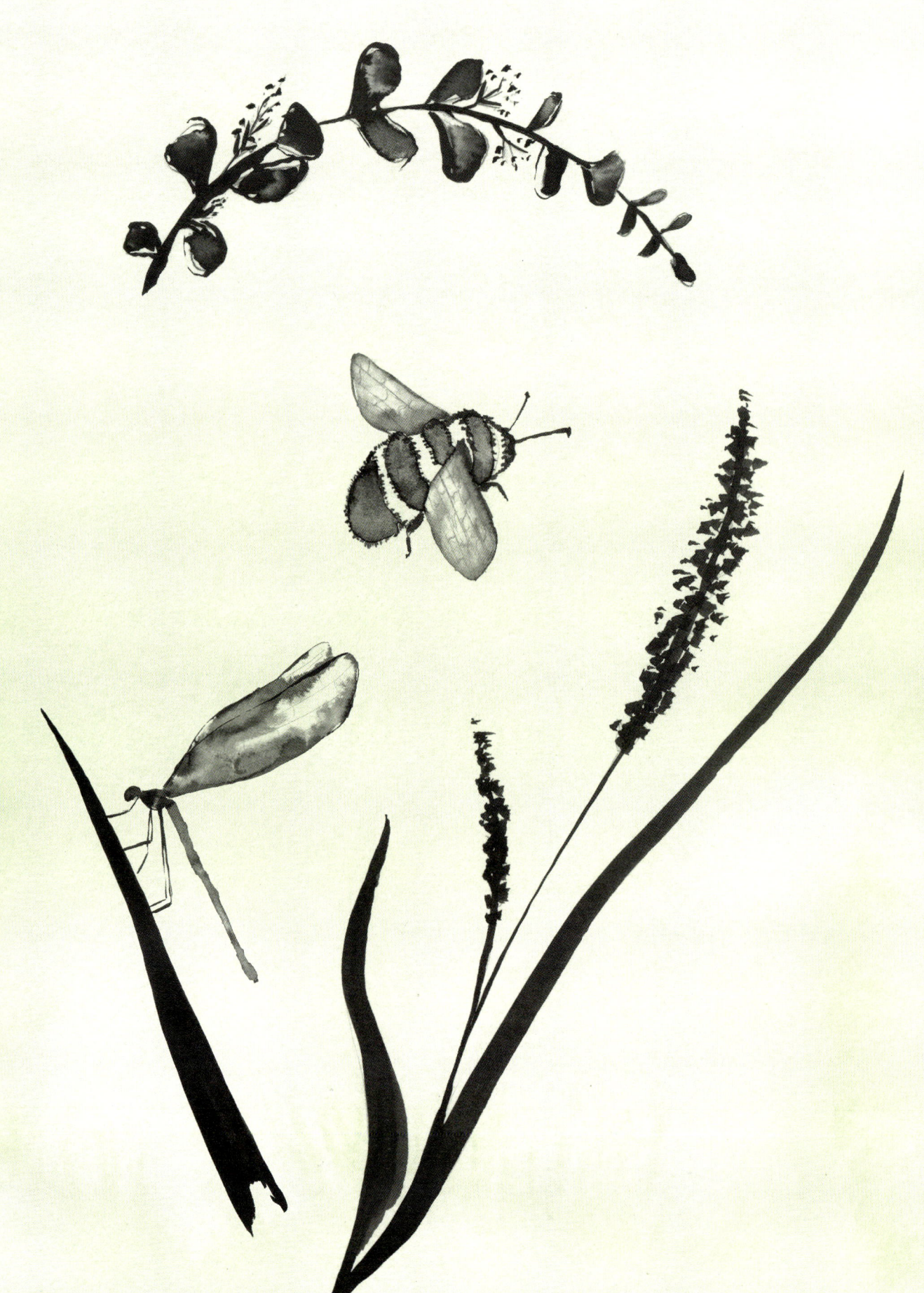

PLANTS, FLOWERS & INSECTS

The projects in this section use some of the basic techniques to create simple but beautiful images. They will help you hone your skills, practice your brushwork, and really understand the combination of water and ink. However, don't underestimate the power of simplicity in art. Just because these are more basic projects in terms of technical elements doesn't mean they are any less powerful as stand-alone pieces. I am constantly striving for simplicity, and I find myself returning to clean lines and uncomplicated images regularly.

NEW BEGINNINGS

As cliché as it may sound, I am always inspired by nature. I very intentionally surround myself with nature because I know how good it makes me feel. I follow the seasons closely and note how they affect my mood, creativity, and general well-being. This little sprout is a sign of spring, of life, of new beginnings. May this simple sprout mark a new beginning for your arts practice, a tiny shoot of creativity.

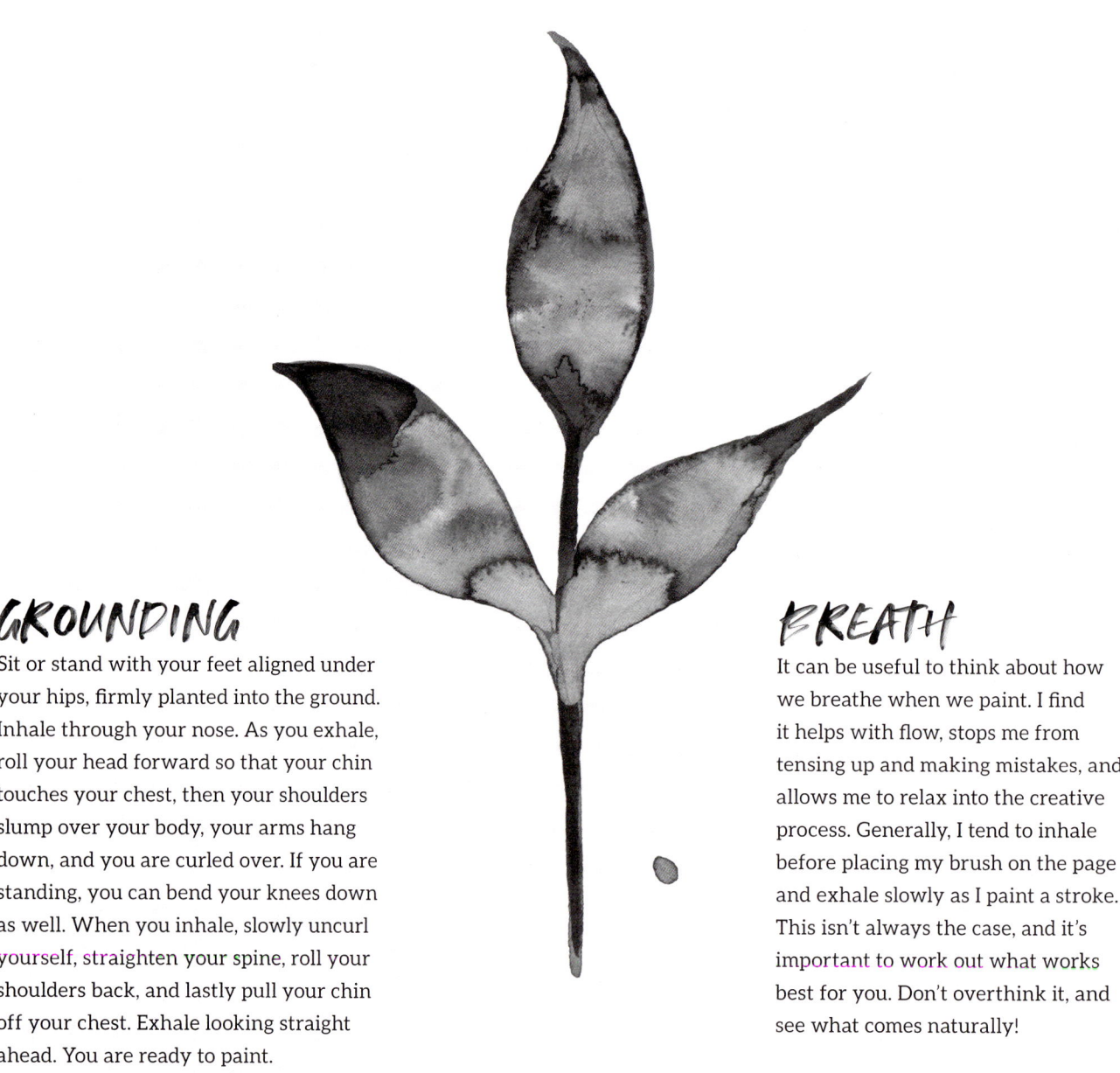

GROUNDING

Sit or stand with your feet aligned under your hips, firmly planted into the ground. Inhale through your nose. As you exhale, roll your head forward so that your chin touches your chest, then your shoulders slump over your body, your arms hang down, and you are curled over. If you are standing, you can bend your knees down as well. When you inhale, slowly uncurl yourself, straighten your spine, roll your shoulders back, and lastly pull your chin off your chest. Exhale looking straight ahead. You are ready to paint.

BREATH

It can be useful to think about how we breathe when we paint. I find it helps with flow, stops me from tensing up and making mistakes, and allows me to relax into the creative process. Generally, I tend to inhale before placing my brush on the page and exhale slowly as I paint a stroke. This isn't always the case, and it's important to work out what works best for you. Don't overthink it, and see what comes naturally!

1

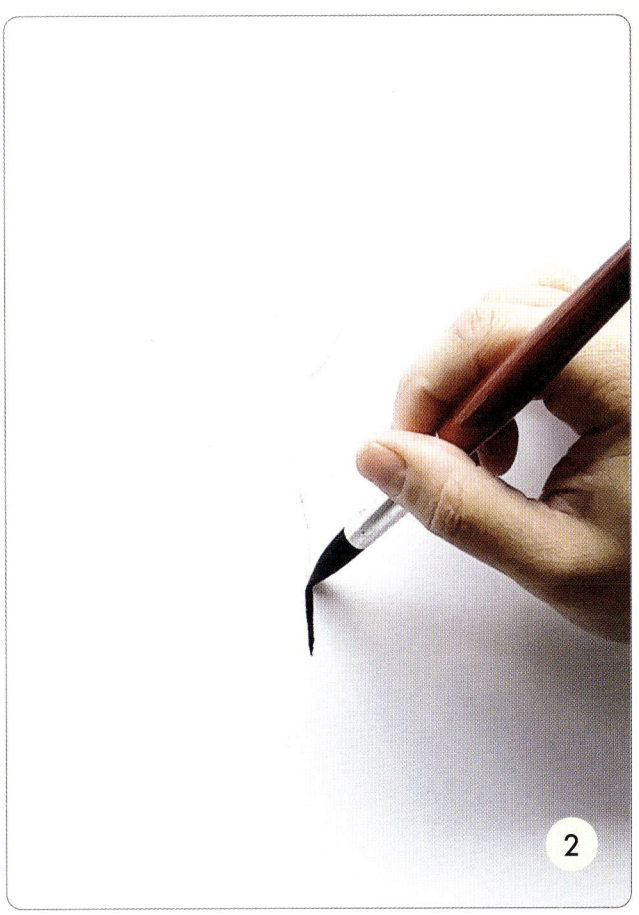

2

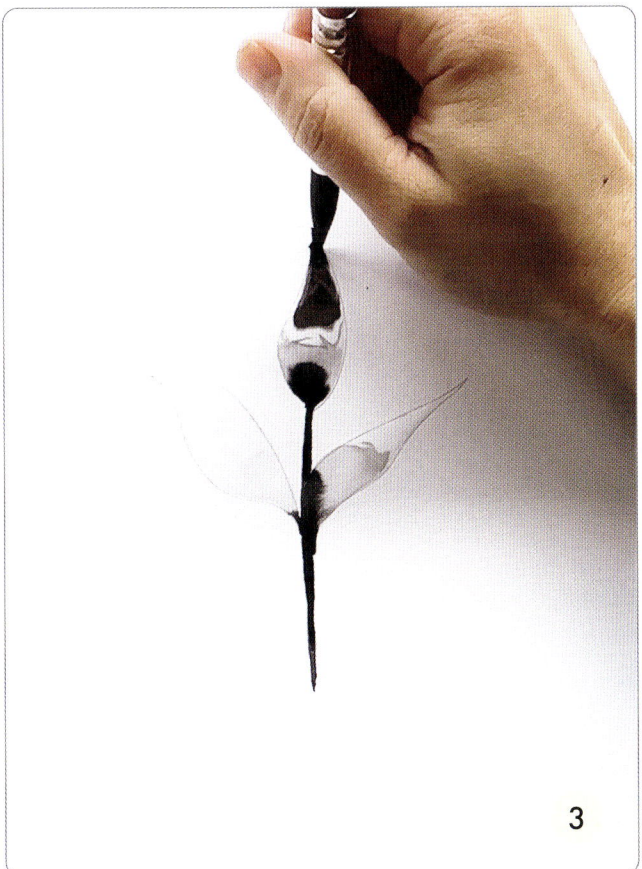

3

1 Trace the outline of the sprout on your page very lightly using your pencil. Dip the water brush into your clean water so it is well soaked. Remove excess water by wiping the brush along the rim of your water jar. Paint water inside the sprout leaves, but don't wet the stem. When you touch the water on each leaf, some of the ink will flow in and move around.

2 Dip the number 12 ink brush into your ink, and remove excess ink by wiping the brush on the rim of the jar. Place the tip of the brush at the bottom of the sprout stem, and paint up the stem until you reach the top leaf.

3 Lift your brush, and place it at the tip of the top leaf. Ink will flow back into the leaf and react with the water.

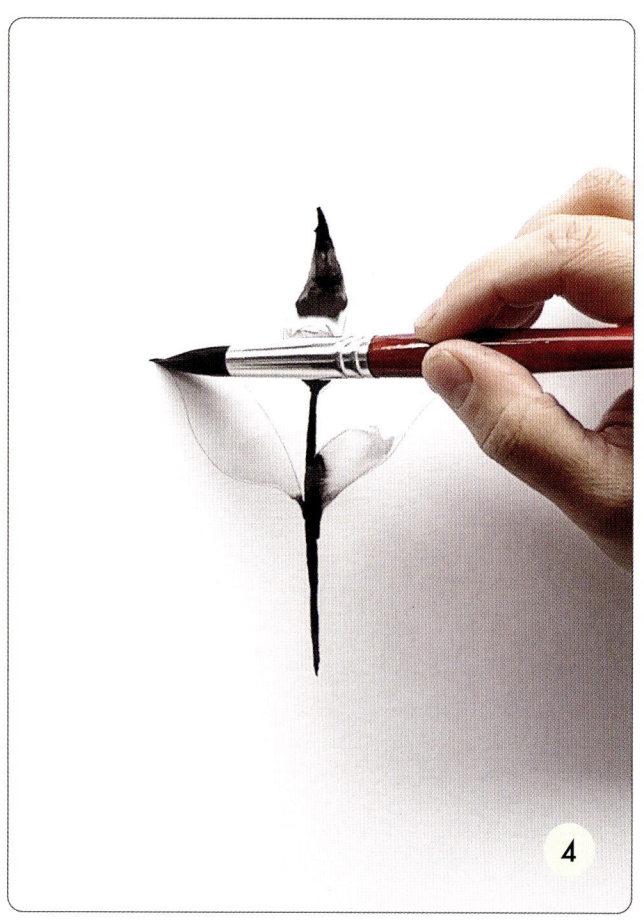

 4 Reload your brush with ink. Touch your brush tip to the left leaf, and watch the ink flow in.

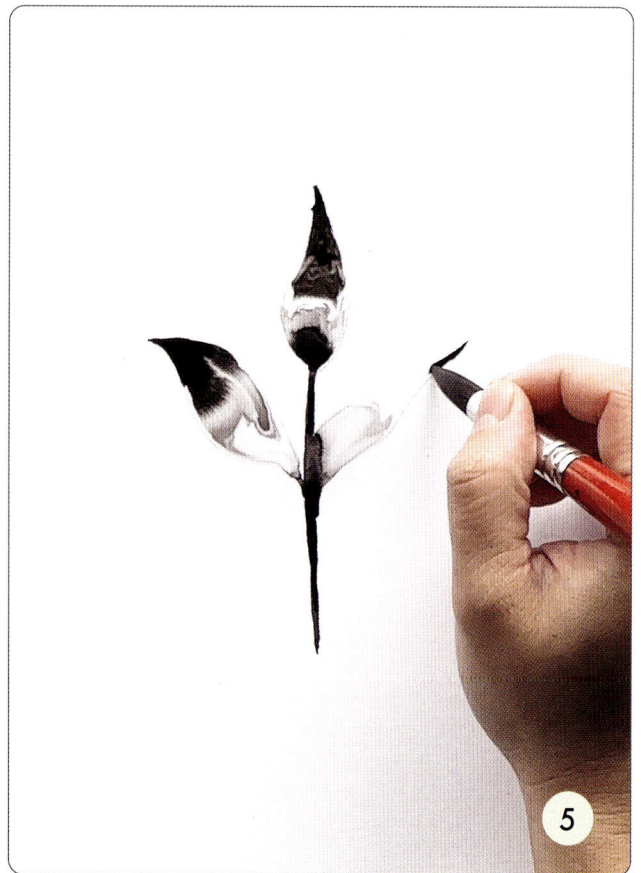

5 Touch the tip of your brush to the right leaf, and allow the ink to flow in. You may want to pull the brush a little farther into the watery part of the leaf to add more ink.

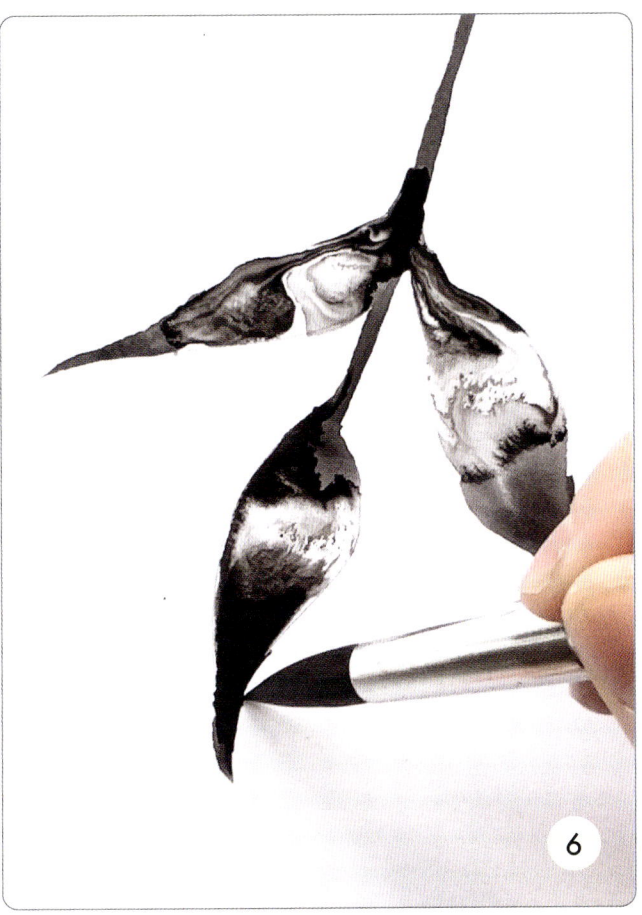

6 Using the tip of the brush, neaten up the edges of the leaves by outlining them lightly. You may prefer to use the finer number 6 ink brush for this. I like to rotate my page around so I can get a better angle and avoid putting my hand in wet ink.

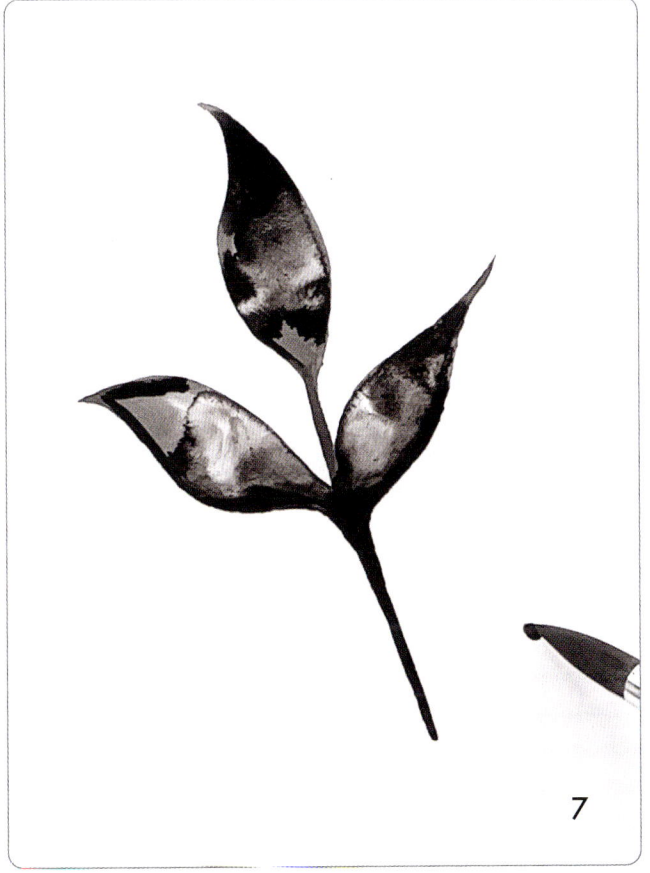

7 I like to add a little dot—almost like a full stop—as a finishing flourish.

IMPERMANENCE

Once again we're drawing inspiration from nature. This time, instead of spring, we are capturing autumn and the crispy leaves mid-fall, caught by the wind. Nothing lasts forever, but the seasons will come again.

GROUNDING

Close your eyes, and listen, breathing gently. Identify sounds you can hear immediately around you—your breath, sounds in the room. Then listen further beyond. What sounds are coming from the room next door? What about outside your window? Can you hear the street, the building next door, the forest beyond? The world? Sit for a moment, and listen to all the things—the sky, the wind, the people, the traffic, the birds. Now work your way backward. Listen to what is on the street, then focus on the room next door, then the space you're in. Bring your focus back to listening to your breath until you feel ready to begin.

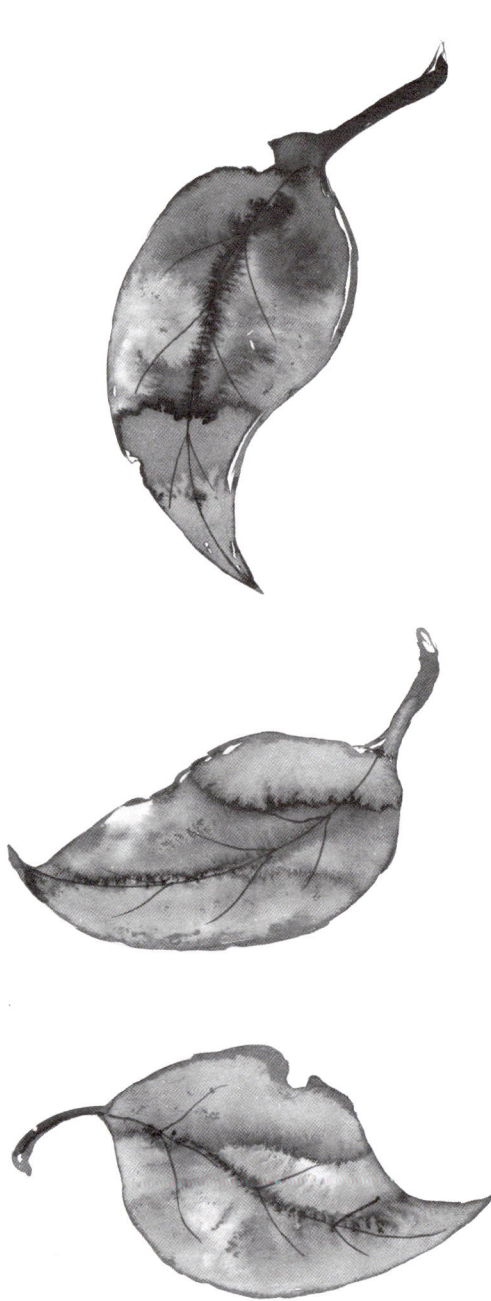

BREATH

This project uses single strokes that flow into the water. There is quite a bit of waiting and watching the ink move by itself. Take purposeful, even breaths while you paint each stroke, and then allow your breathing to relax into a rhythm as you watch the ink move.

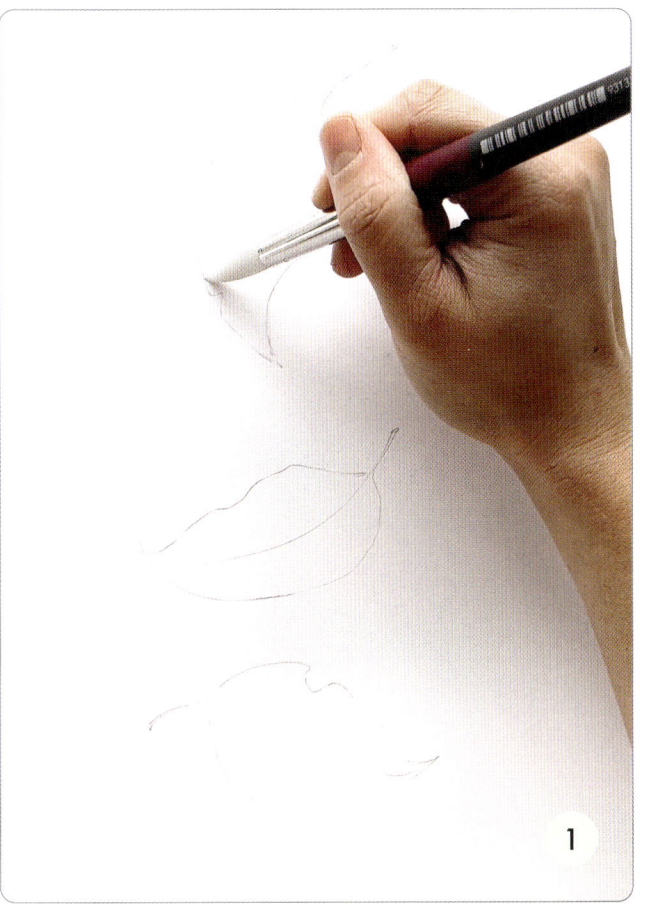

1 Trace the outline of the leaves on your page very lightly using your pencil. Dip the water brush into your clean water so it is well soaked. Remove excess water by wiping the brush along the rim of your water jar. Paint water inside each leaf, but leave the stem dry. If you feel like you can't paint each of the leaves before the water dries, you can do one at a time.

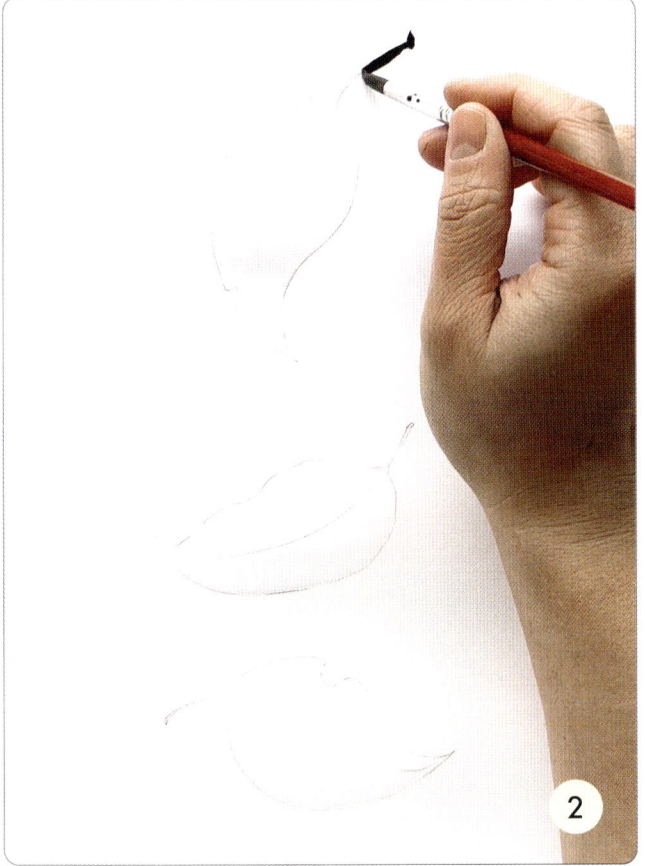

2 Dip the number 6 ink brush into your ink, and remove excess ink by wiping the brush on the rim of the jar. Place the tip of the brush on the top leaf stem. Painting lightly to keep a relatively fine line, pull the brush down into the water of the leaf, all the way to the tip. Watch how the ink moves.

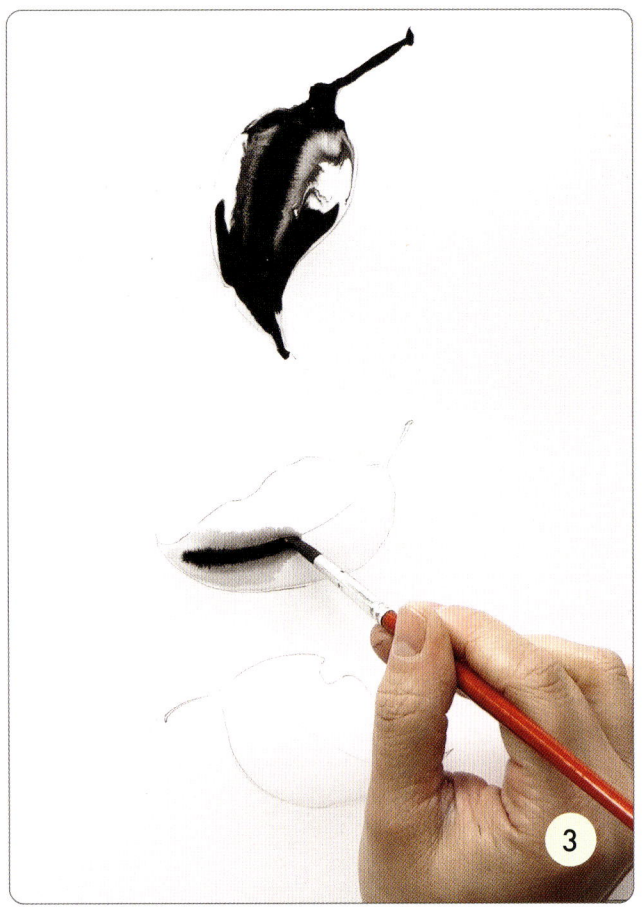

3 Your brush might be quite wet, so dab it on a paper towel, and reload it with ink. For the second leaf, I am starting at the tip of the leaf. That is because I'm right-handed, and I find it easier to pull the brush from left to right. If you are left-handed, you can start from the tip of the stem, or rotate the page so you have a better flow. Pull the brush through the water to the tip of the stem. Watch how the ink moves.

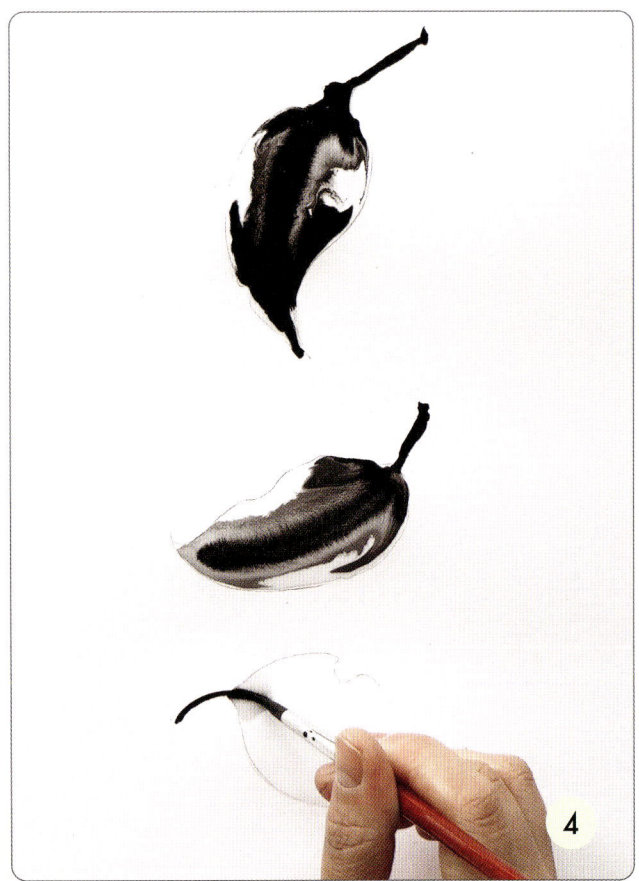

4 If necessary, dab and reload your brush with ink. On the third leaf, I am starting at the stem (if you are left-handed, you may prefer to start at the leaf tip). Once again, pull the brush along the stem, through the water, and to the tip of the leaf. Watch how the ink moves.

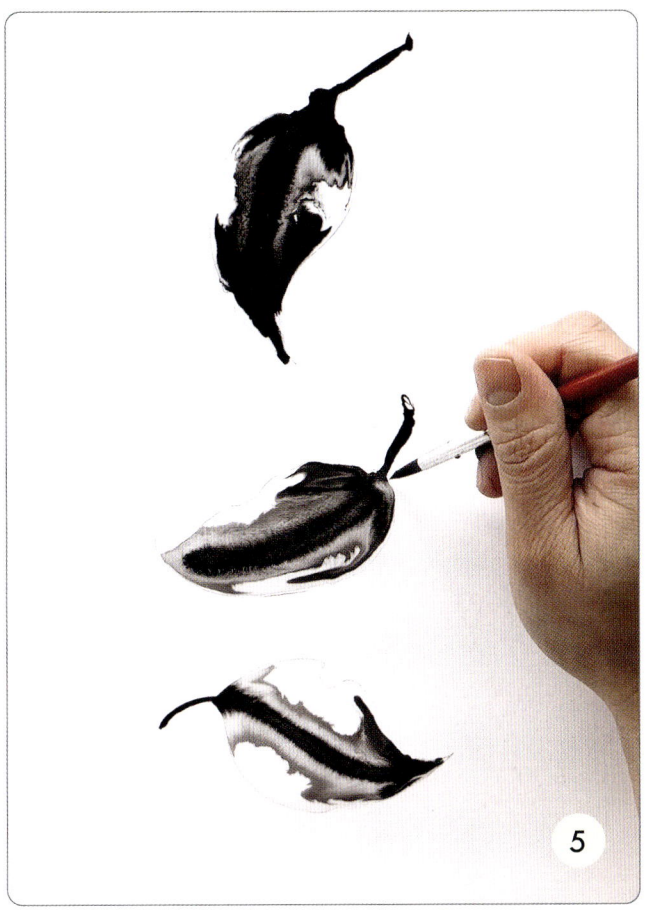

5 Use the tip of your brush to neaten up any edges, but be careful not to add too much ink to your leaves, or they will lose the beautiful texture from the water-and-ink reaction.

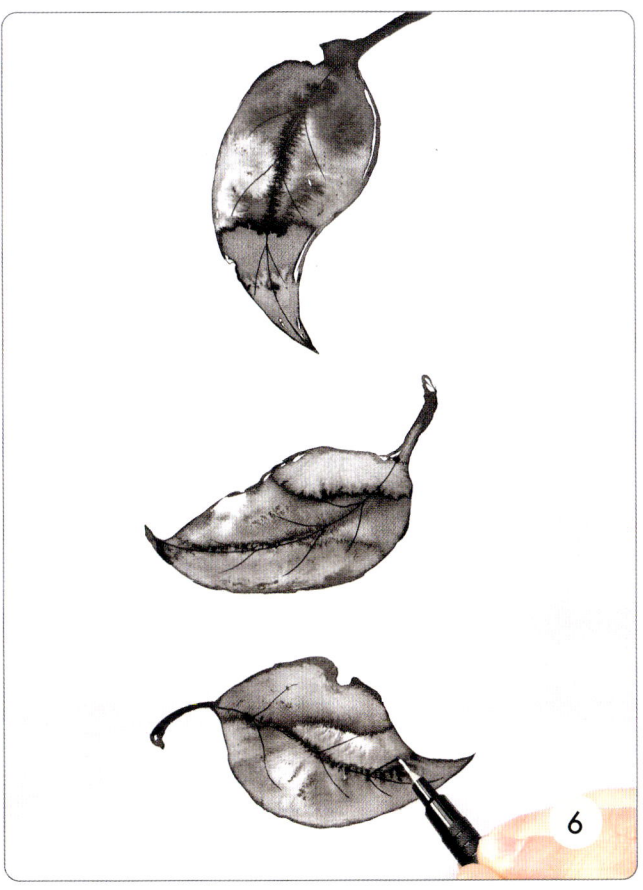

6 Once your leaves are completely dry, you can add some vein details using a fineliner pen.

MAGNOLIA

Magnolias are one of the early signs of spring that I look for.
Amongst the cherry blossoms and narcissus, magnolias grandly announce
the end of winter and promise longer, lighter, warmer days. They are a
beautiful flower and simple to paint. If you enjoy painting magnolias, look
for photos of them online, and see if you can paint them in ink too!

GROUNDING

Make yourself a hot drink. Wrap your
hands around the cup, and breathe in
the steam. Take small sips of your drink
while you feel the warmth your hands
and your body radiate.

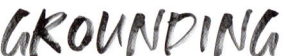

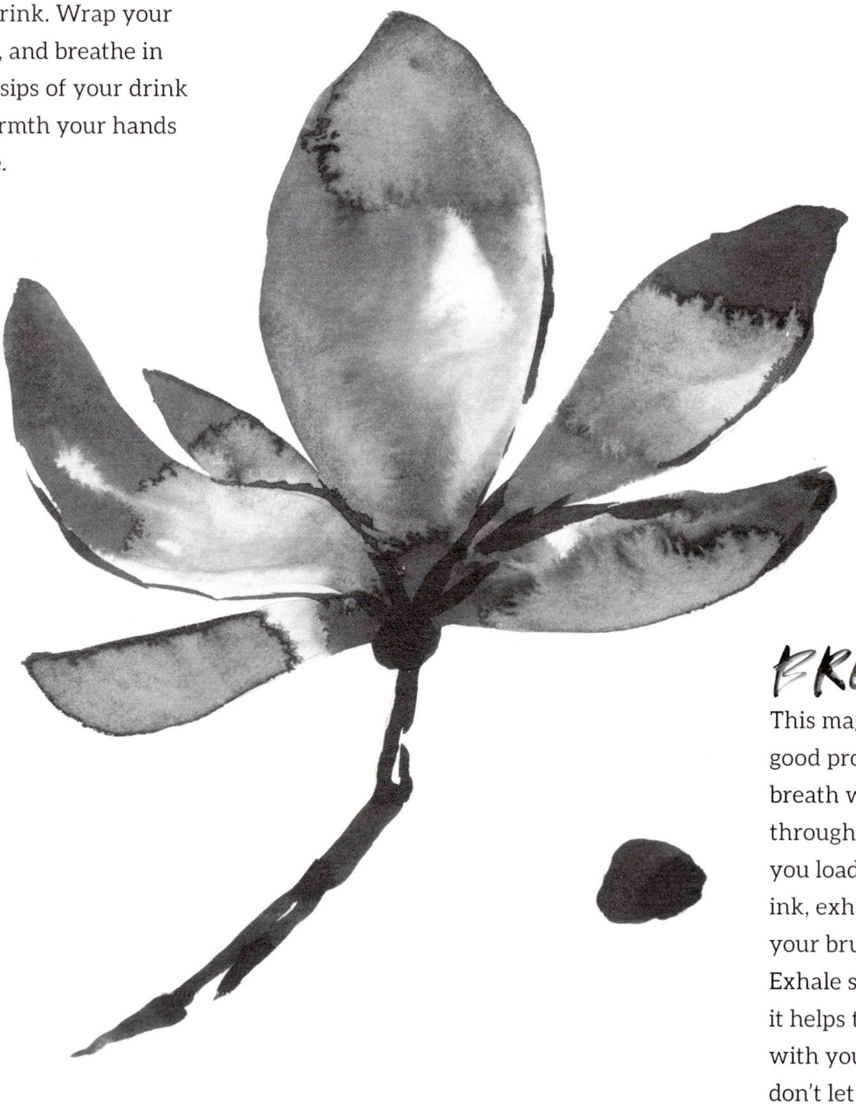

BREATH

This magnolia flower is a
good project to practice
breath work. Try inhaling
through your nose when
you load your brush with
ink, exhaling as you touch
your brush to the page.
Exhale slowly; sometimes
it helps to make an O shape
with your mouth so you
don't let all your breath out
at once. Just be sure not to
blow your ink around!

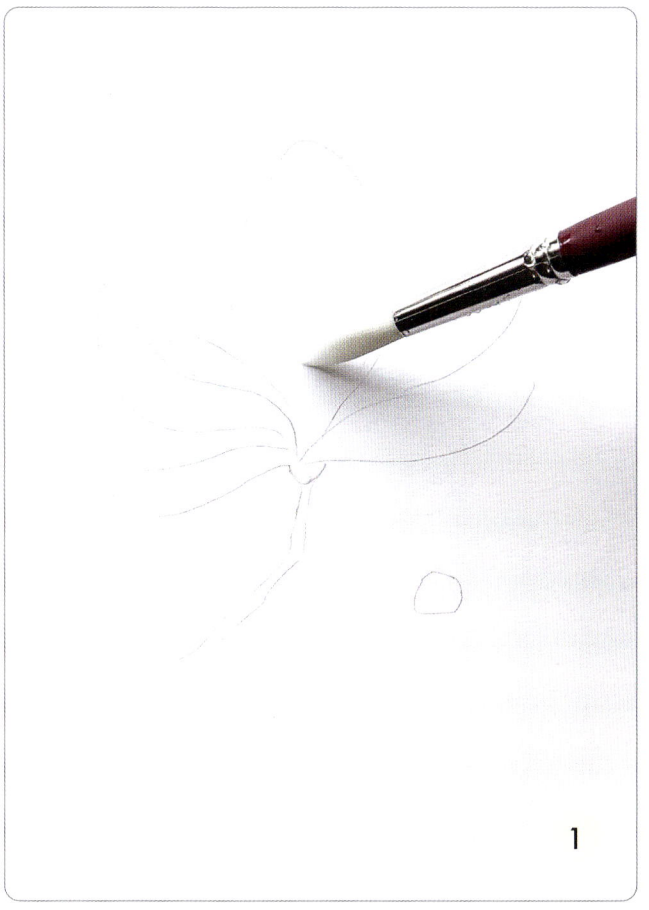

1

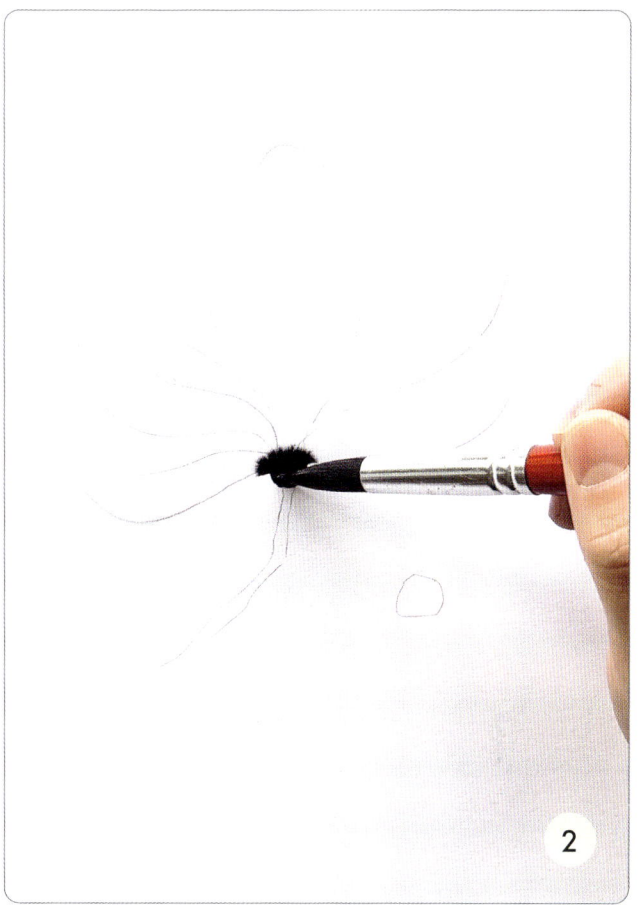

2

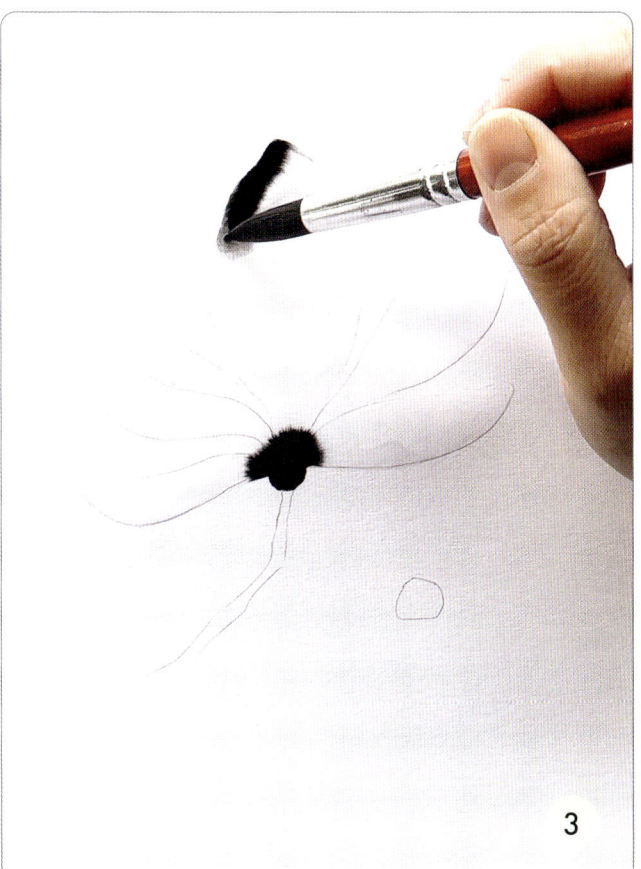

3

1 Trace the outline of the magnolia flower on your page very lightly using your pencil. Dip the water brush into your clean water so it is well soaked. Remove excess water by wiping the brush along the rim of your water jar. Paint water inside the flower petals and bud, but don't wet the stem.

2 Dip the number 12 ink brush into your ink, and remove excess ink by wiping the brush on the rim of the jar. Place the tip of the brush at the top of the base bud of the flower, and hold it to the page, allowing the ink to spread into the water.

3 Reload the brush with ink, and touch it to the tip of the middle petal, pulling the brush down the side of the petal about halfway. The ink may spread into other petals, but that is fine.

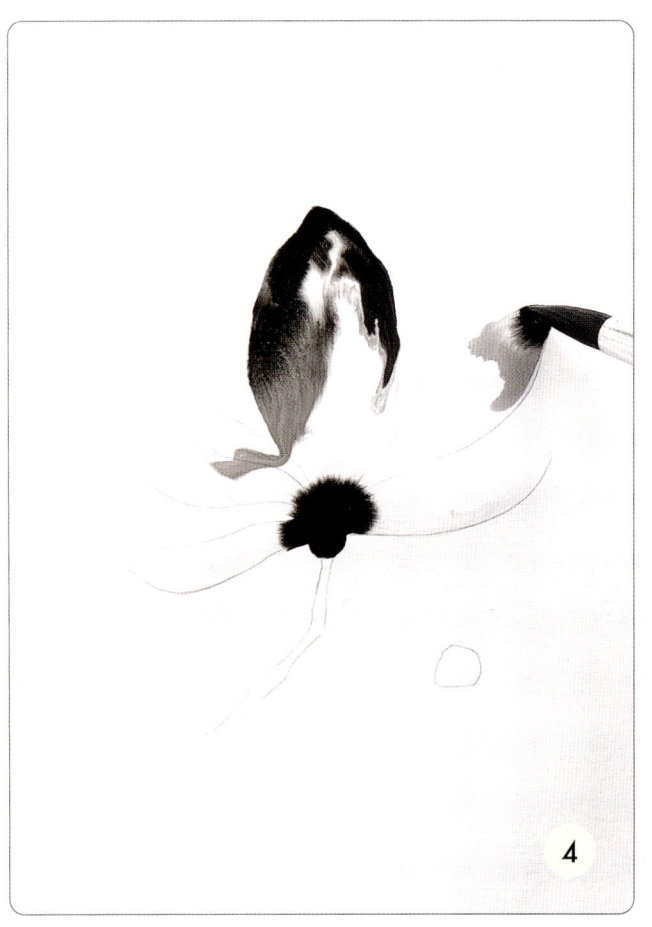

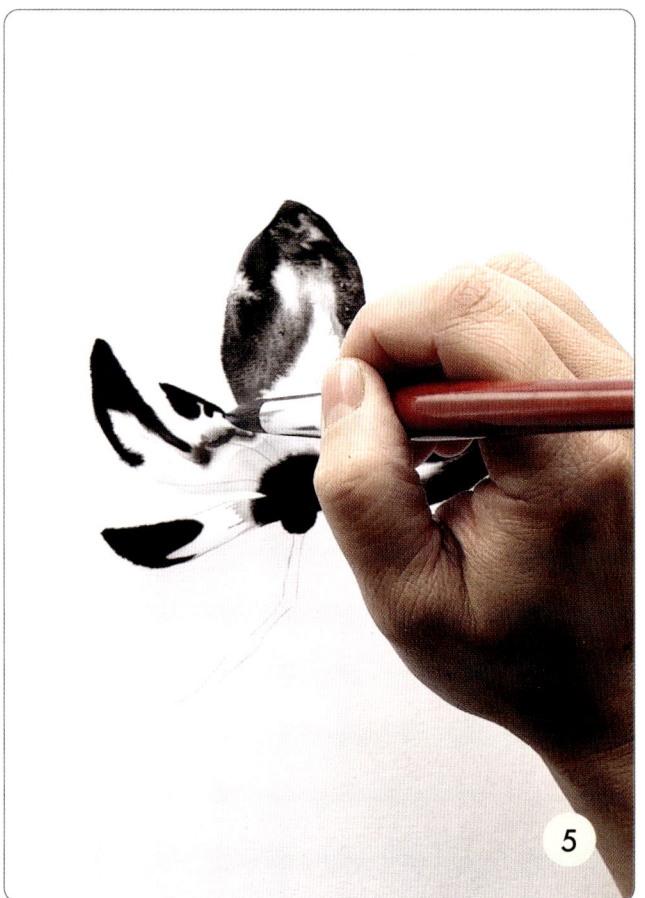

4 Hold the ink brush to the other petals, painting along some of the petal edges, so that ink seeps into the water-filled areas. I like to start at the tip of each petal and watch the ink flow into the rest of the flower.

5 Repeat this with each of the petals.

6 Allow the flower to dry. It doesn't need to be perfectly dry, about 80 percent. Using your number 12 ink brush, paint onto the dry paper along the pencil mark of the flower stem. I like to start at the bottom and paint up to the flower.

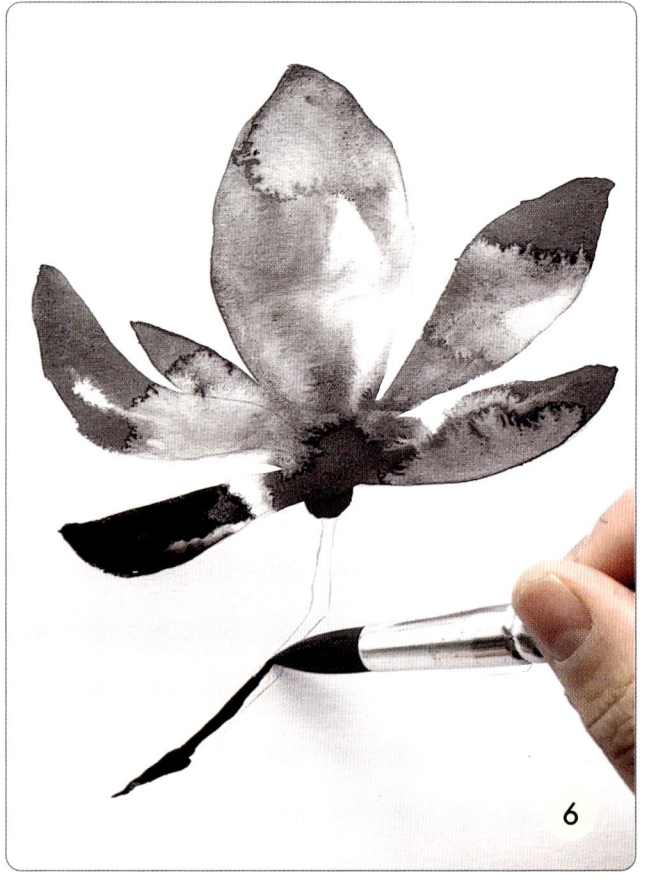

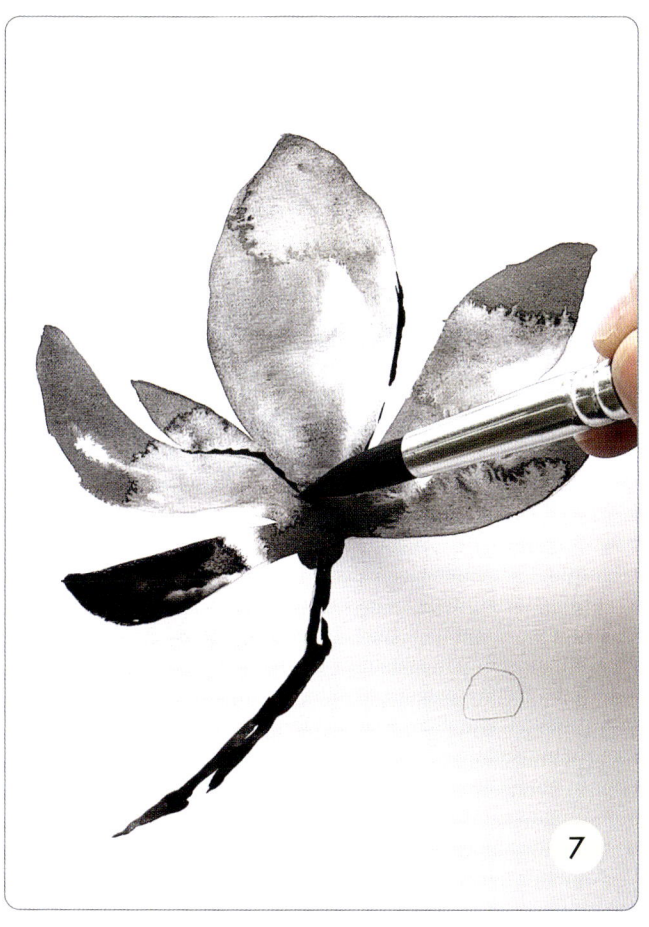

7 Using the tip of the brush, add in some fine lines to redefine the petals. You may prefer to use the number 6 ink brush or a fineliner pen for this.

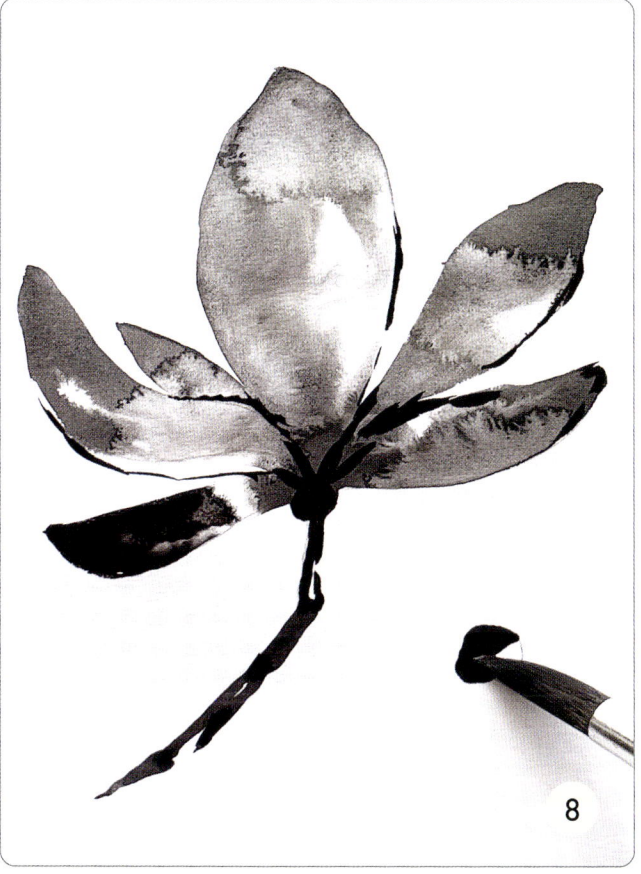

8 I sometimes like to add an inky blob to a painting that needs a little something extra to feel finished. You might like to add one to your magnolia flower, but you can also leave it off if you prefer.

TINY DRAGON

Dragonflies are so delicate and beautiful that sometimes they look like they are made of glass. They are a true sign of summer, like long days, warm evenings, and the gentle hum of insects in the garden.

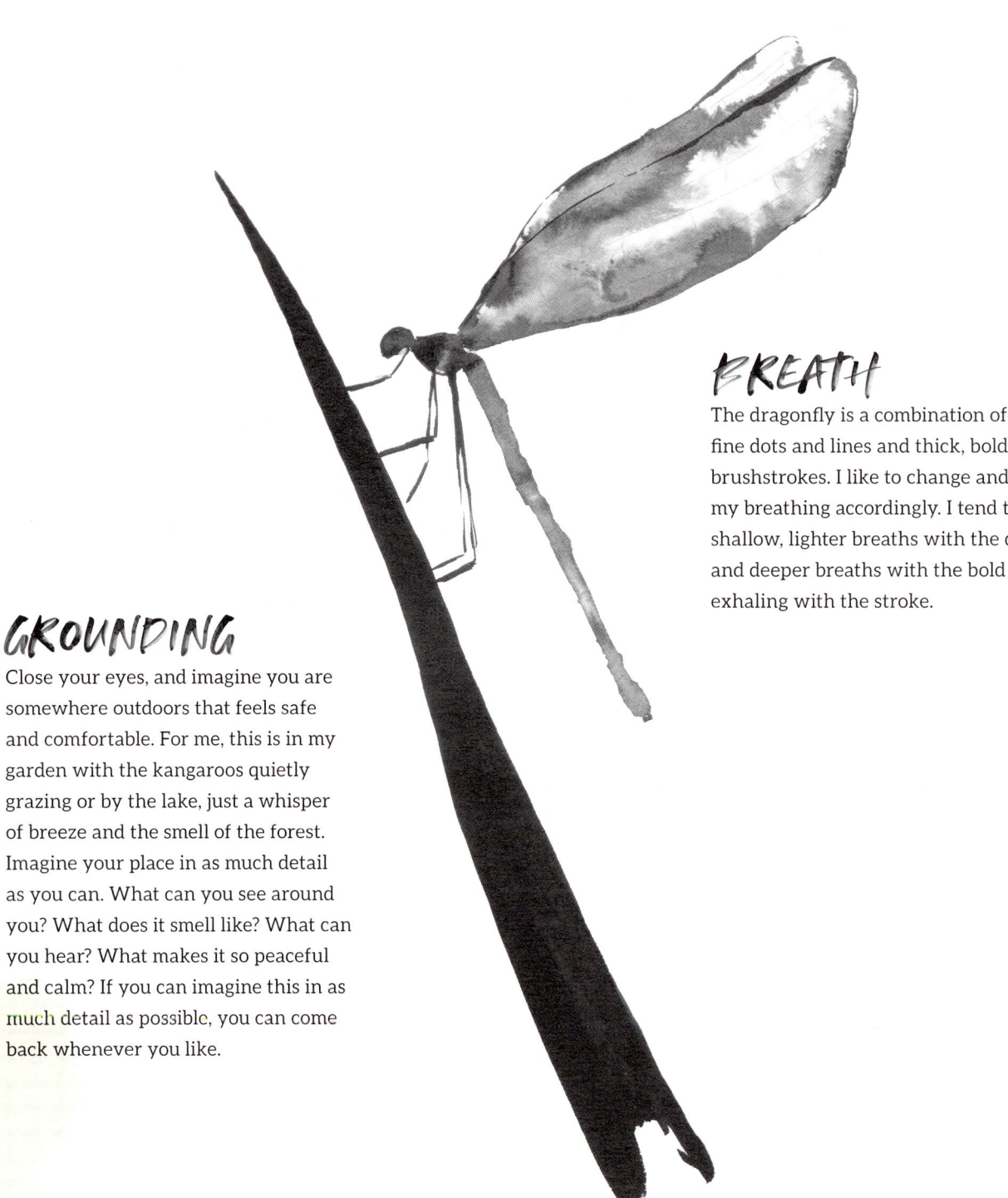

BREATH

The dragonfly is a combination of fine dots and lines and thick, bold brushstrokes. I like to change and adapt my breathing accordingly. I tend to take shallow, lighter breaths with the dots and deeper breaths with the bold lines, exhaling with the stroke.

GROUNDING

Close your eyes, and imagine you are somewhere outdoors that feels safe and comfortable. For me, this is in my garden with the kangaroos quietly grazing or by the lake, just a whisper of breeze and the smell of the forest. Imagine your place in as much detail as you can. What can you see around you? What does it smell like? What can you hear? What makes it so peaceful and calm? If you can imagine this in as much detail as possible, you can come back whenever you like.

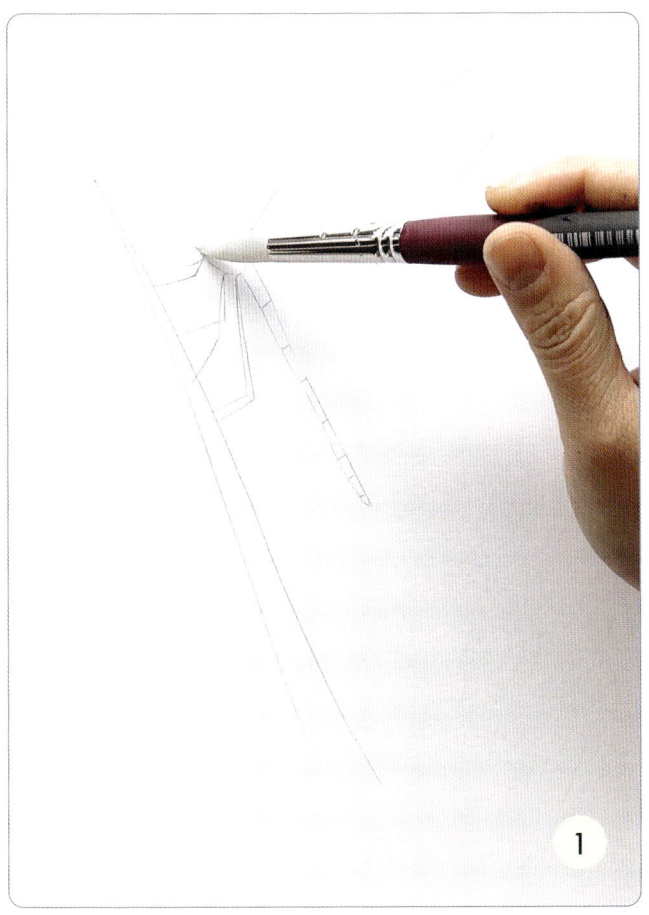

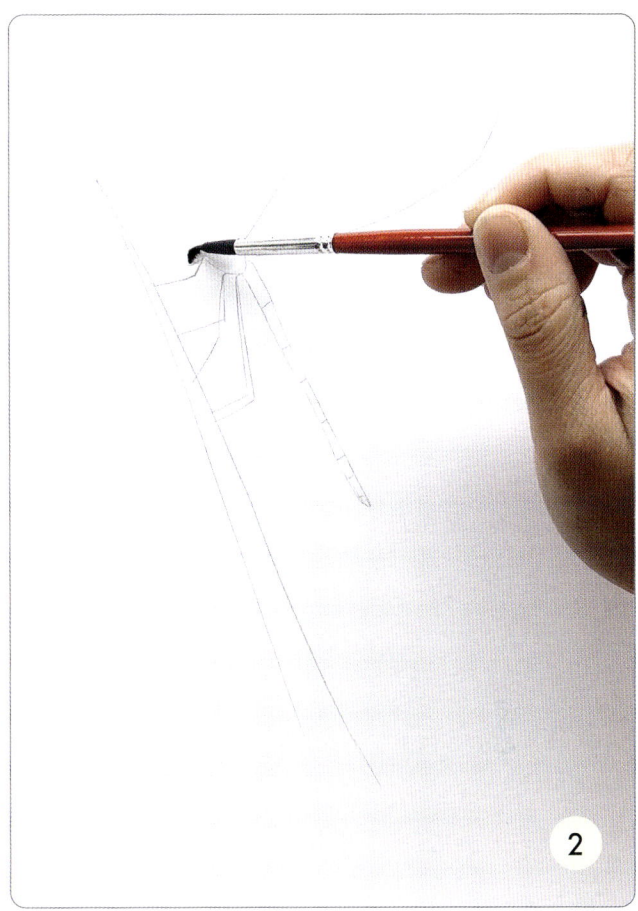

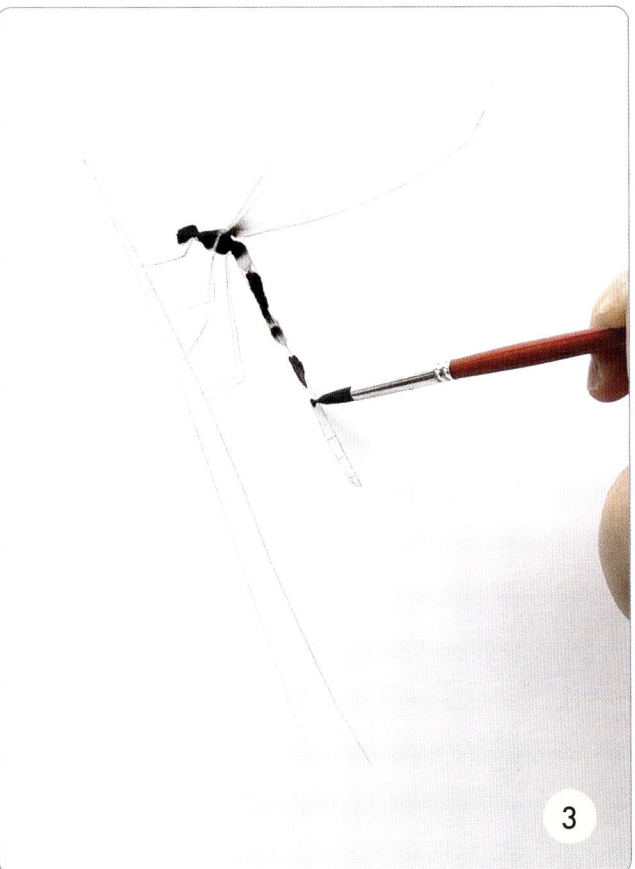

1 Trace the outline of the dragonfly on your page very lightly using your pencil. Dip your water brush into the water, and remove excess by wiping it on the rim of the jar. Paint water onto the head, body, and wings of the dragonfly. Leave the legs and blade of grass dry.

2 Dip your number 6 ink brush into the ink, and remove excess ink by wiping the brush on the rim of the jar. Using the tip of the brush, place a dot of ink on the dragonfly's head, and pull the brush down into the middle body section. The water will start to spread into the tail and the wing, but that is fine.

3 Using the tip of the number 6 ink brush, continue down the tail, placing a dot of ink in each segment. They will bleed into each other a little.

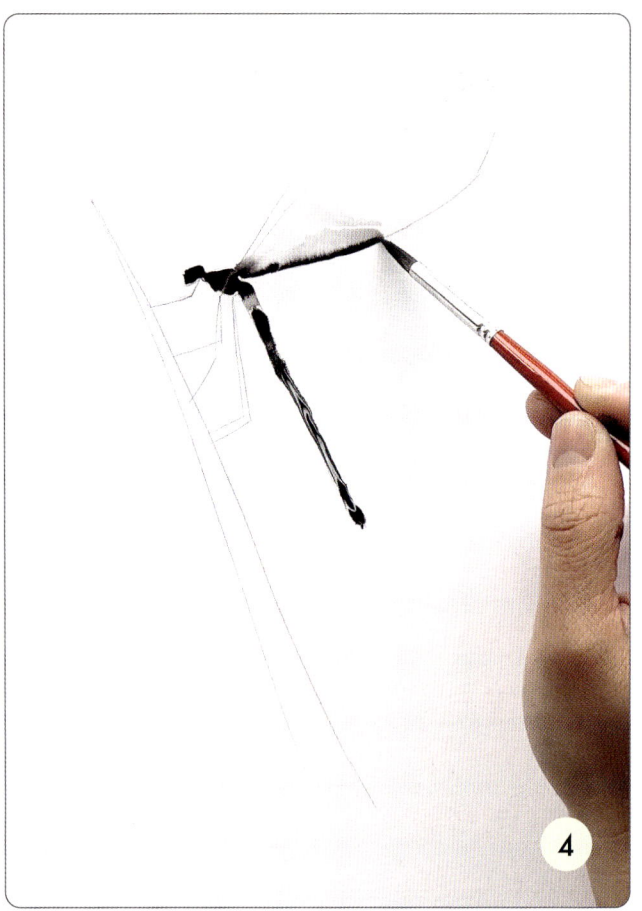

4 Still using the very tip of the brush, hold your hand very lightly, and paint along the pencil outline of the wings. The ink will start to bleed into the watery center of the wings. When this dries, it will give a light and transparent appearance.

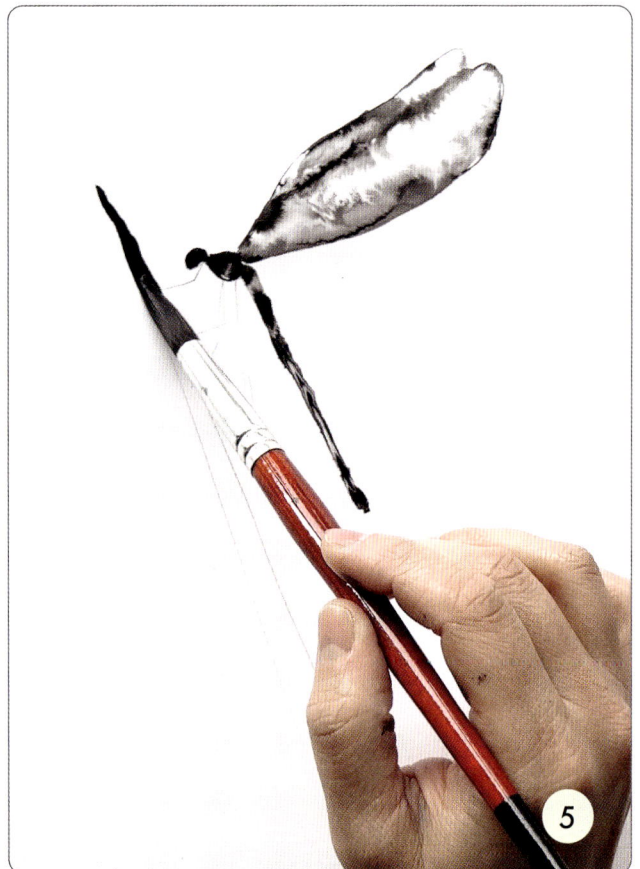

5 Dip your number 12 ink brush into the ink, and remove the excess by wiping it on the rim of the jar. Place the tip of the brush at the tip of the grass, and pull the brush down the length of the blade, putting slightly more pressure on the brush as you move down to create a thicker line.

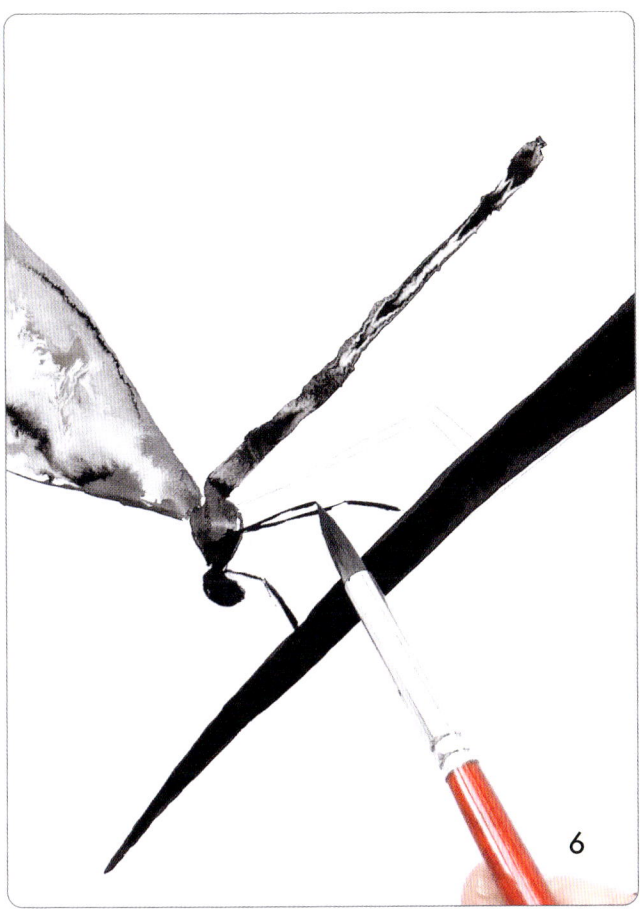

6 Using your number 6 bush again, reload it with ink, and paint fine lines along the dragonfly's legs. I like to rotate the paper so that the legs are at a more comfortable angle to paint. Be sure to keep your hand nice and light above the paper so you get a very fine line. If you find this too difficult with the brush, you can use a fineliner pen. Set the dragonfly aside to dry.

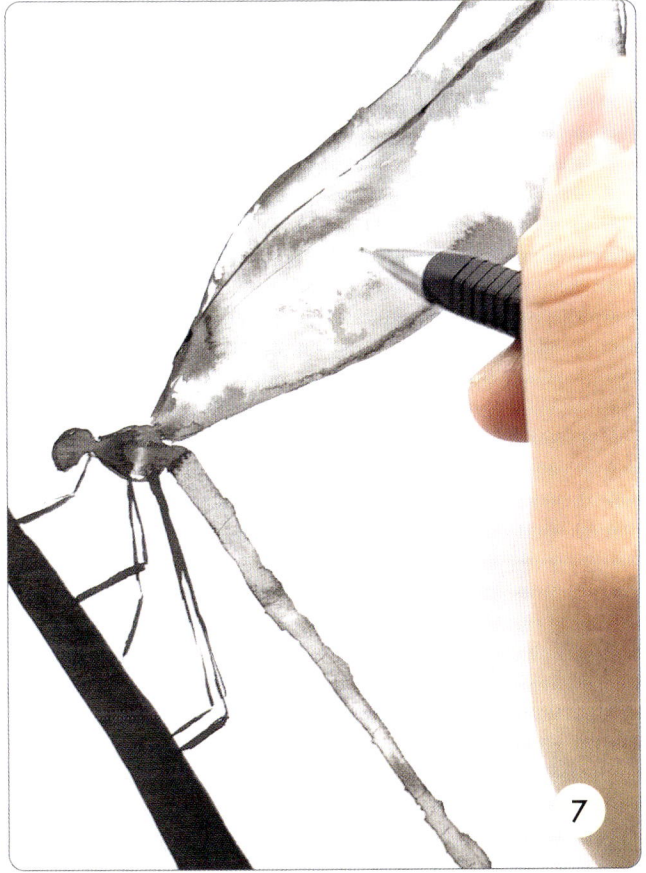

7 Once the dragonfly is completely dry, use a very sharp pencil or mechanical pencil to lightly draw some line textures onto the wings. You can make up whatever texture you like; just be sure to draw it on very lightly. It should be barely visible.

IRIS

I think iris flowers are beautiful. I have hundreds across my garden.
They do have a tendency to spread like weeds, but they are so pretty that
I don't mind! They are also begging to be painted in ink with their fluid,
delicate petals. If you master one, you could do a whole page full of them!

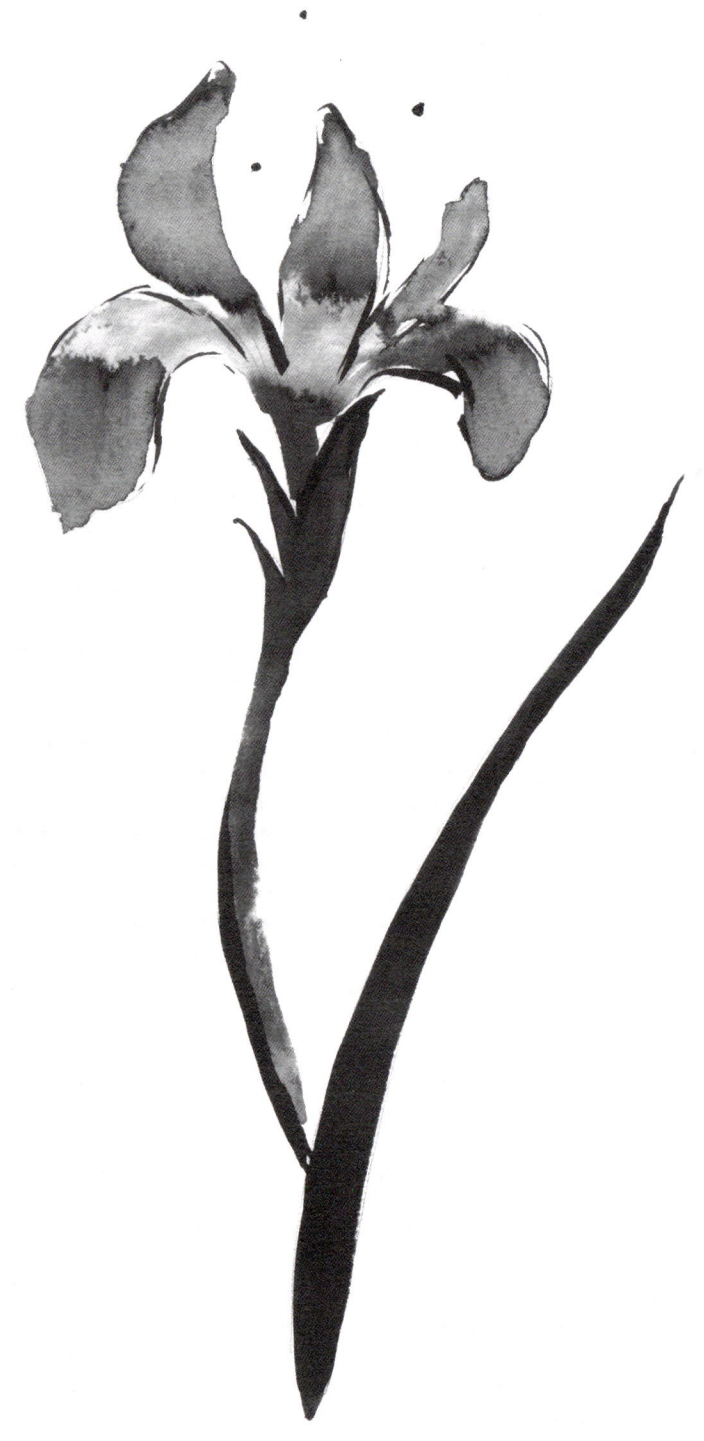

GROUNDING

Sometimes when I first get into
the studio, I'm not ready to paint
straightaway. I need time to prepare.
I clear my space, wipe down my desk,
and cut pieces of paper down to size.
It not only gets me ready to paint in
a practical sense, but it also eases me
into the rhythm of my creative space. It
prepares me in every sense. Take some
time now to prepare your physical
space so you are ready to paint.

BREATH

I like to take long, even breaths with this
project. For most of the strokes, the brush
is held to the page for a longer length of
time. Try inhaling before you place the
brush to the page, and while the brush is
on the page, do one full exhalation and
inhalation. This one is a good project for
practicing intentional breathing.

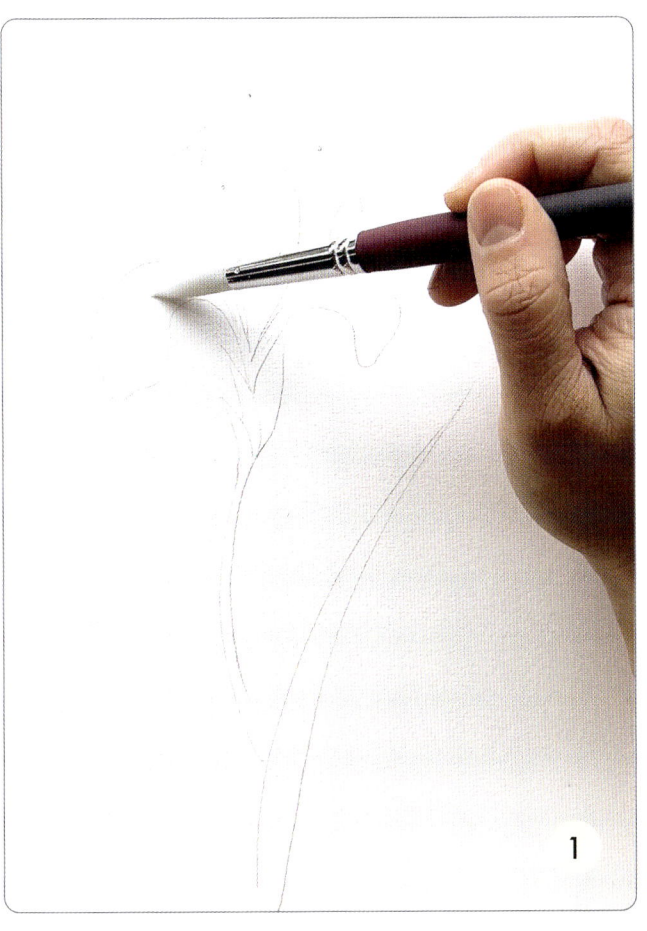

1 Trace the outline of the iris on your page very lightly using your pencil. Dip your water brush into the water, and remove the excess by wiping it on the rim of the jar. Paint water on the flower petals and along the whole stem. Leave the leaf dry.

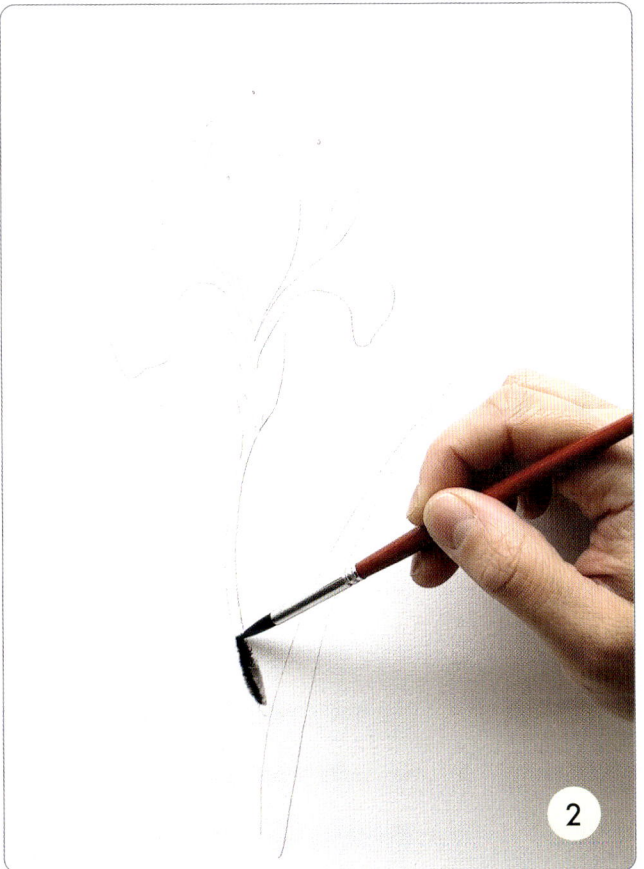

2 Dip your number 6 ink brush into your ink, and remove the excess by wiping it on the rim of the jar. Starting at the bottom of the stem, lightly drag your brush up the stem until you reach the base of the flower where the petals meet. Lift the brush from the page. Some of the ink will move into the watery petals—this is what you want to happen.

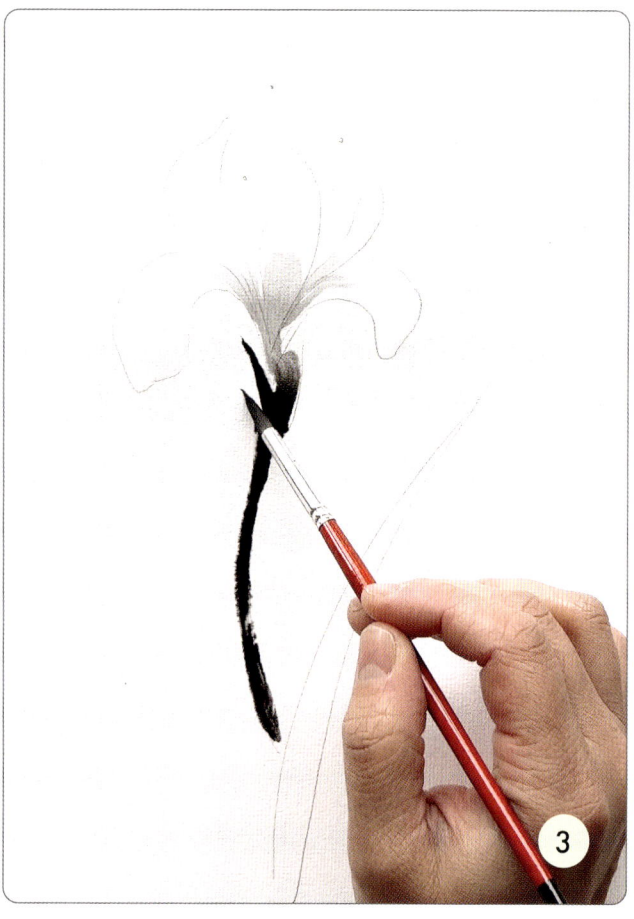

3 Using the tip of the brush, paint the sepal (the outer parts of the flower bud). You will find that the brush is just the right shape to paint these in one stroke.

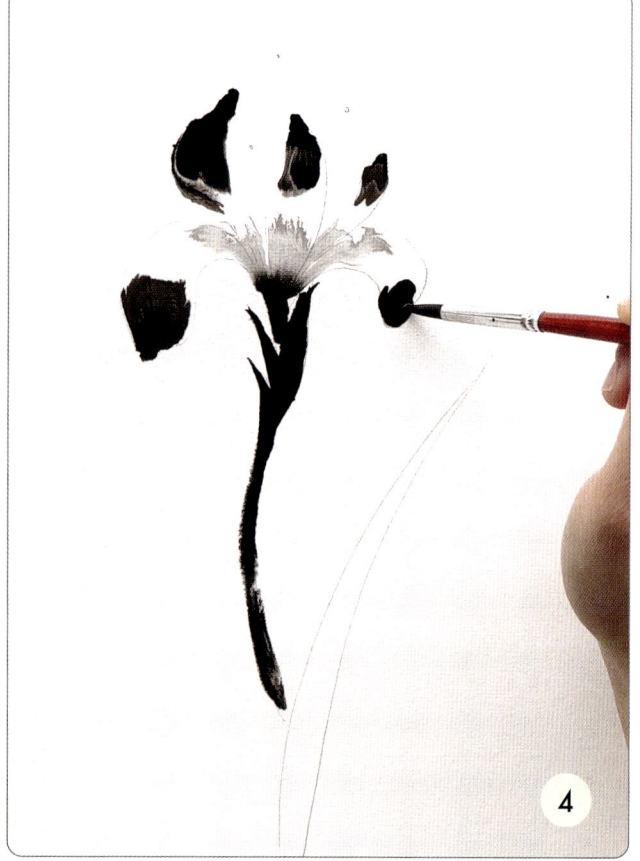

4 Reload the brush with ink by dipping it into the jar and wiping the excess off on the rim. Place the tip of the brush at the end of each petal, and hold it in the water for a count of three. You will see the ink moving into the rest of the flower.

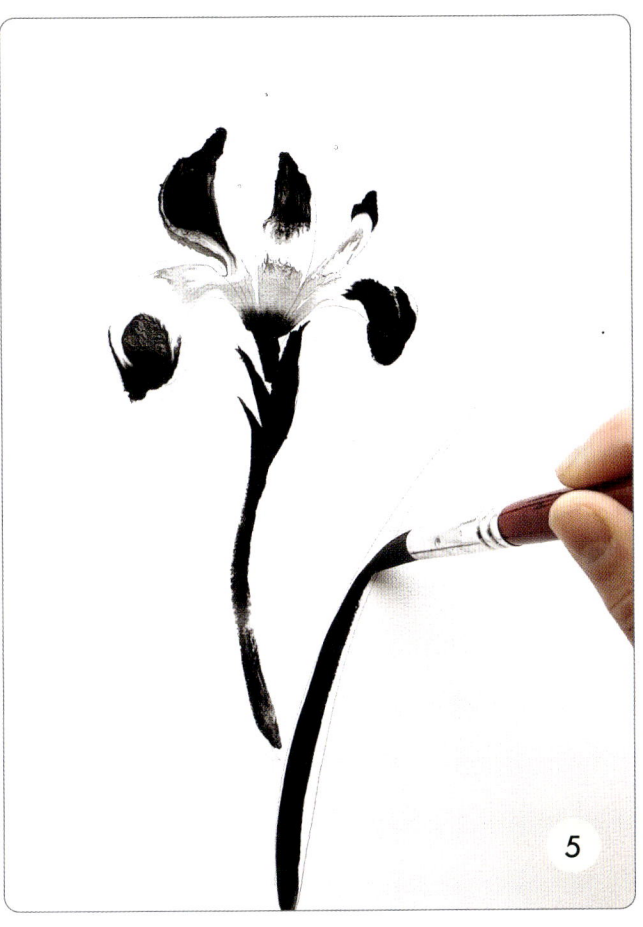

5 Dip the number 12 ink brush into the ink, and remove any excess by wiping it on the rim of the jar. Place the brush at the bottom of the leaf, and push down to paint a thick line. As you pull the brush up the leaf, press down less on the paper, and the line will naturally become thinner. Lift your hand from the page completely as you reach the tip of the leaf. Leave the painting to dry.

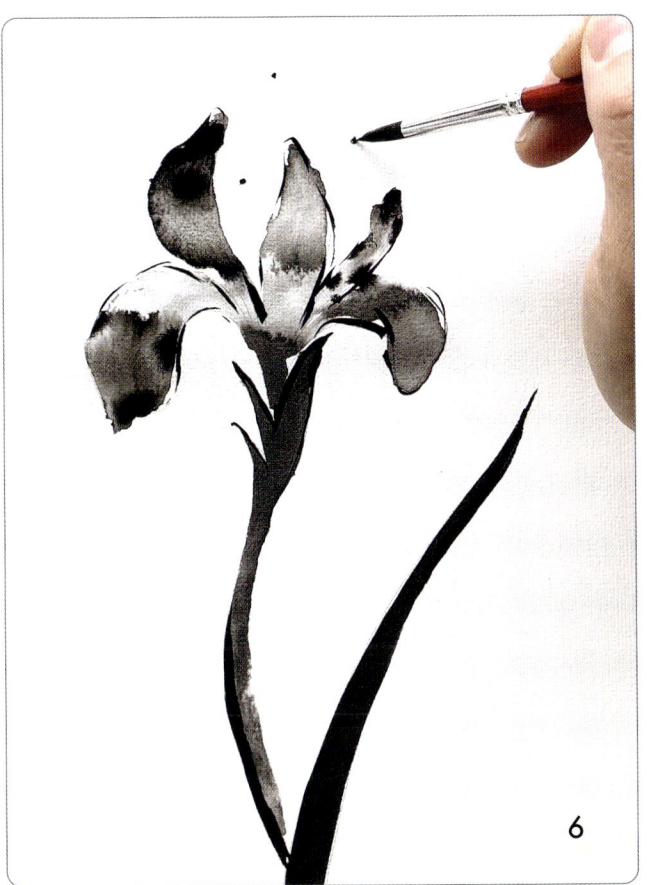

6 When the iris is about half dry, use the number 6 ink brush to neaten the edges of the petals. Using the tip of the brush and painting very lightly, cover any pencil lines that you can still see. Finish by touching the very tip of your brush to the paper to make the three dots.

EUCALYPTUS WREATH

I love the smell of gum leaves. After the rain, early in the morning, on a warm summer evening, or a crisp winter night, I step out into my garden on the edge of the Australian bush. I reach out and break off a small branch of eucalyptus, and it smells like home.

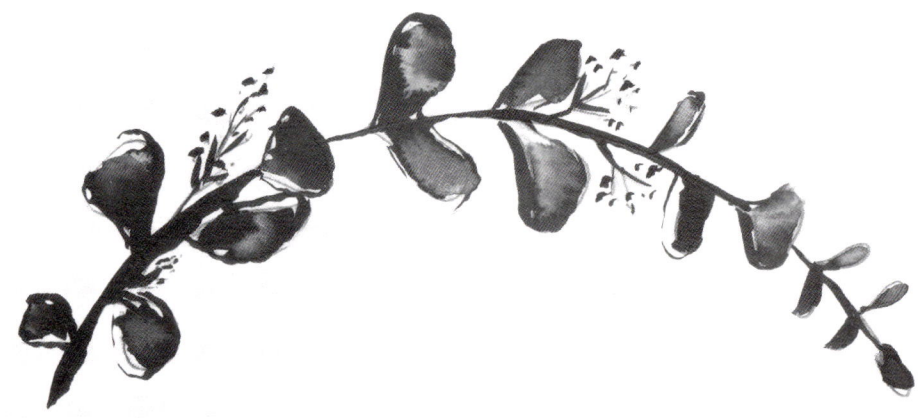

GROUNDING

Close your eyes, and find a comfortable sitting position. Take ten slow breaths, and with each breath, whisper something that reminds you of home. For me, it's gum leaves, my mum's apple tart, and Japanese barley tea. What is it for you?

BREATH

Remember to inhale when your brush is poised, ready to paint, and to exhale slowly as you place the brush on the paper and paint your line. In this project, there are a number of fine lines. When painting these, I like to hold my breath, as it seems to steady my hand. When I lift the brush from the page, I then exhale slowly. Sometimes when I exhale, it helps to look up from the page (I like to look out the window and beyond).

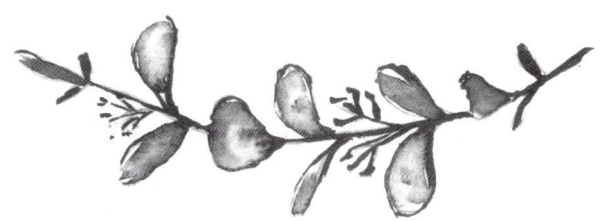

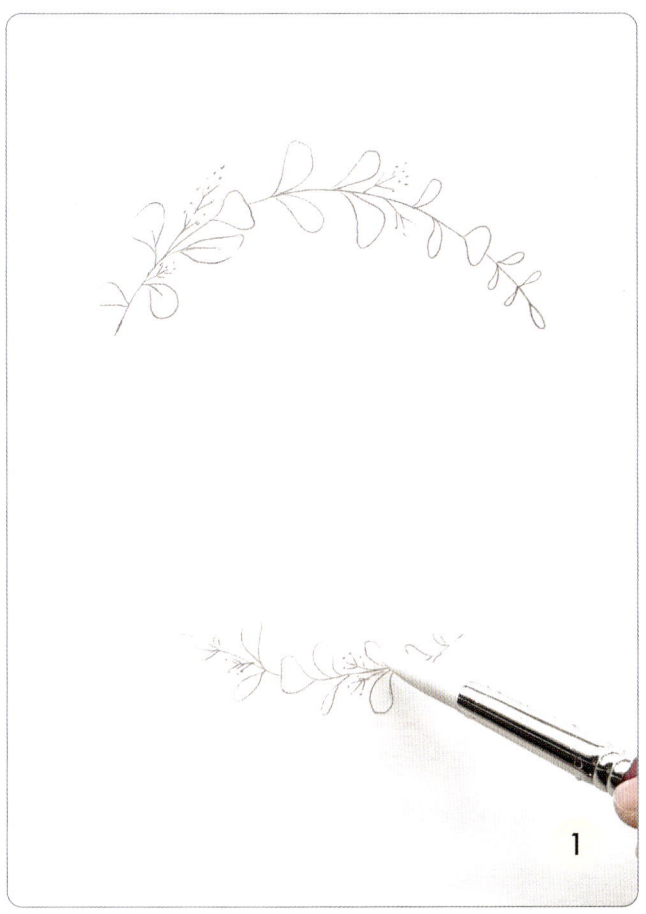

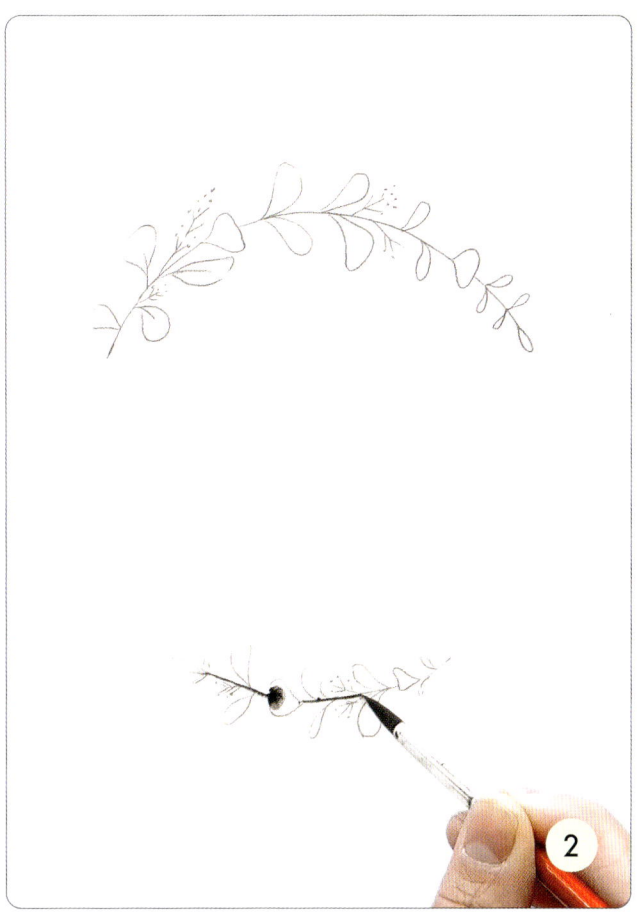

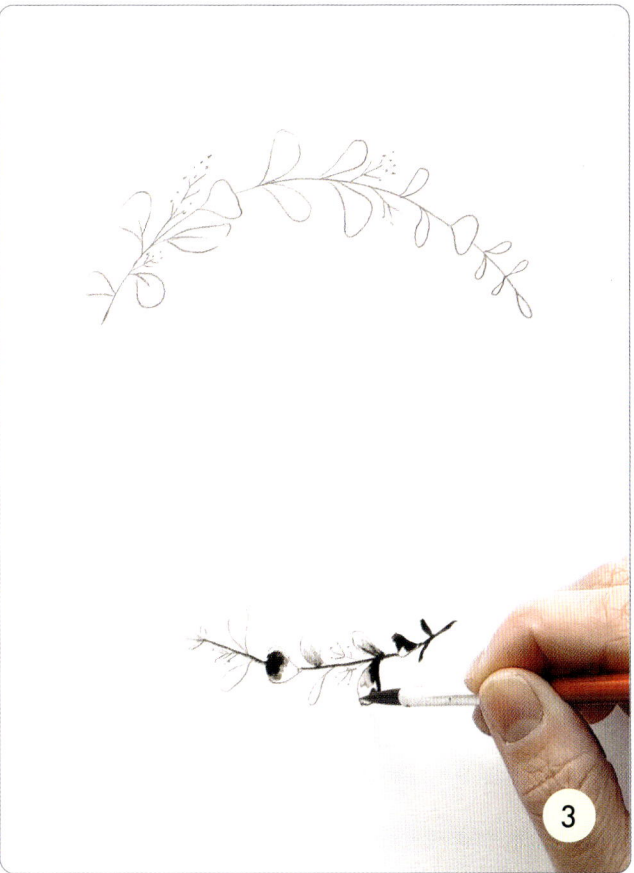

1 Trace the outline of the eucalyptus wreath on your page very lightly using your pencil. Dip the water brush into your clean water so it is well soaked. Remove excess water by wiping the brush along the rim of your water jar. Paint water inside the outlines of the eucalyptus leaves on the bottom branch. Do not paint any water on the stem or the tiny flowers—these remain dry.

2 Dip the number 6 ink brush into your ink, and remove excess ink by wiping the brush on the rim of the jar. Holding your hand quite high over the page, use just the tip of the brush to paint the stem of the bottom branch. You can do this in one slow stroke, or if you find it easier, you can break it up into parts. I am right-handed, so I paint left to right, but if you are left-handed, it will be easier to paint right to left.

3 Make sure your brush doesn't have too much ink on it. Wipe off any excess if needed. Using the very tip of the brush, lightly outline each of the leaves. Some of the ink will bleed into the water, and some will remain crisp and strong.

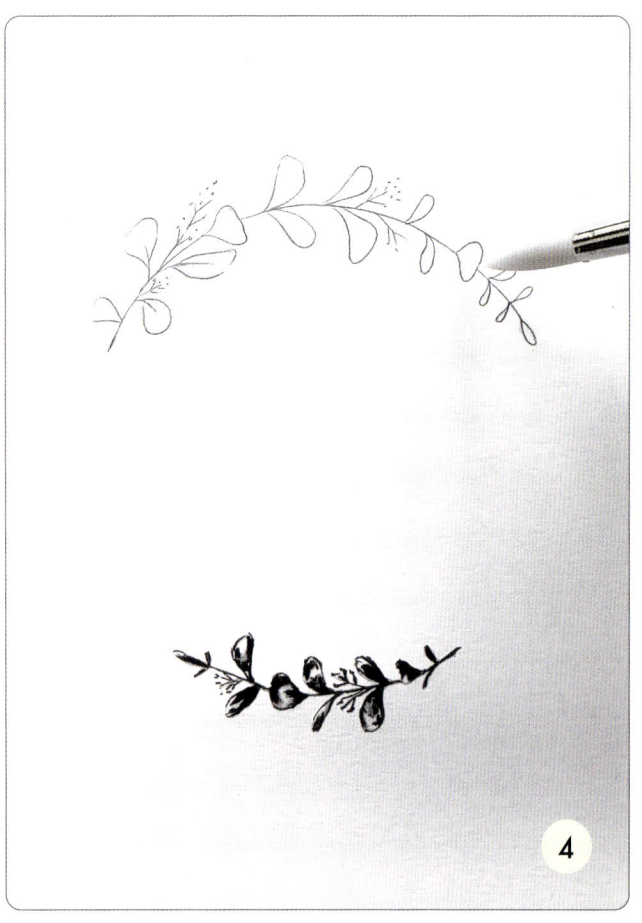

4 Use your water brush to paint water inside the leaves of the top branch.

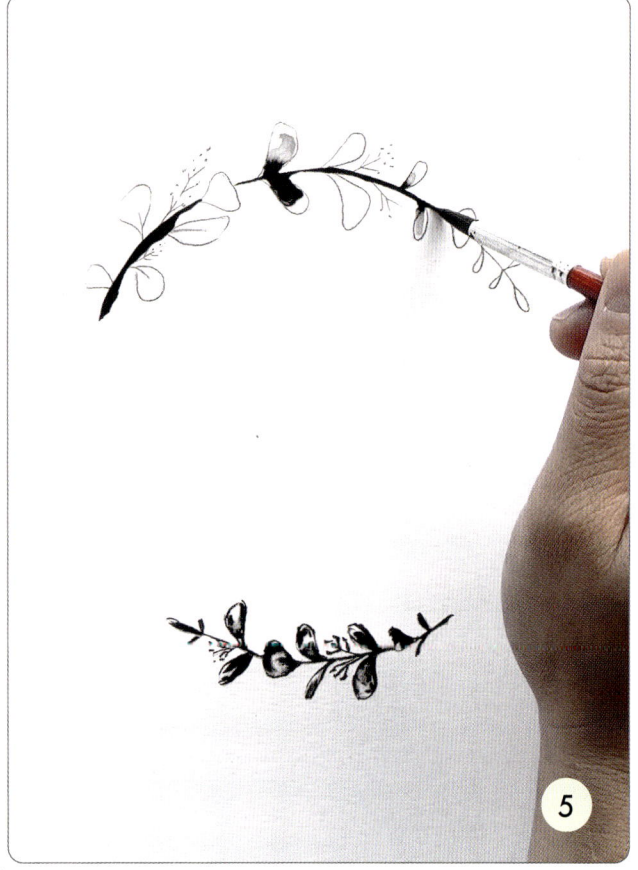

5 Dip the number 6 ink brush into your ink, and remove excess ink by wiping the brush on the rim of the jar. Holding your hand high above the page and using just the tip of the brush, paint a fine line along the top branch stem.

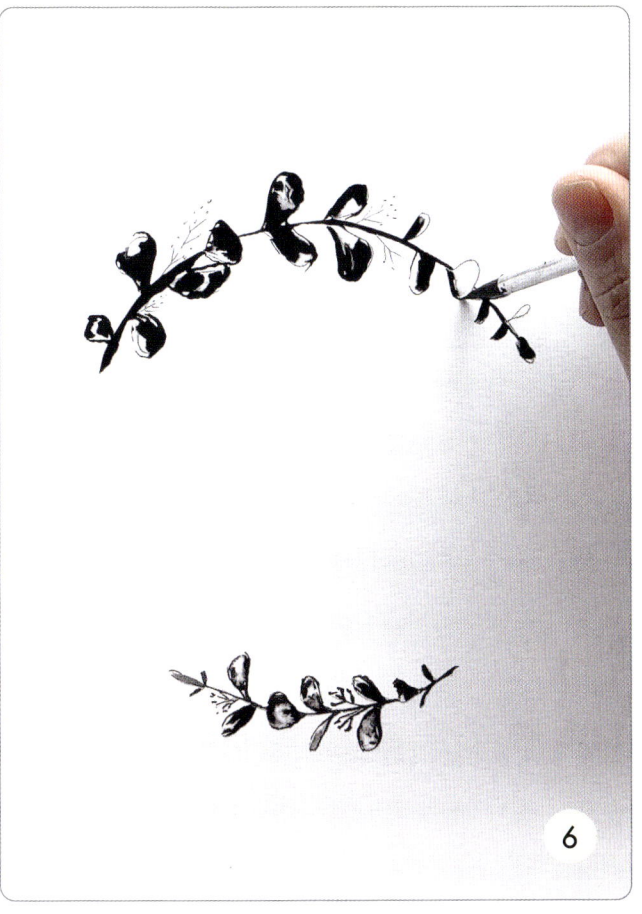

6 Remove any excess ink from your brush, and then using the very tip, lightly outline each of the leaves, just as you did with the lower branch.

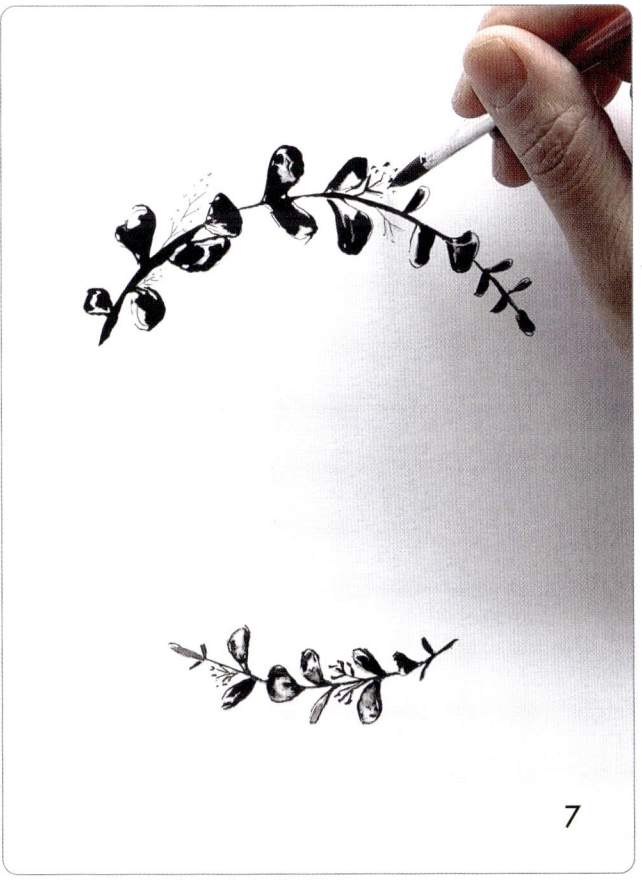

7 Make sure there is very little ink on your brush—you want it quite dry for this part. Positioning your hand high above the page, paint with the very tip of the brush to add in the little flower details.

QUEEN OF THE LAVENDER

This project is a celebration of bees. They flock to my garden in spring and summer with such enthusiasm that whole bushes and garden beds hum with their activity. They are fascinating to watch and are such an important part of my little home ecosystem.

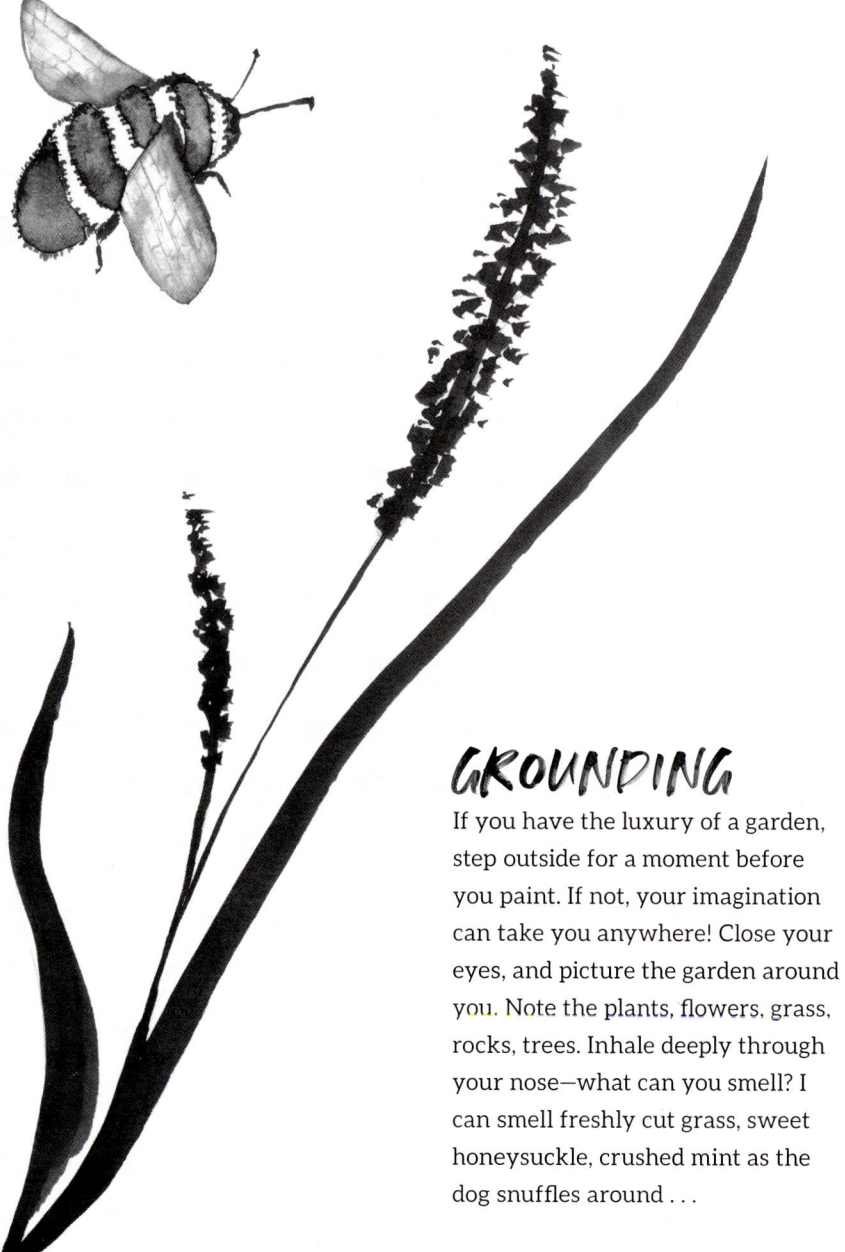

BREATH

This project combines long, flowing brushstrokes with short stippling marks. Adjust your breath to match your brushstrokes, exploring how deeply you inhale and how slowly you exhale.

GROUNDING

If you have the luxury of a garden, step outside for a moment before you paint. If not, your imagination can take you anywhere! Close your eyes, and picture the garden around you. Note the plants, flowers, grass, rocks, trees. Inhale deeply through your nose—what can you smell? I can smell freshly cut grass, sweet honeysuckle, crushed mint as the dog snuffles around . . .

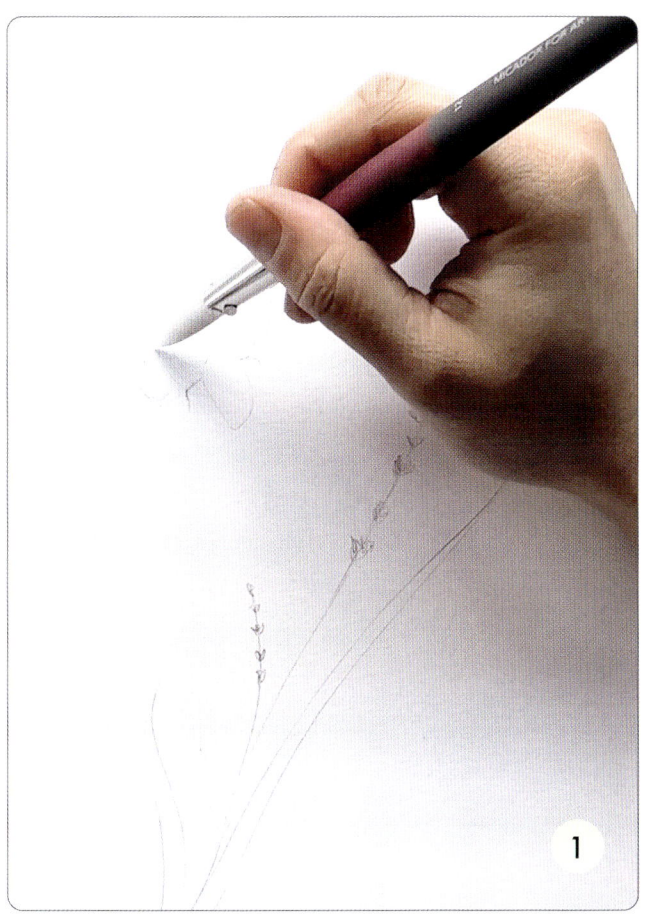

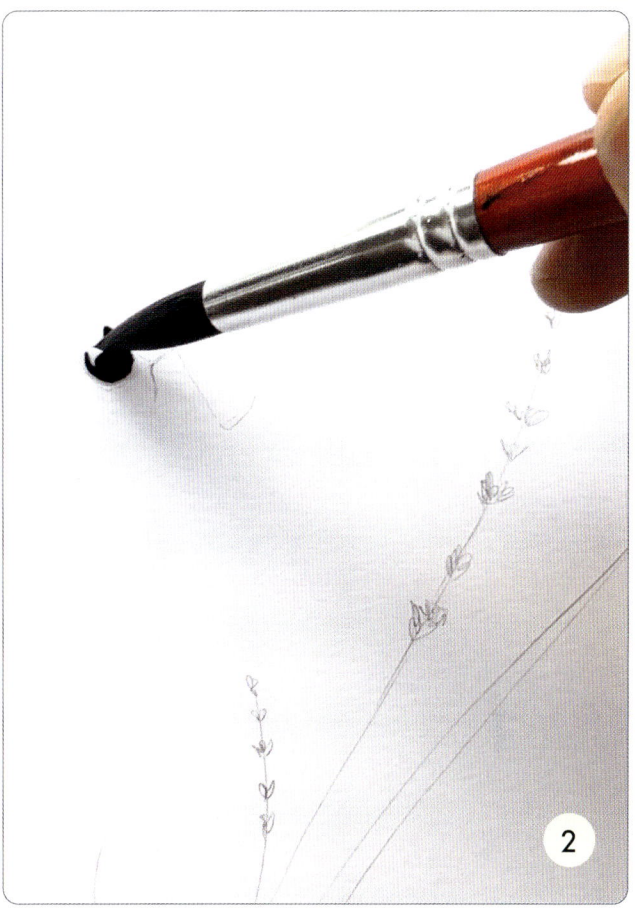

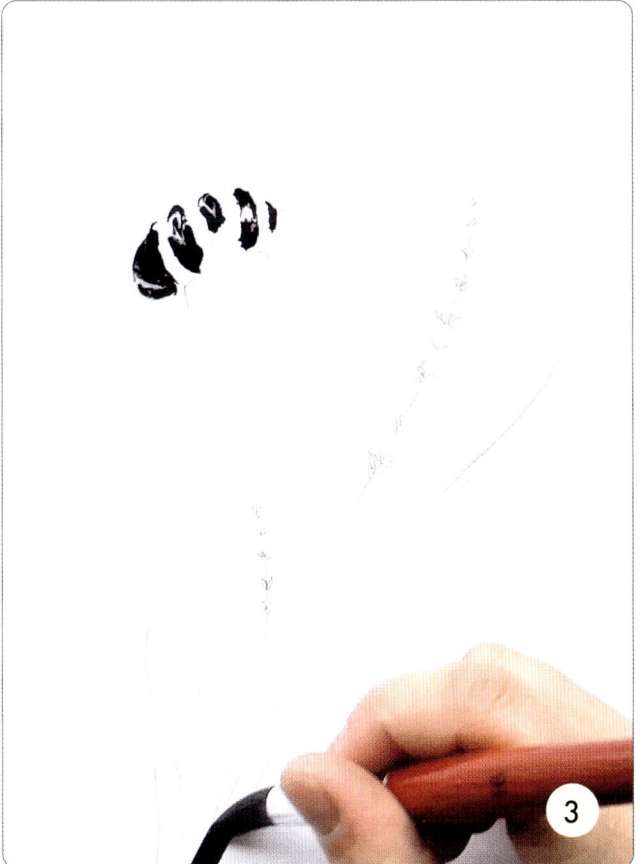

1 Trace the outline of the bee and flower on your page very lightly using your pencil. Dip the water brush into your clean water so it is well soaked. Remove excess water by wiping the brush along the rim of your water jar. Paint water inside every second stripe of the bee's body. You want to have water in the sections on each end of her body.

2 Dip the number 12 ink brush into your ink, and remove excess ink by wiping the brush on the rim of the jar. Drop ink onto each wet section of the bee by placing the tip of the brush on the water. If you find the number 12 ink brush too cumbersome, you can use the number 6. The larger sections of the bee's body will need more touches from the brush to make them black; the smaller section may only need one light touch.

3 Reload your number 12 ink brush, and using long, sweeping brushstrokes, paint over the pencil lines to create the leaves and stems of the lavender plant.

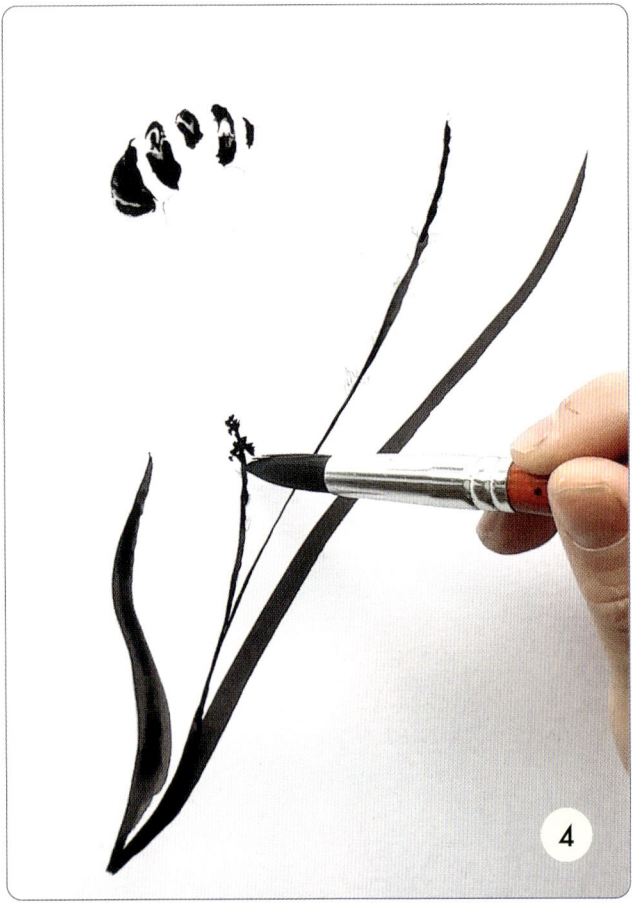

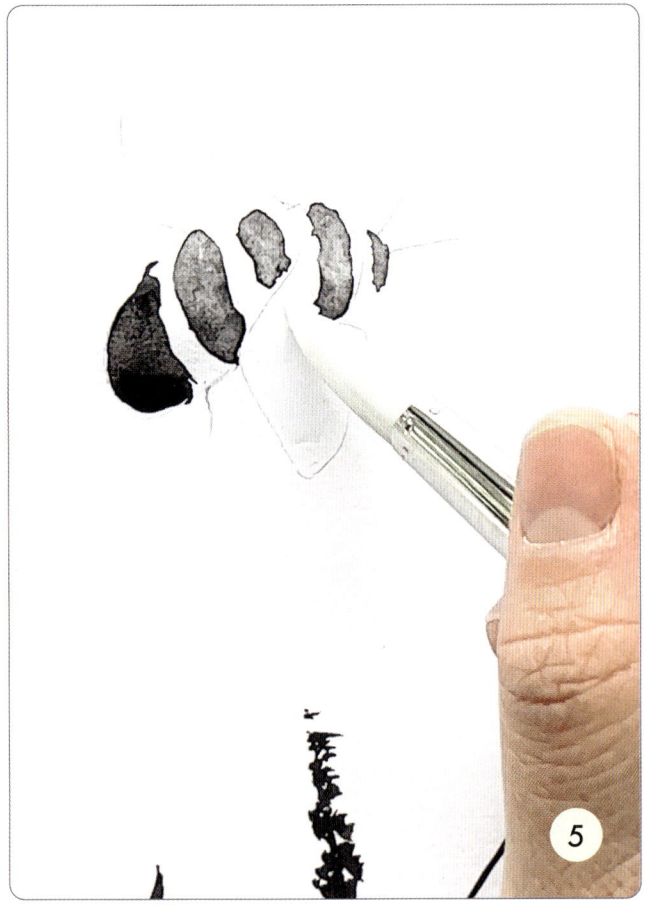

4 Using the tip of the number 12 ink brush, lightly dab irregular dots to create the flowers around the stem.

5 Once the body of your bee has dried, use your water brush to paint clean water in the bee's wings.

6 Dip the number 6 ink brush into the ink, and then remove most of the ink from the brush by dabbing on a paper towel. You don't want much ink on your brush at all. Using just the tip of the brush and holding your hand high above the page, lightly paint over the pencil outline around the edge of the wings. The ink will move into the center of the wings; allow it to move without touching it.

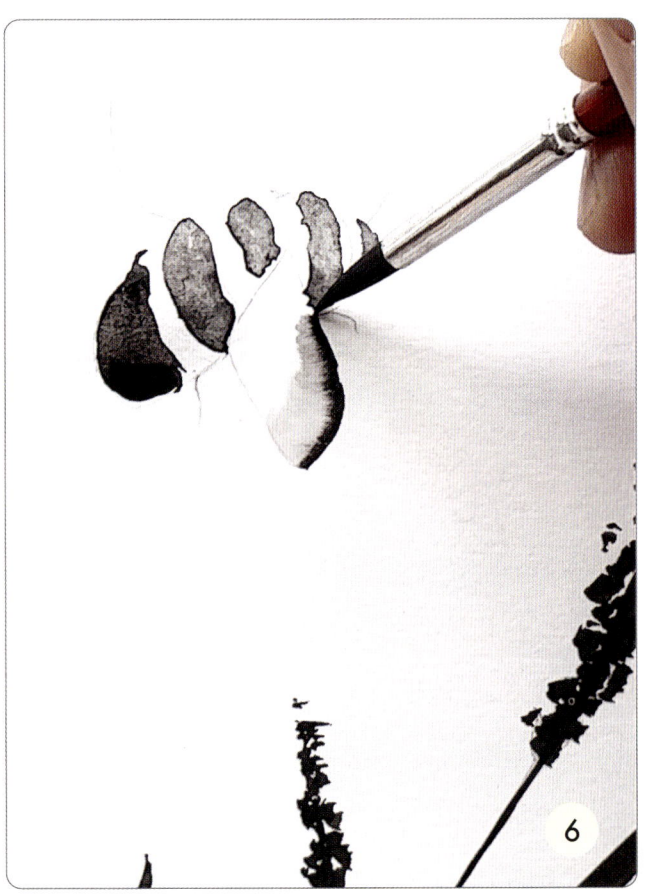

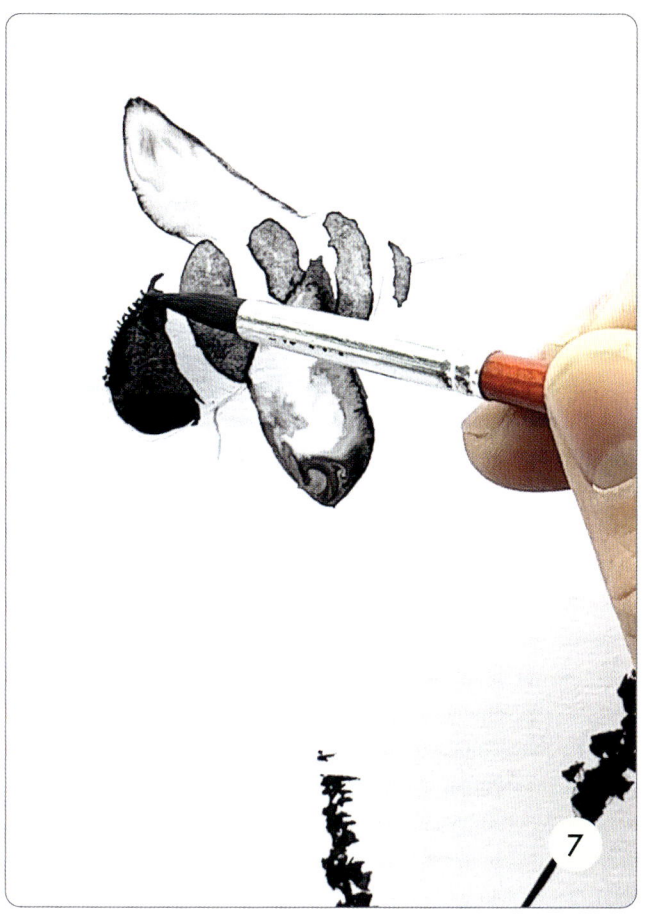

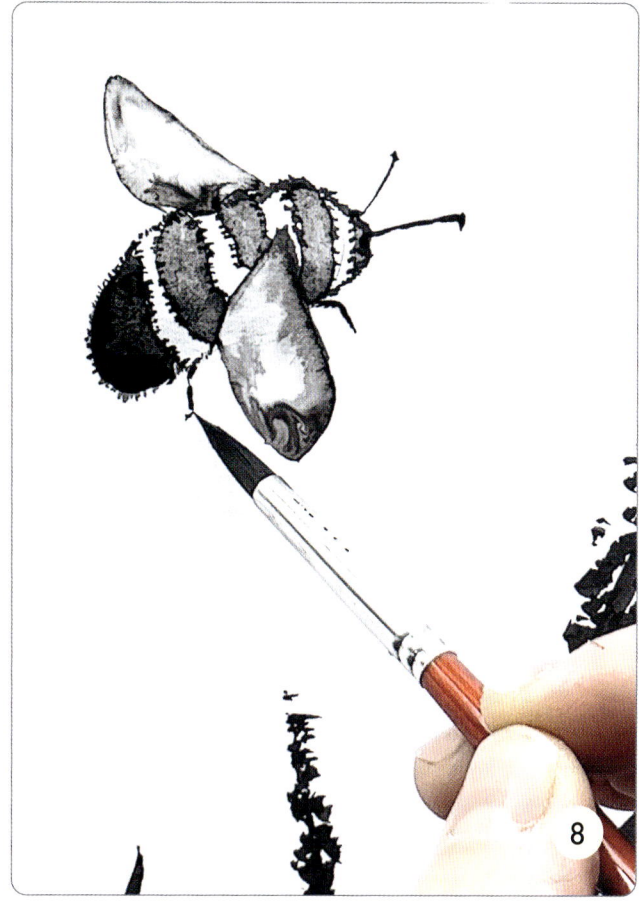

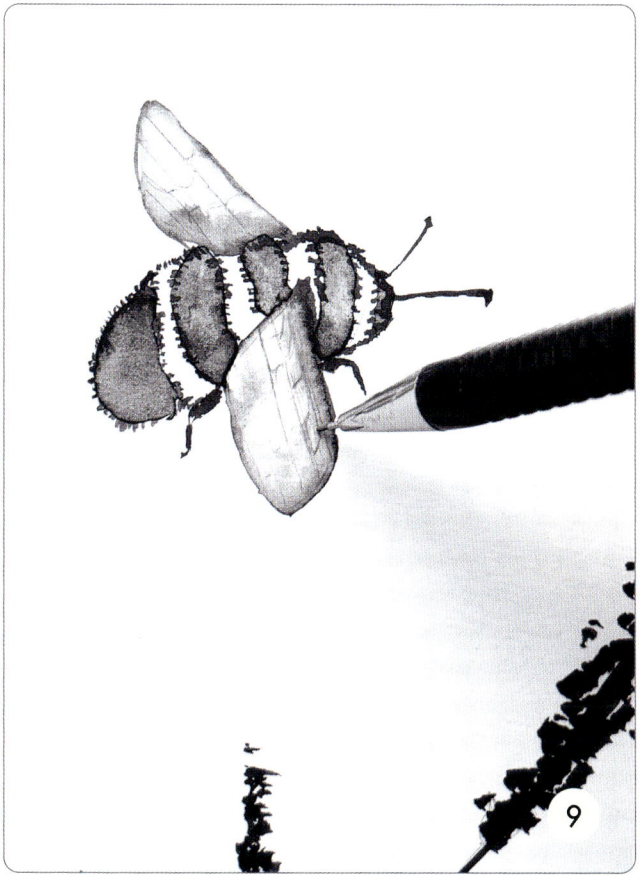

7 Now return to the black segments of the bee's body. Using the tip of the number 6 ink brush, add tiny hairs using very small brushstrokes around the edge of each black section. I make these tiny marks by having most of the brush on the already painted body so only the tip overlaps the edge.

8 Still using the number 6 ink brush with very little ink, paint in the fine details of the legs and feelers. Hold your brush lightly above the page, and it will be easier to get a fine line. If you have trouble using the brush, you can use a fineliner pen for this part.

9 Once your bee is completely dry, use your pencil to lightly draw lines on the bee's wings. I use a mechanical pencil, but you can also use a regular pencil—just make sure it is very sharp.

BUTTERFLY AMONG THE FLOWERS

Here we have the ephemeral and beautiful butterfly. Out in the real world, its beauty lasts such a short time, but here on the page, you can capture it permanently. The butterflies in my garden are particularly attracted to the bright and beautiful coneflowers with circular centers. If you have a favorite flower, you can easily swap it out for the ones on the template. Scan the QR code to watch me paint this project!

GROUNDING

If you can, position yourself near a window or a doorway, something you can look through to outside and beyond. Close your eyes, with your chin tucked to your chest. Take three deep breaths in this position. On the fourth breath, lift your chin, and open your eyes, looking out to the farthest point you can see. Breathe. Lower your eyes slightly, and focus on something a little closer, in the middle ground of your vision. Now lower your eyes again, and focus on your hands—move them around, watch how they move, think about the complex things they can do. They are truly extraordinary!

BREATH

This project has quite a few repetitive strokes for the petals and long fine lines for the stems. Before you begin, settle into an even breathing rhythm. I find this helps avoid tension when painting detail. It underpins the entire way I approach painting: how tightly I hold my brush, my posture, how close I bring my face to the page.

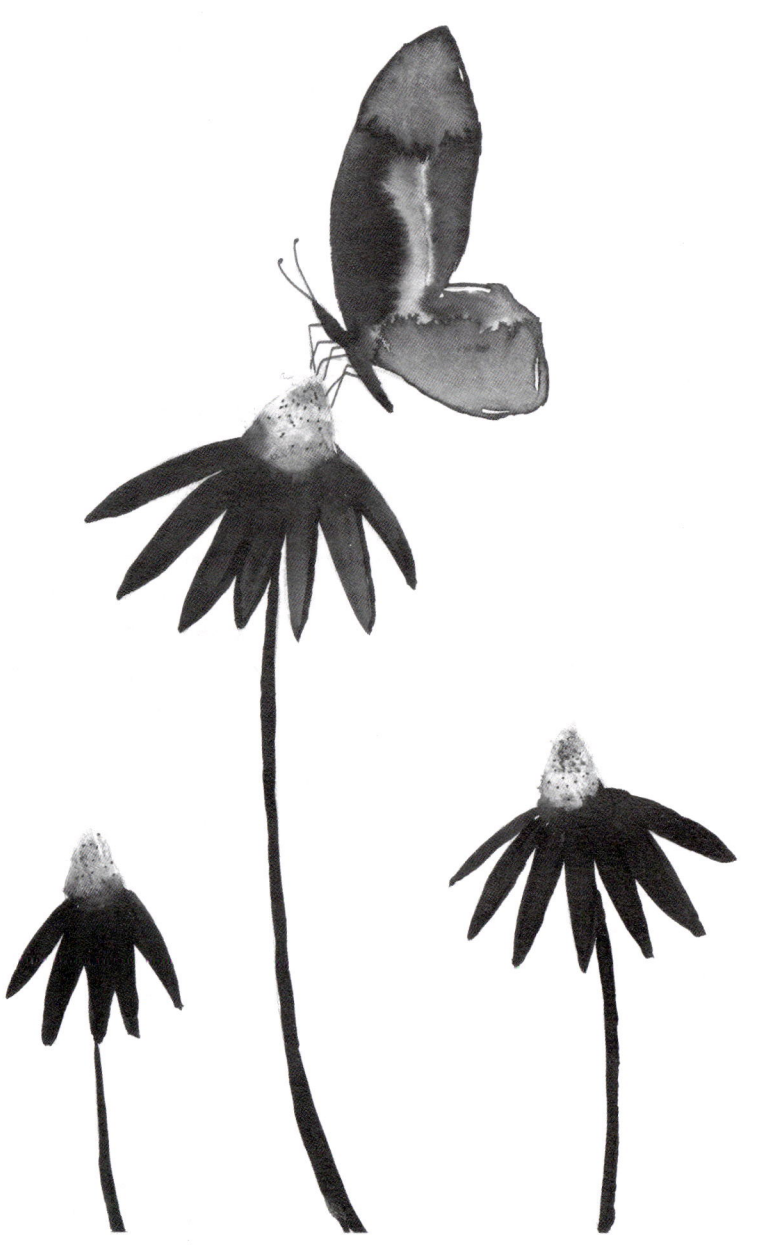

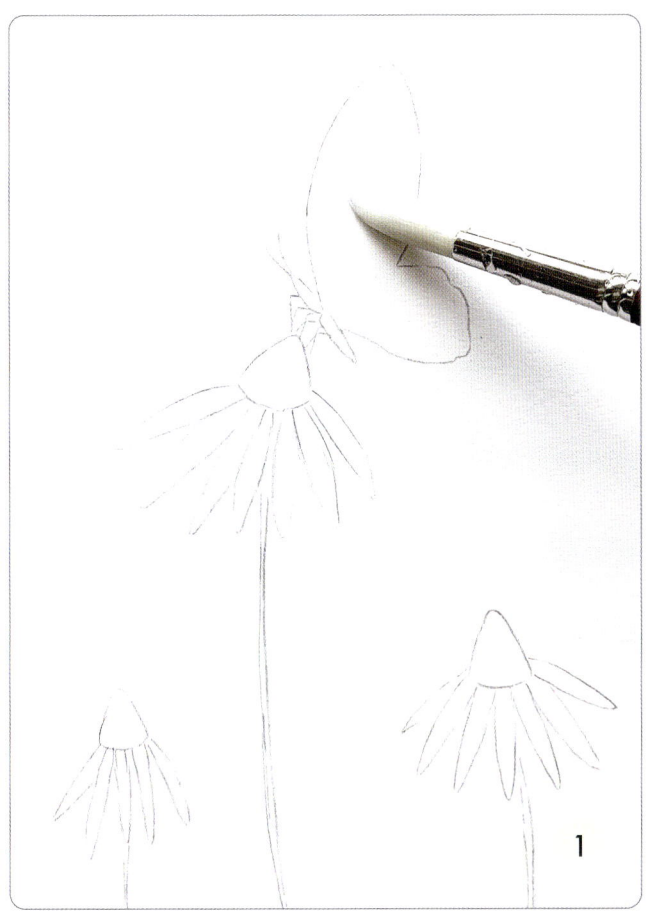

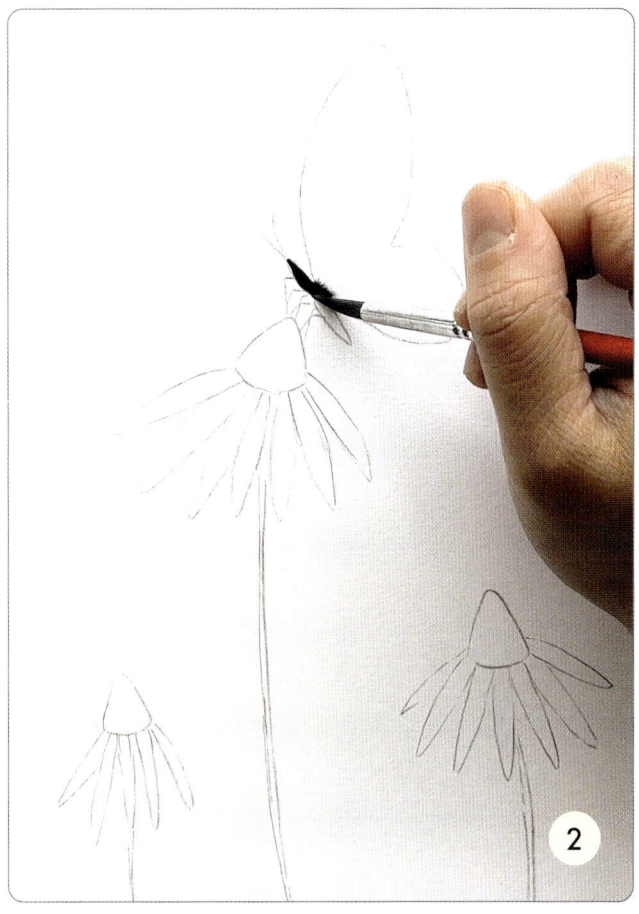

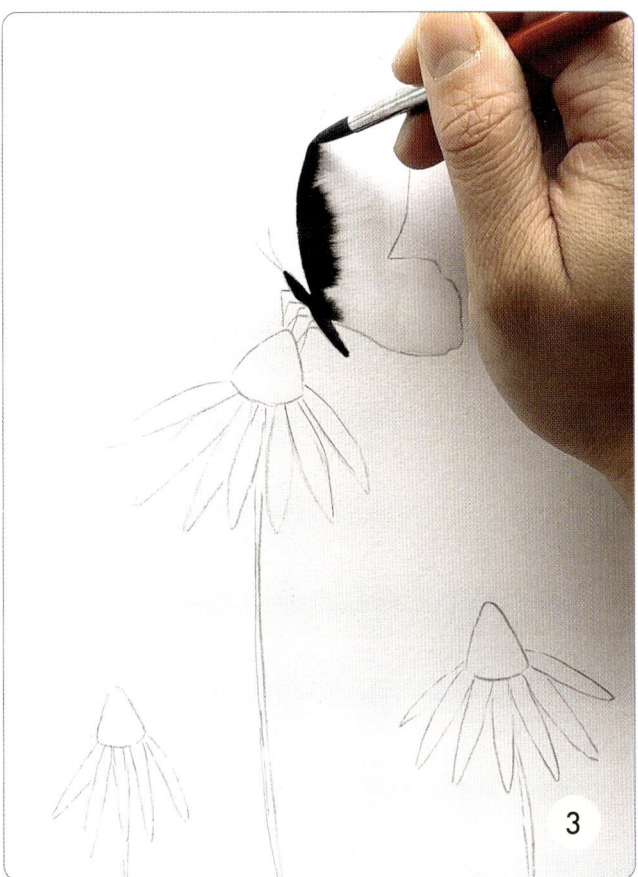

1 Trace the outline of the butterfly and flowers on your page very lightly using your pencil. Dip the water brush into your clean water so it is well soaked. Remove excess water by wiping the brush along the rim of your water jar. Paint water on the wings of the butterfly. Leave the body dry. Paint the cone centers of the flowers. Leave the petals and stems to dry.

2 Dip the number 6 ink brush into your ink, and remove excess ink by wiping the brush on the rim of the jar. Place the tip of your brush at the top of the butterfly's body. Paint a solid brushstroke to fill the butterfly's body. As the brush touches the water on the wings, the ink will bleed into the wings. Let the ink move freely through the water on the wings.

3 Holding your hand high above the page and using just the tip of the brush, paint an ink line around the edge of the wing, covering the pencil line. Some of this line will bleed into the water.

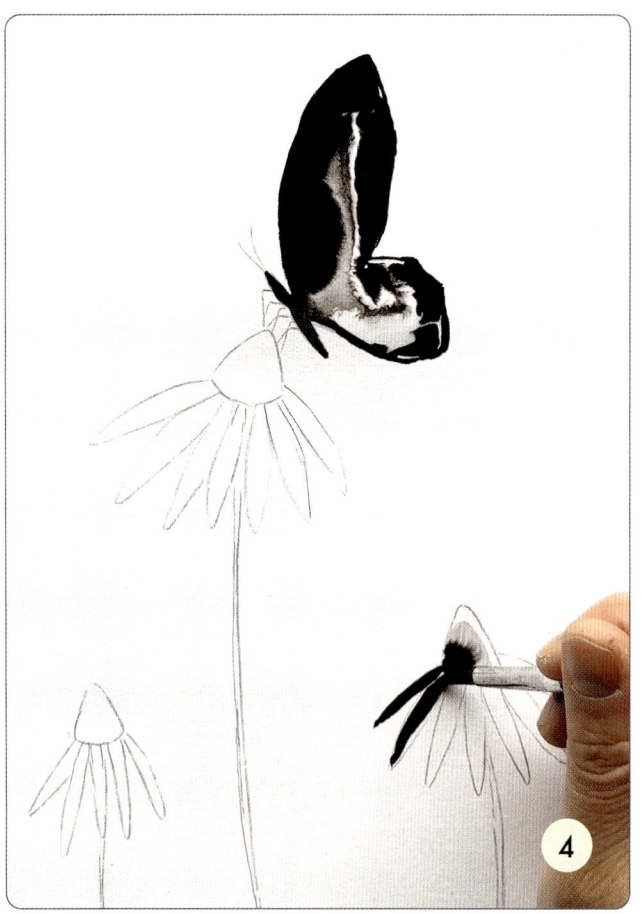

4 Wipe any excess water off the ink brush; it may have absorbed some water from the wings. Reload the brush, and paint in the petals. Start from the outside tip of the petal, and pull the brush inward, touching the brush just to the edge of the cone center so that ink bleeds into the water.

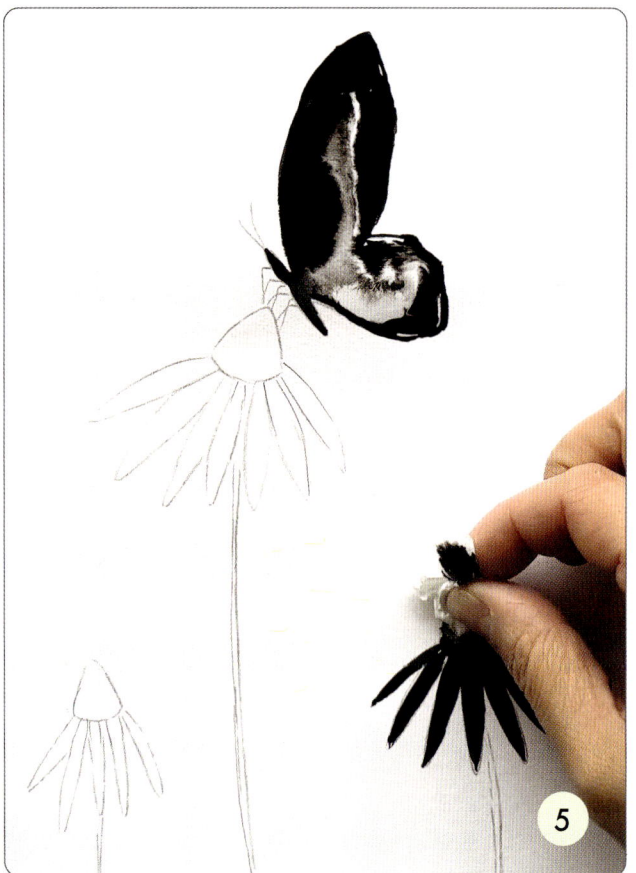

5 Take a small piece of paper towel, and dab some of the ink away from the cone center, creating a soft, fluffy texture.

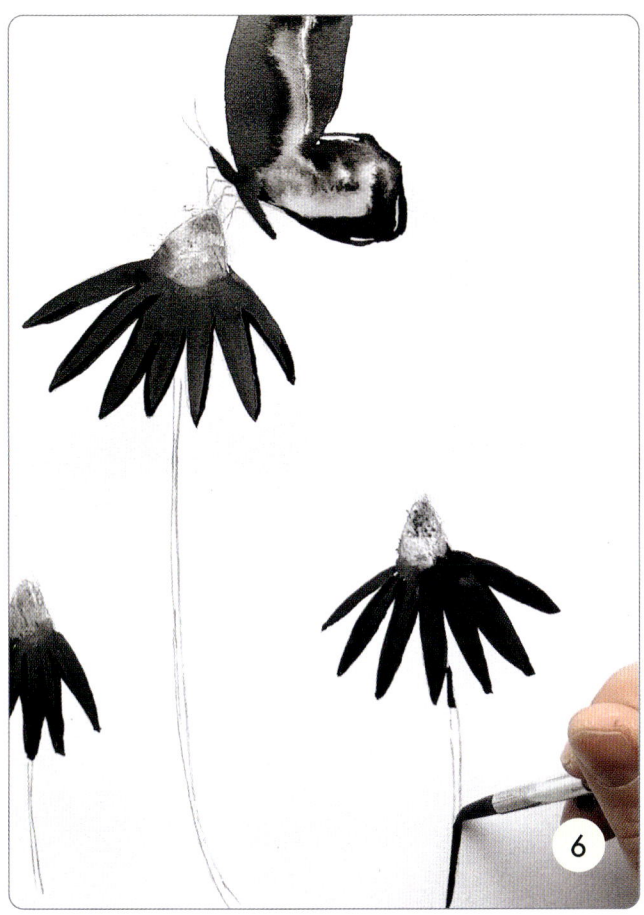

6 Reload your number 6 ink brush, and paint long strokes to make the flower stems. Keep your hand high and light on the page to paint a fine, steady line. Sometimes I find it easier to rotate the page so I am painting the line from a different angle.

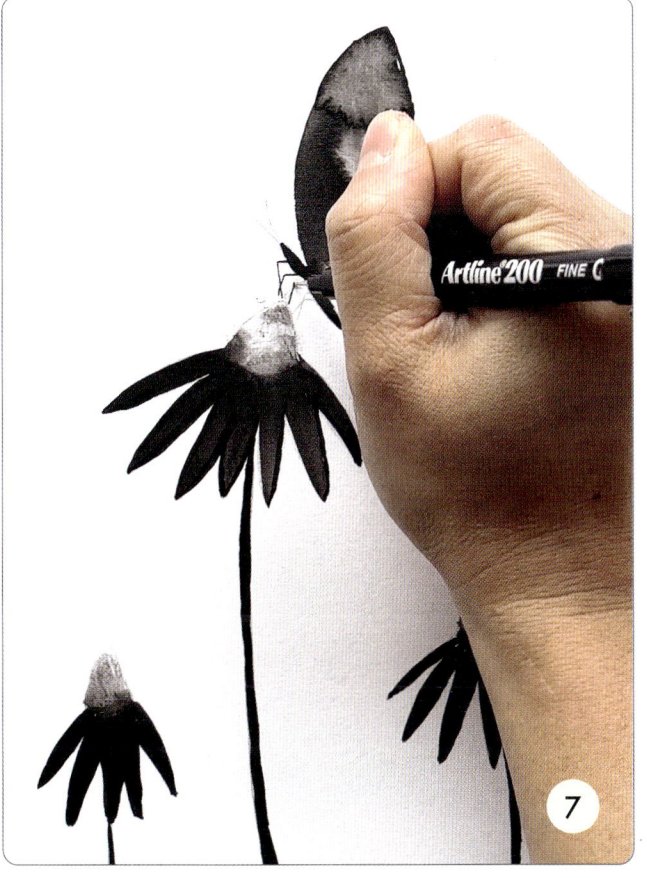

7 When the butterfly and flowers are completely dry, use a fineliner pen to draw in the legs and antennae, and then add some fine dots on the cone centers as a finishing touch.

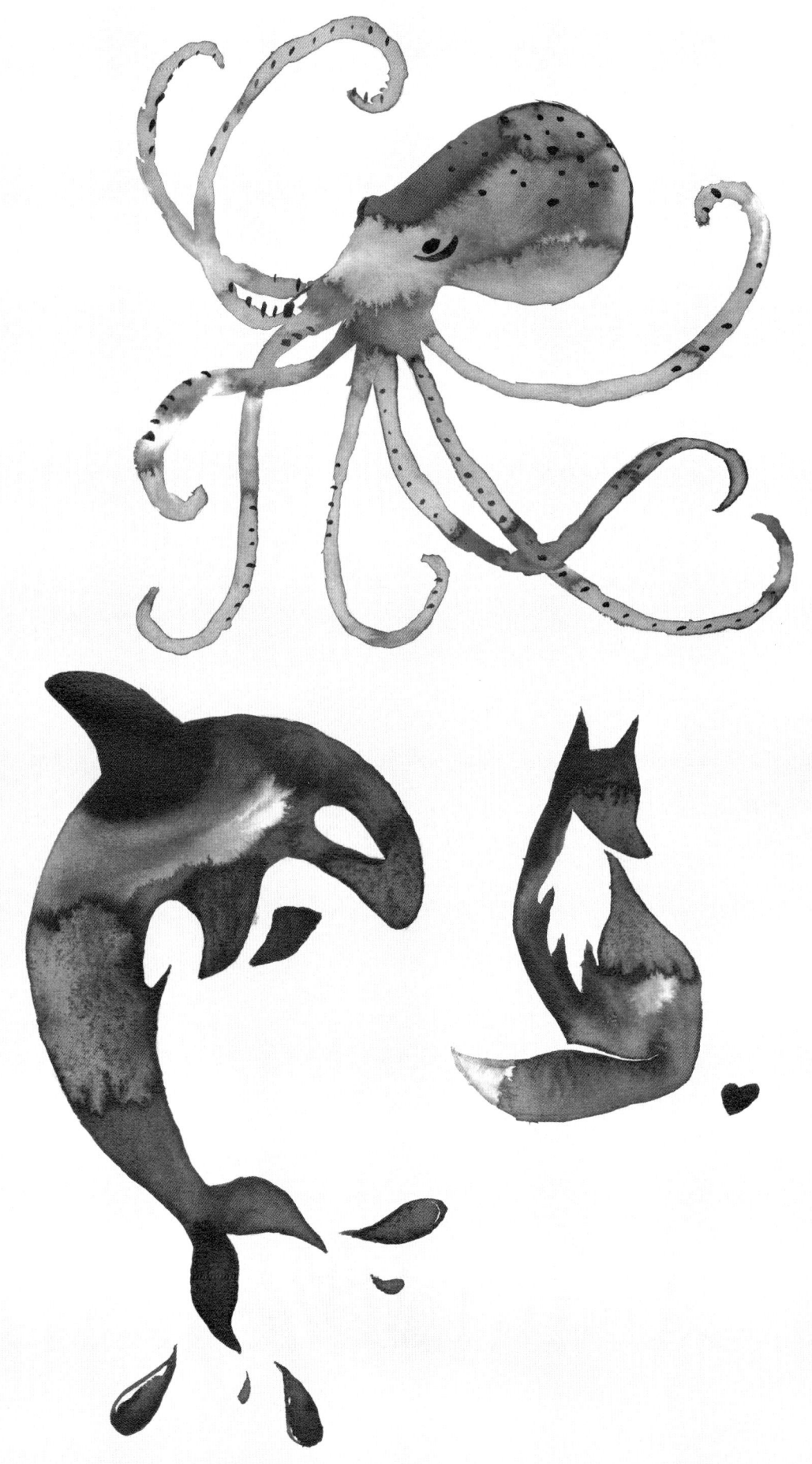

52

ANIMALS

I've grouped all the animals together in this chapter, but as with the plants, flowers, and insects of the previous section, the animals get a little more challenging as you go. From *Chat Noir* to Chonky Narwhal, you will begin to make more creative decisions around how much ink to add and how many touch-up brushstrokes you need. My biggest advice is to pause before adding more ink. It has a life of its own, and some of the best results come when you don't touch it too much and allow it to take shape naturally. The final projects in this chapter, beginning with Luminescence and ending with Miss Blackbird's Garden, bring a new level of intricacy. There are multiple elements, multiple layers, and more complex brush work. The key thing to remember with these projects is patience. Allow the ink to really move through the water before painting a new brushstroke, wait for things to dry properly before adding a new layer, and break the image down into manageable parts if you find them overwhelming. Go slow. Remember to breathe.

CHAT NOIR

Cats are glorious to paint and draw, and sumi ink captures their sleek, elegant nature so well. Black cats have a particular allure to them.

GROUNDING

Place your hands palms-down on the table in front of you. Inhaling through your nose and exhaling through your mouth, slowly roll your shoulders backward five times and then forward five times. Keep your palms on the table the whole time.

BREATH

Most of this project is painting fine lines along the pencil edges. I find this is made easier by breathing out slowly while I paint along the lines. Sometimes this means pacing how much breath I release—I find it easier to breathe out through slightly pursed lips or to count as I exhale.

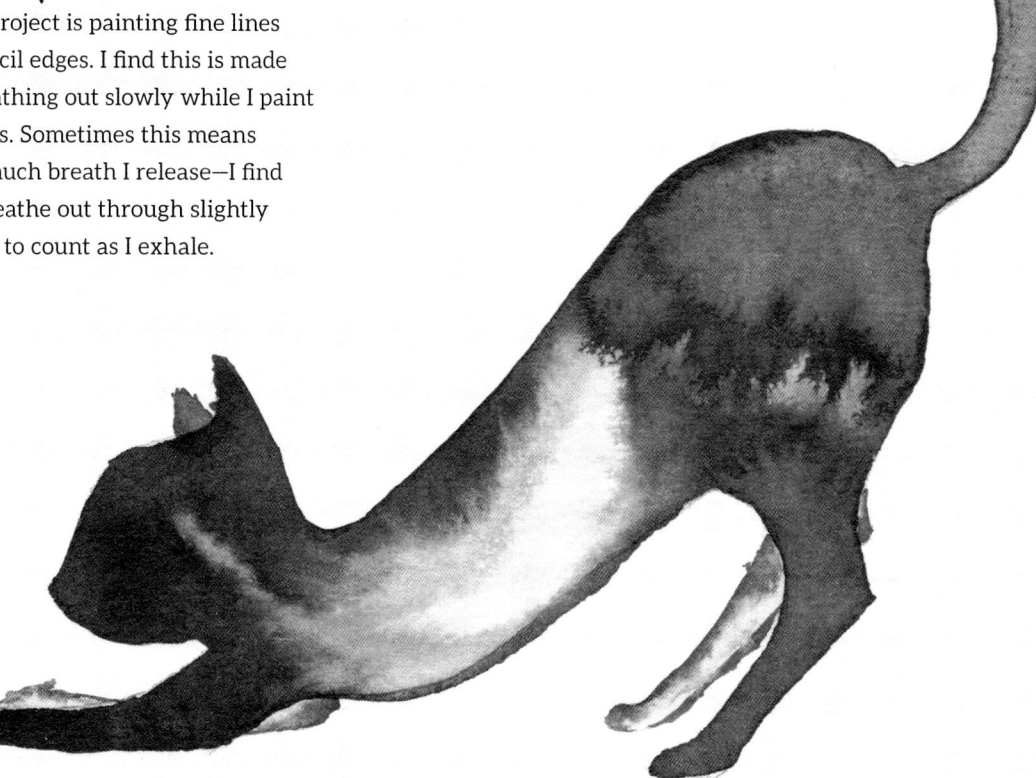

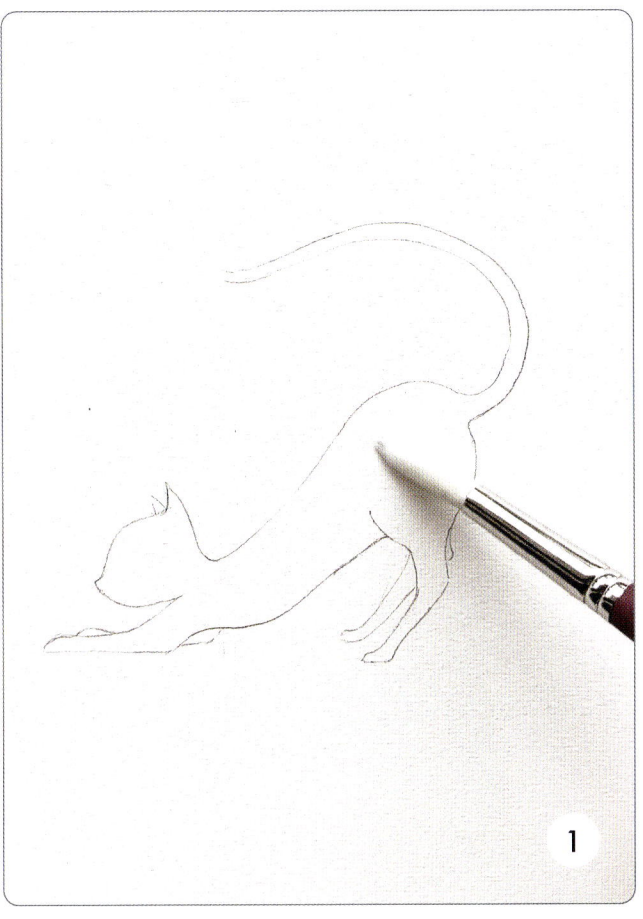

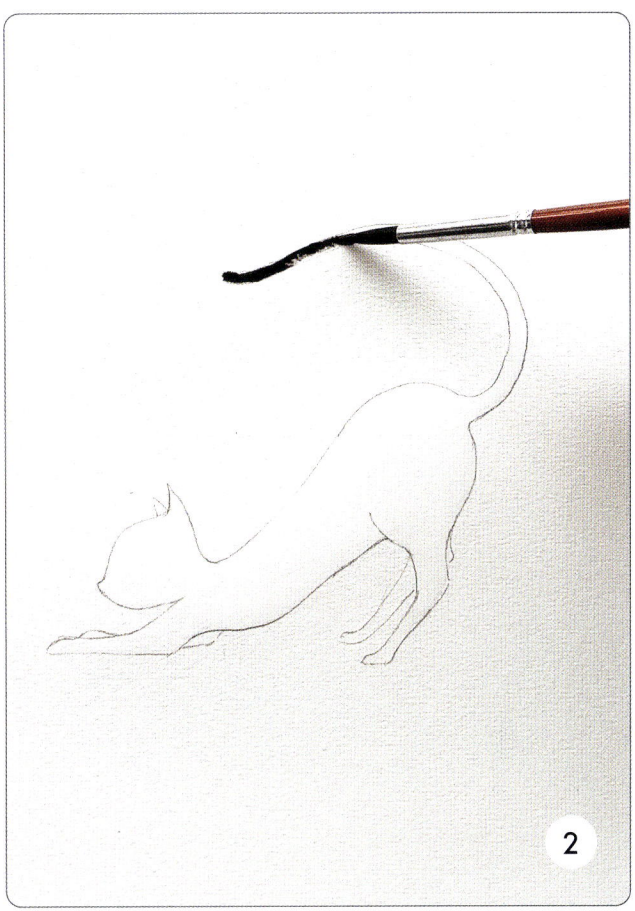

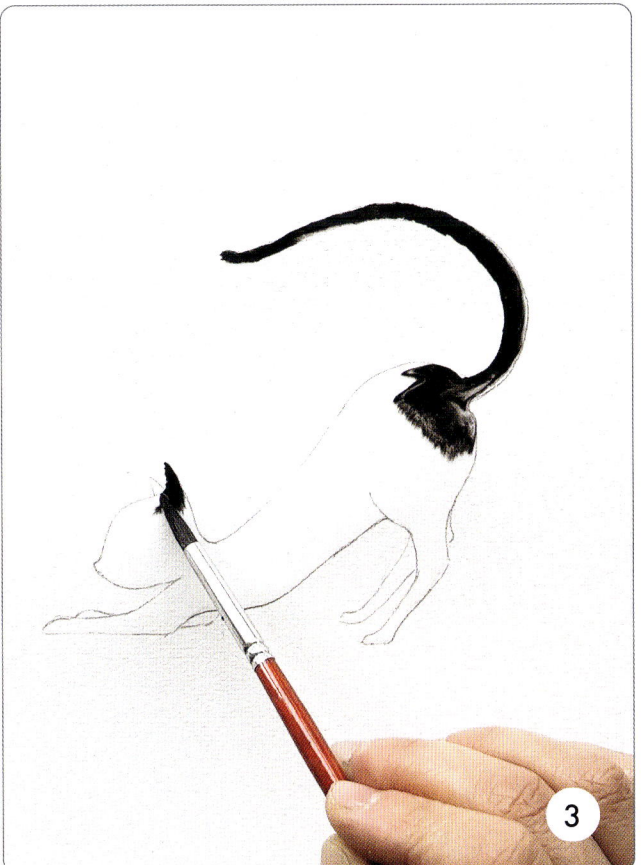

1 Trace the outline of the cat on your page very lightly using your pencil. Dip your water brush onto the water, and remove any excess by wiping it on the rim of the jar. Paint water onto the main body and tail of the cat, leaving the cat's right-hand paws and ear dry.

2 Dip your number 6 ink brush in the ink, and remove excess ink by wiping it on the rim of the jar. Pull the brush down through the tail until you reach the cat's bottom. Lift the brush as the ink moves into the water of the main body.

3 Using the tip of the brush, paint ink onto the wet ear. Then pull the brush down along the cat's forehead and nose, all the way under the chin. The ink will move into the water you have already painted on the face.

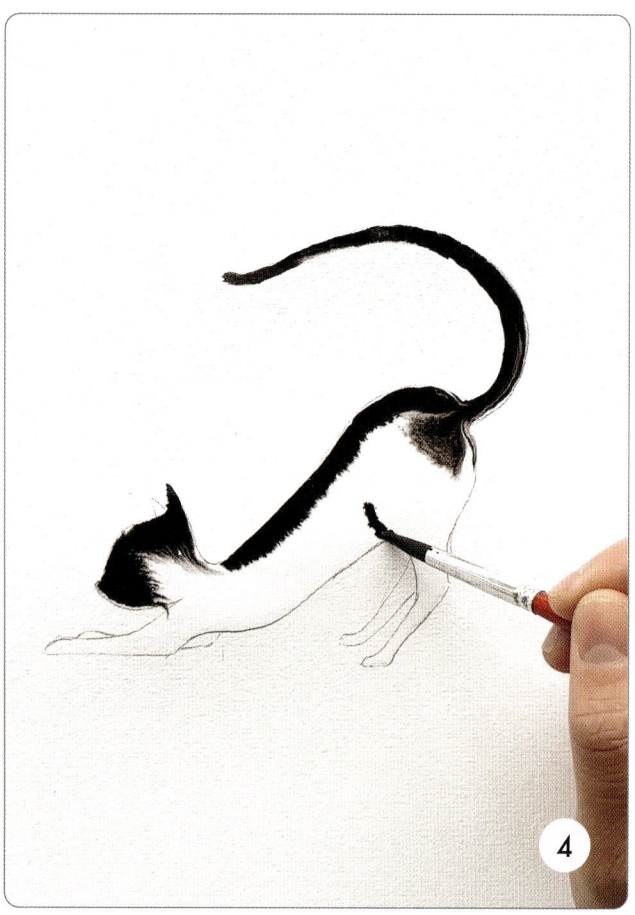

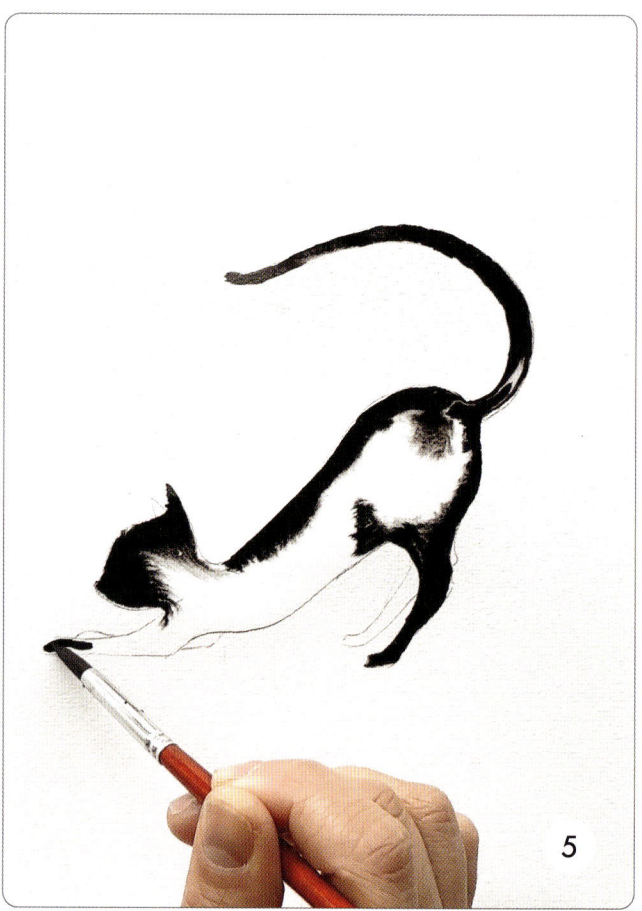

4 Reload your number 6 ink brush with ink, and remove the excess ink. Place the tip of the brush on the pencil line of the cat's upper thigh, and pull the brush all the way down to the paw. If the ink hasn't naturally spread along the pencil line connecting the cat's leg and tail, you can fill this in now.

5 Place the tip of the brush on the tip of the front paw, and paint along the bottom of the paw line, all the way up the chest and underbelly to the back leg.

6 Clean up any lines you have already painted by gently passing the number 6 ink brush along the edges. I find it often helps to rotate my page, as I can have my hand at a better angle. Put the painting aside to dry.

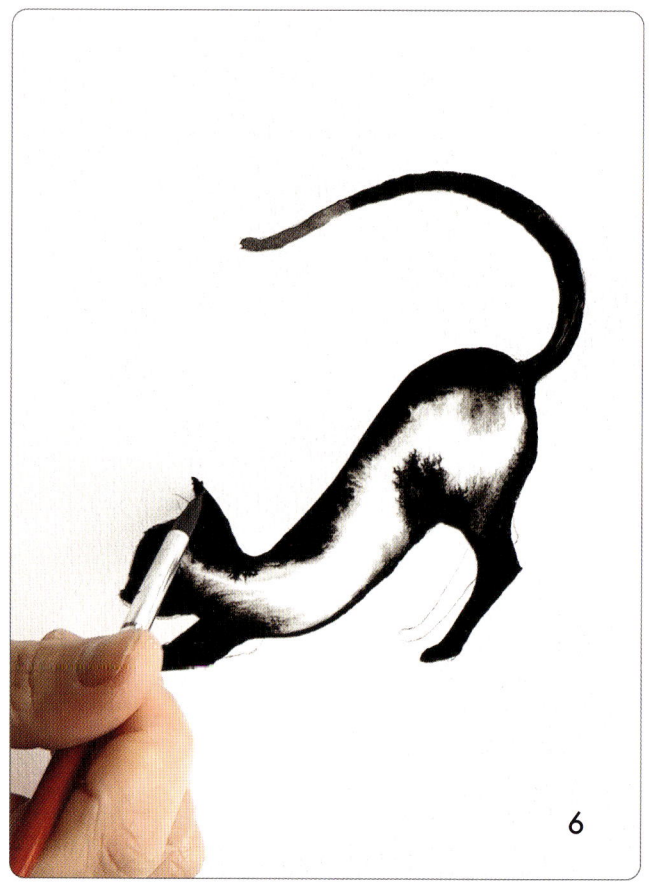

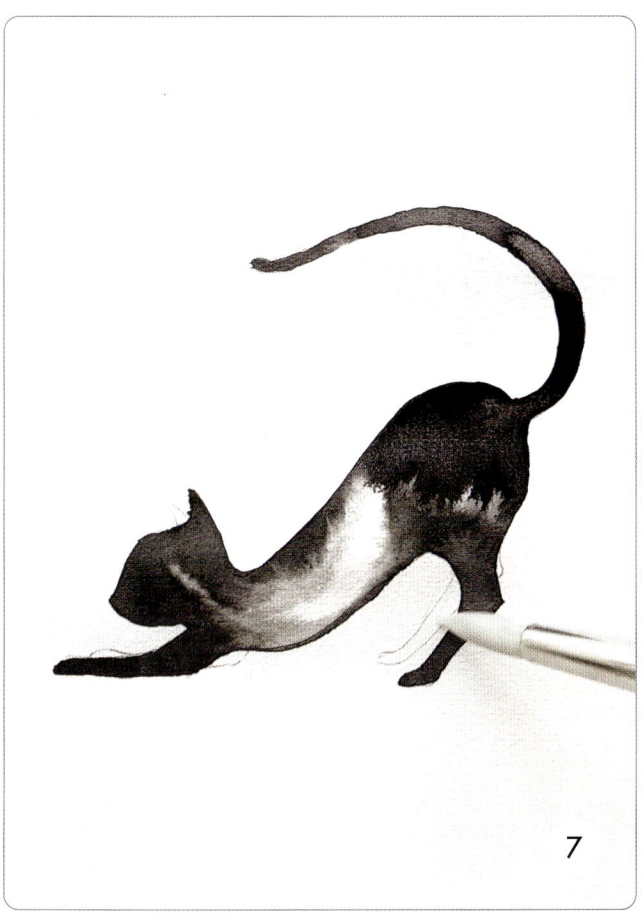

7 Once dry, take your water brush, and paint water on the remaining leg and ear.

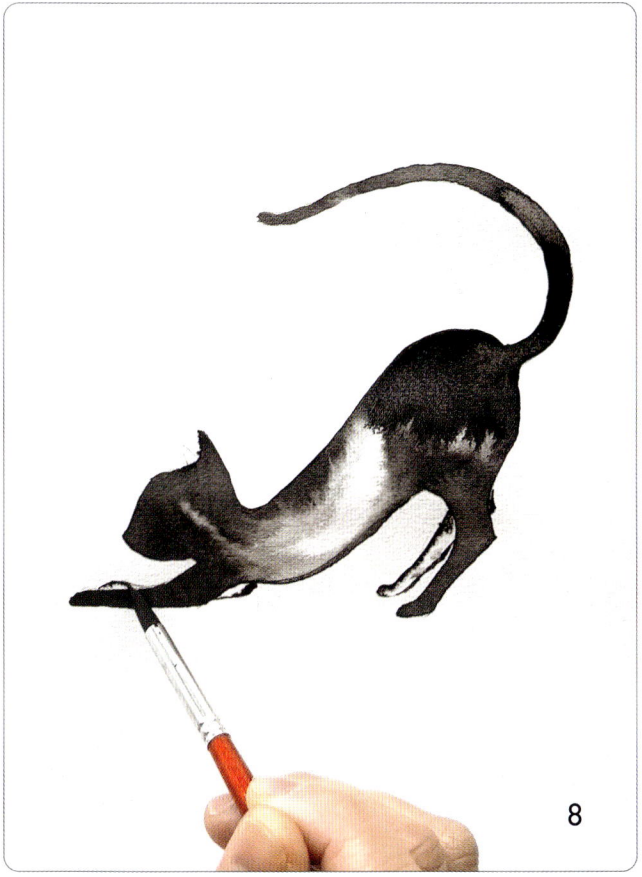

8 Dip your number 6 ink brush in the ink, and remove any excess. Very lightly, paint a fine line around the remaining paws and ear so the ink fills in the water you just painted. Be careful not to have too much ink on your brush for this part, as the legs and ear are very small details.

FRANK THE SAUSAGE DOG

Dogs bring me such joy. I love going to a dog park and seeing all the pups running around, playing, wrestling, adventuring. It's a guaranteed dopamine boost for me, and I always come away feeling happier. This project celebrates the joy of pups—this is Frank, he is a sausage dog, and he is loving life. Scan the QR code to watch me paint this project!

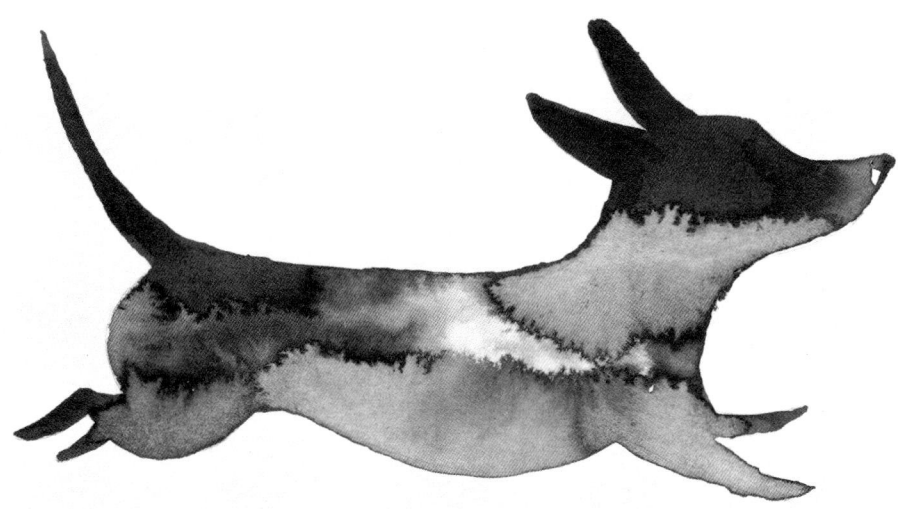

GROUNDING

While sitting in your chair, plant your feet firmly on the floor. Gently stamp each foot on the floor, alternating them to create a steady rhythm. Match your breath with this rhythm. Inhale for four stamps, hold for four stamps, exhale for four stamps. You might try speeding up your stamping or slowing it down. Breathe and stamp for at least one full minute before you start this project.

BREATH

There are a couple of fine lines in this project, and when I paint these, I like to hold my breath—I find it gives me a steadier hand. If you are going to hold your breath while you paint, remember to inhale deeply and exhale slowly. Each time I've painted a line holding my breath, I like to exhale and then pause my painting, taking a few breaths in and out to reestablish my breathing.

1 Trace the outline of the dog on your page very lightly using your pencil. Dip the water brush into your clean water so it is well soaked. Remove excess water by wiping the brush along the rim of your water jar. Paint water inside the pencil lines of the dog, except for the tips of his paws and his tail; leave these dry.

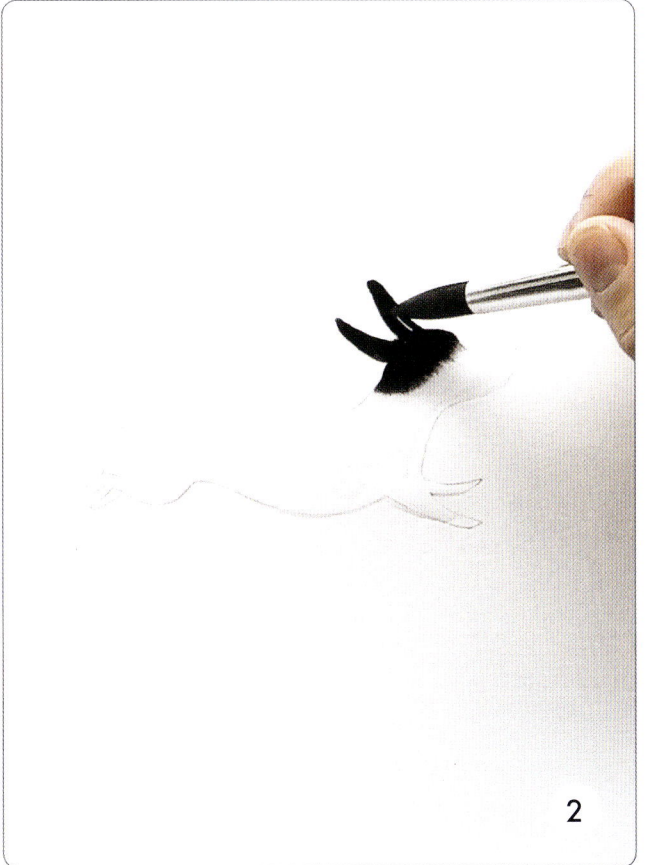

2 Dip the number 6 ink brush into your ink, and remove excess ink by wiping the brush on the rim of the jar. Start by placing the tip of the brush at the tip of the dog's ear, and pull the brush down until you reach his head. Repeat with both ears.

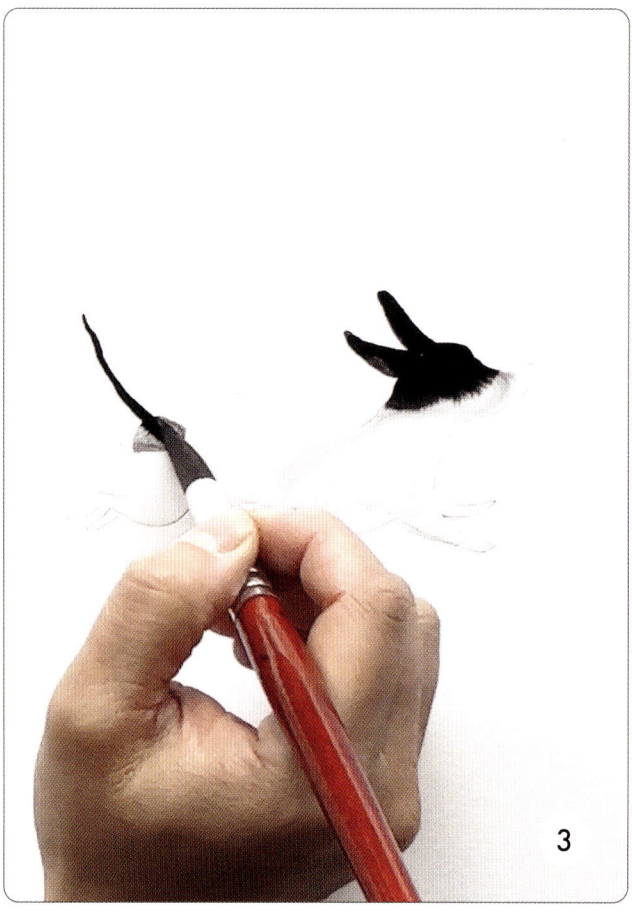

3 Still using your number 6 ink brush, make sure it doesn't have too much ink on it. Wipe it on a paper towel to remove excess ink if need be. Place the very tip of the brush at the tip of the dog's tail, which does not have water on it. Pull the brush down toward the dog's body until you reach his bottom. The ink will start to spread through the water on his body.

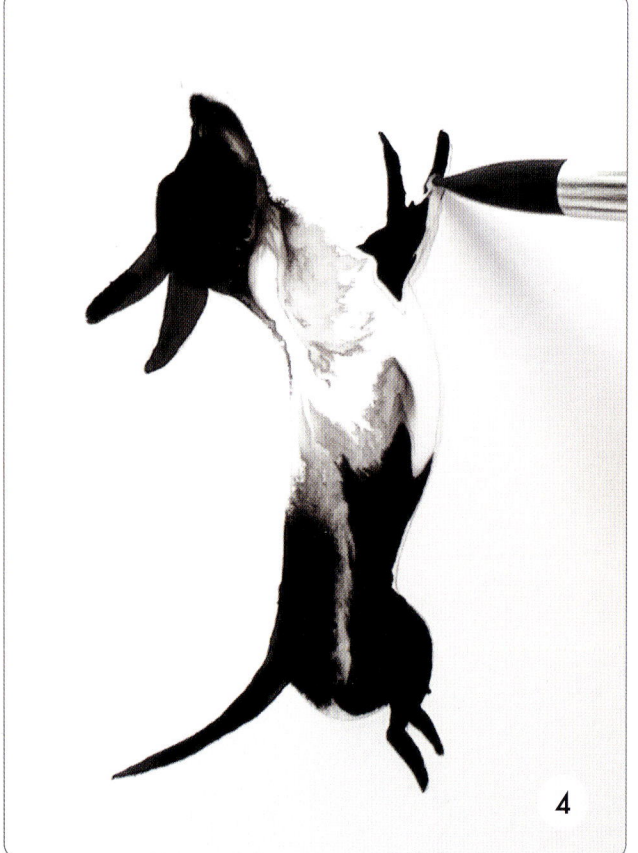

4 Using the fine tip of the brush, paint in the tips of the dog's paws, pulling the brush toward his body, stopping when the ink and the water touch. Sometimes with small strokes like the paws, I like to rotate the page to get a better angle. Take the time to observe how the ink moves within the water. You can always add more ink if you feel there are too many white spaces, but be sure to only add a small amount at a time or your dog could end up completely filled in.

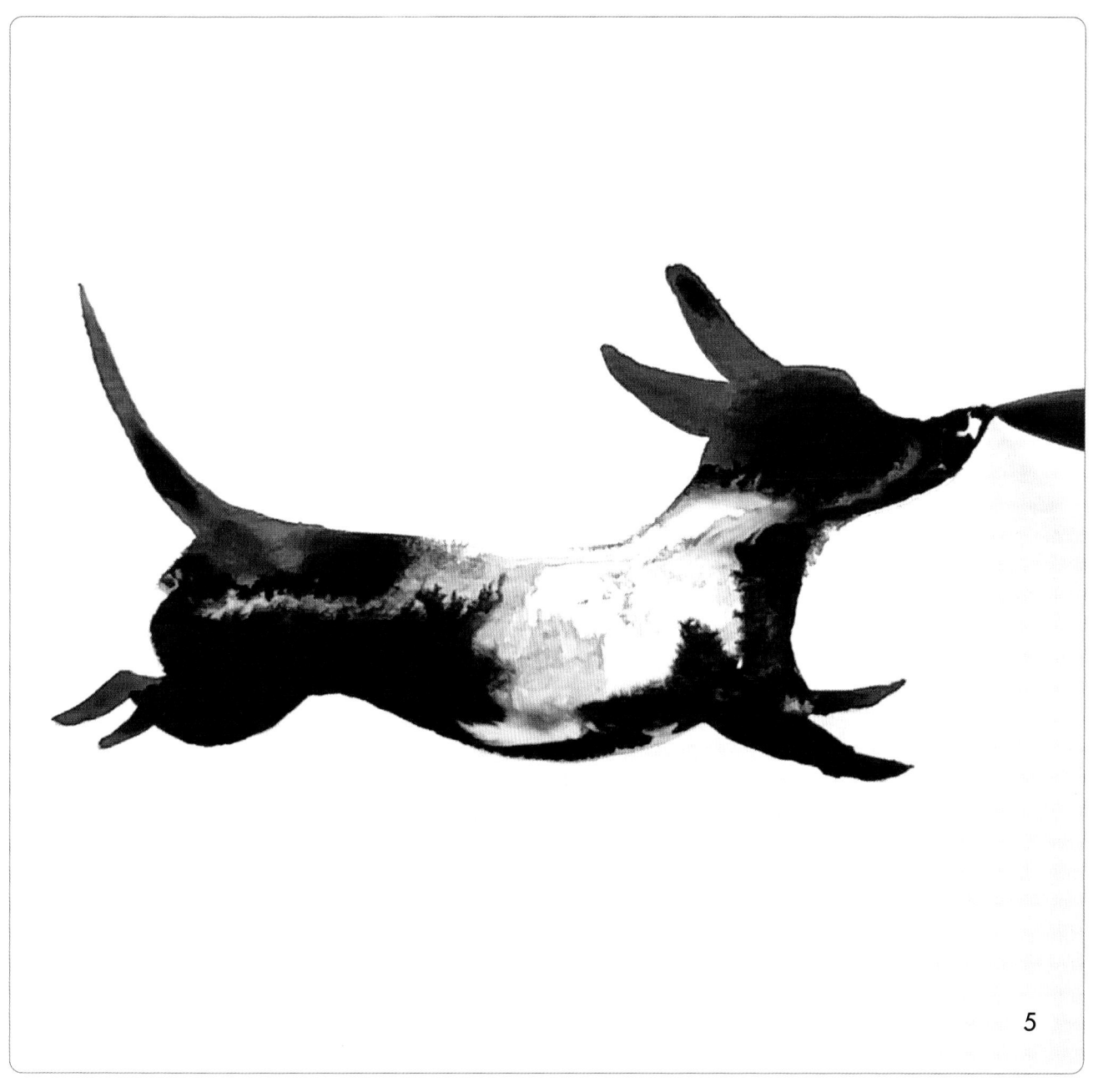

5

5 Holding your hand high above the page, paint a tiny dot on the end of the dog's nose. You will want quite a dry brush for this, so make sure there isn't too much ink on it. Tidy up any other edges or lines that you need to fix.

WILD

The wolf is one of those characters that wears many hats: villain, hunter, mystic, protector. Perhaps part of its allure is that it can shapeshift, powerfully adapt to its surroundings, move through the shadows, command the wild . . .

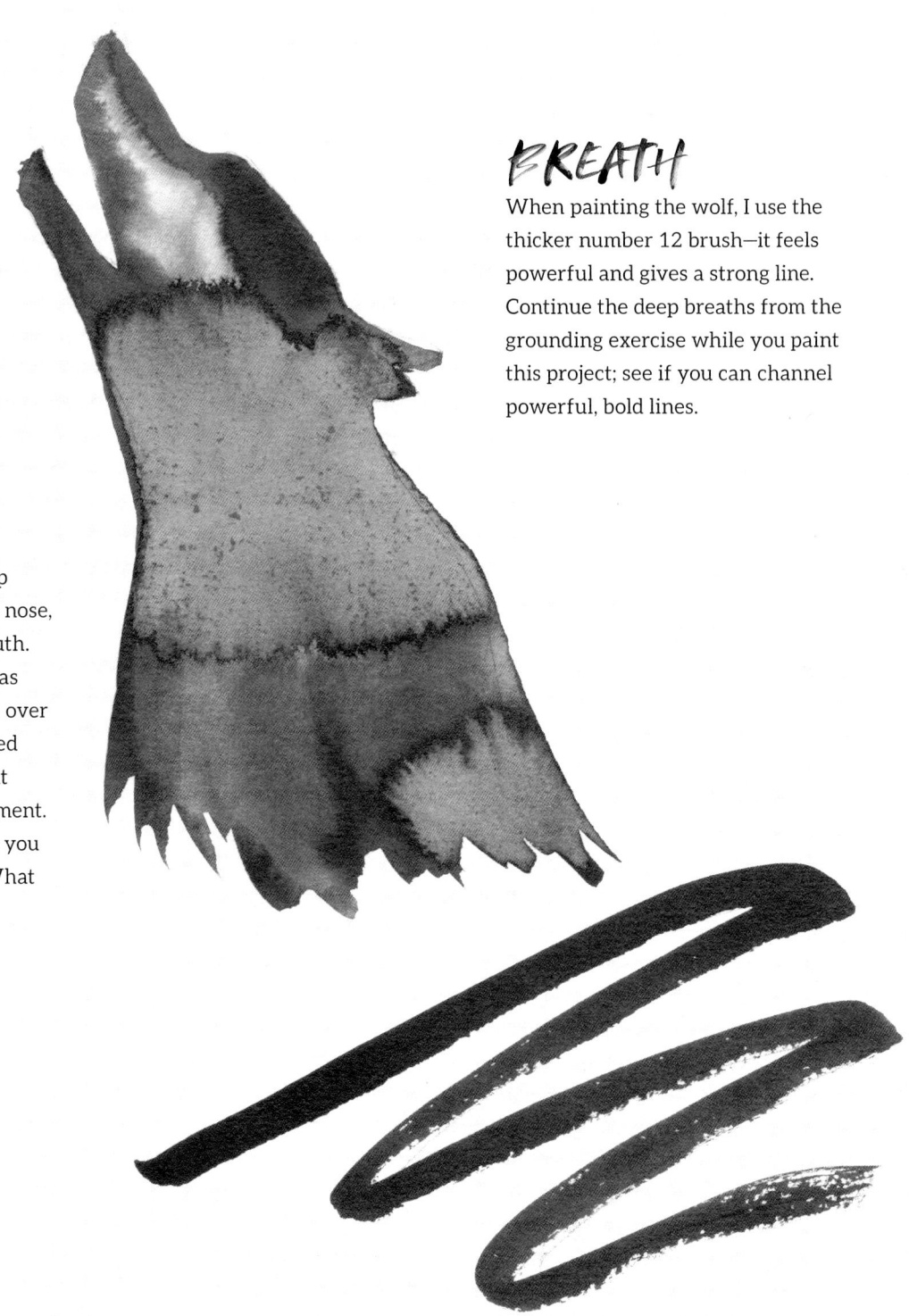

BREATH

When painting the wolf, I use the thicker number 12 brush—it feels powerful and gives a strong line. Continue the deep breaths from the grounding exercise while you paint this project; see if you can channel powerful, bold lines.

GROUNDING

Close your eyes and take deep breaths—inhale through your nose, and exhale through your mouth. Imagine you are as powerful as the wolf. Feel the wind ripple over your fur. Feel your feet planted firmly on the ground, but light enough to take off at any moment. What can you see? What can you hear? What can you smell? What makes you powerful?

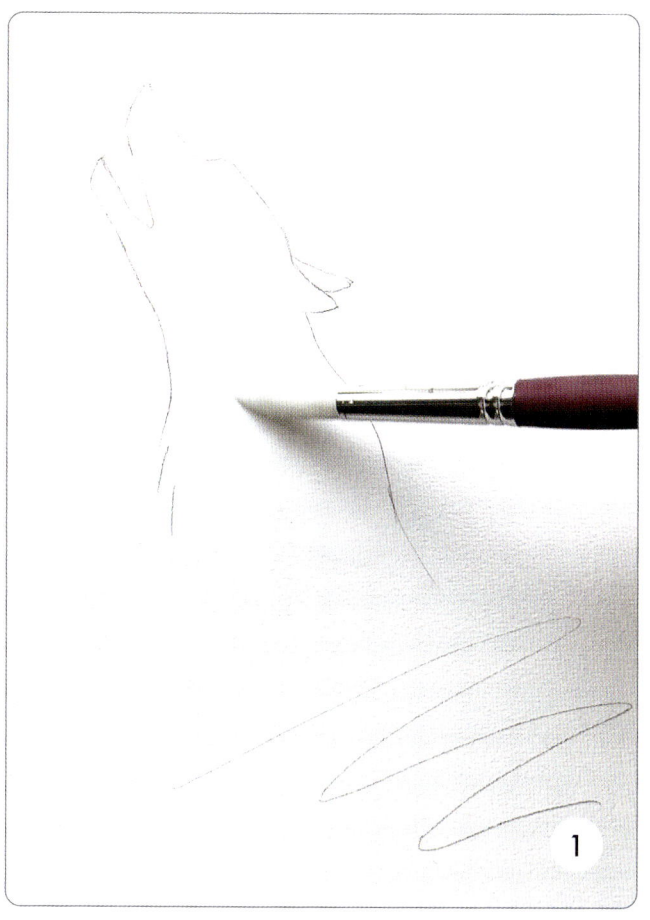

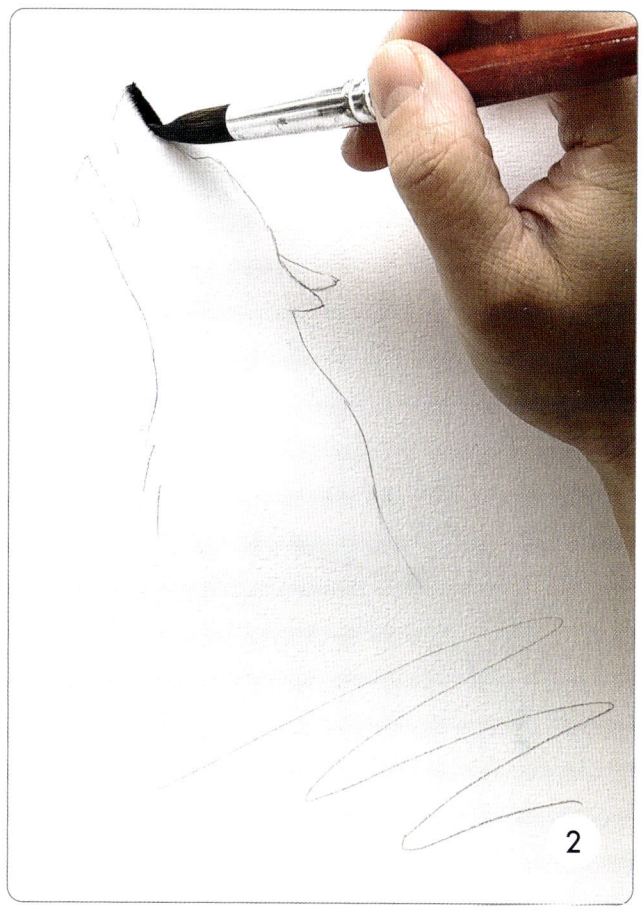

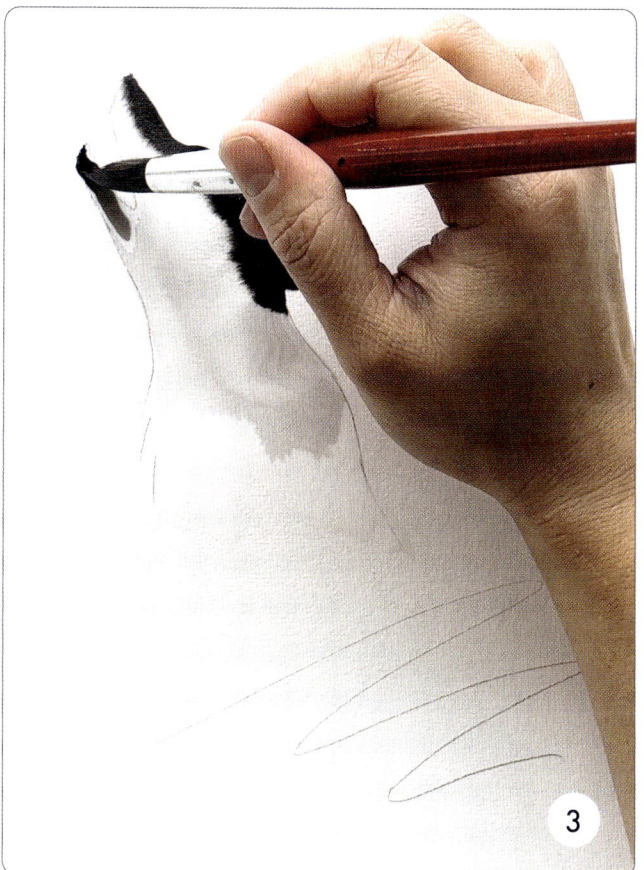

1 Trace the outline of the wolf on your page very lightly using your pencil. Dip your water brush into the water, and remove excess by wiping it on the rim of the jar. Paint water onto the whole wolf. Keep your brushstrokes light as you come to the bottom of the neck where the lines end.

2 Dip your number 12 ink brush into the ink, and remove any excess by wiping the brush on the rim of the jar. Place the tip of the brush on the tip of the wolf's nose. Pull down along the snout, head, and all the way to the rip of the ear, following the pencil line.

3 Place the tip of the brush on the tip of the wolf's lower jaw. Pull the brush down all the way under the chin and to the end of the chest.

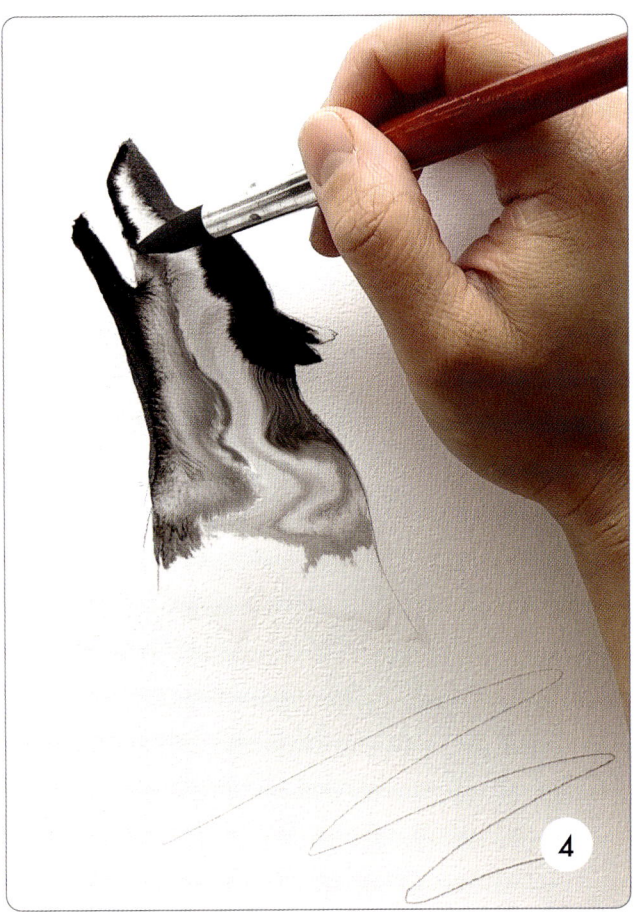

 Using the very tip of the brush, paint a fine line along the pencil mark of the wolf's upper jaw.

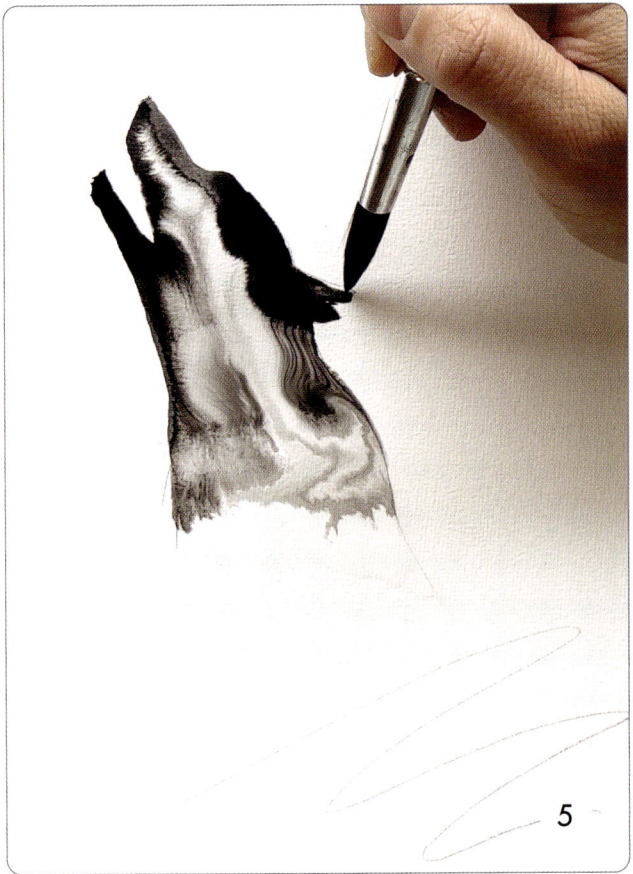

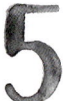 Using the very tip of the brush, paint ink onto the second ear.

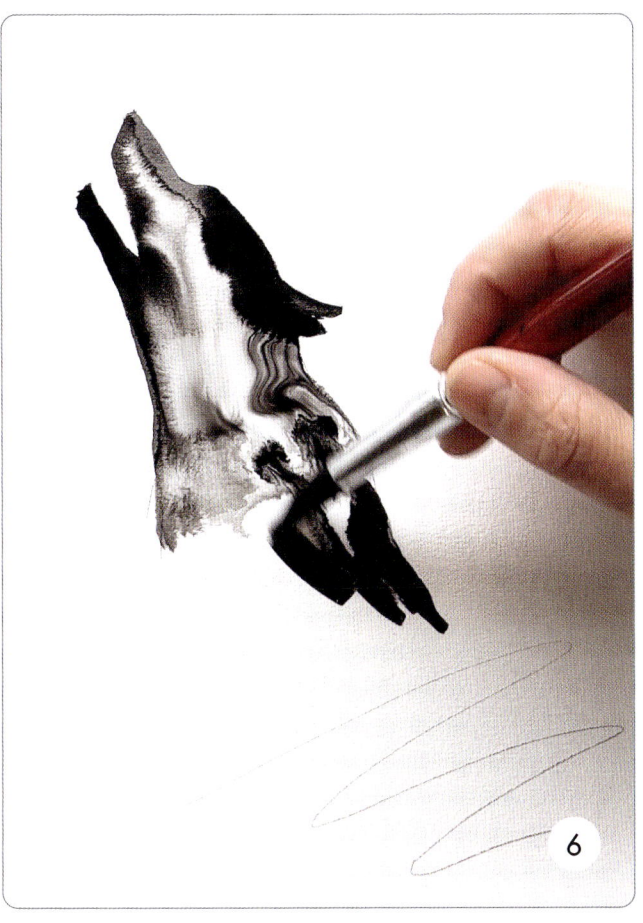

6 Paint four or five brushstrokes starting from the base of the neck, drawing the brush up to the wet area. Try to keep your hand and the brushstrokes loose.

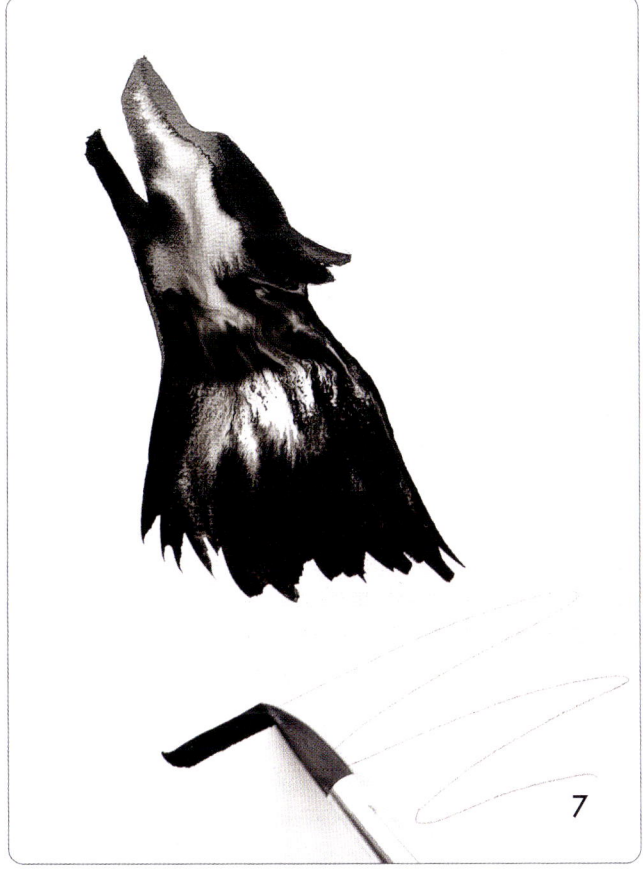

7 Reload the brush with ink; you want it quite full. Paint a broad, bold line along the squiggle under the wolf, using the flat side of the brush. Start from the top left, and work your way down to the bottom right of the line. I find this easiest to do in a single, relatively quick stroke.

SPRING EQUINOX

This little bunny is a symbol of spring, fertility, and life. It uses the technique of drawing patterns over the top of the dried ink texture with a fineliner pen. If you like this technique, you can use it on any number of the other projects—just make sure your ink layer is completely dry before you go in with your pen!

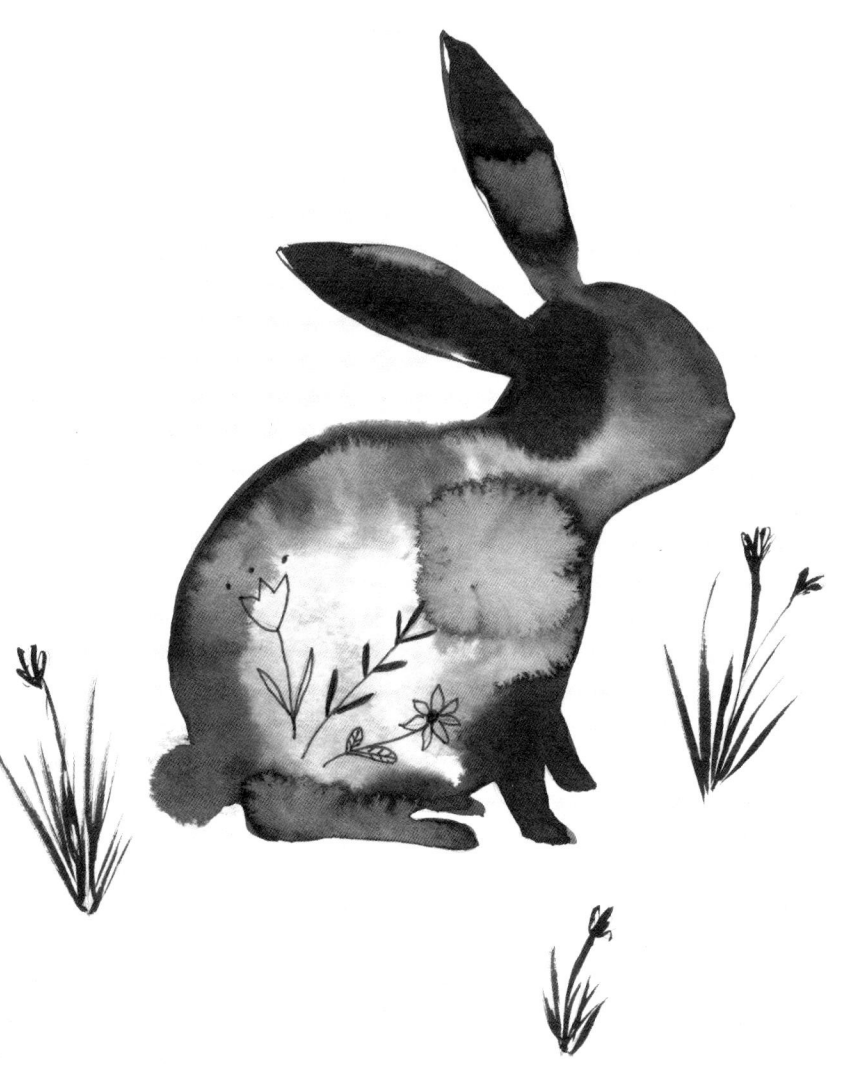

GROUNDING

Before you begin, do a scan of your body. Starting with the very top of your head, notice how your scalp feels. Travel down through your brain, your nose, the back of your neck. Consciously acknowledge each body part that you mentally scan over. How does it feel? Does it hurt? Does it itch? Does it feel like nothing? Move down your body, through your chest, your hips, your legs. Notice which parts of your body are in contact with other objects. Are you sitting? Which parts of your body push back against the chair? Do your feet touch the ground? Can you feel the ground pushing back? Once you have scanned through your whole body, take a deep breath, and feel every part of your body fill with oxygen. Exhale slowly. You are ready to begin.

BREATH

By this stage in the book, you might have found your own comfortable breathing rhythm. If this is the case, go with what is comfortable for you; eventually it should feel very natural. With this project, I like to exhale when painting the broad brushstrokes for the ears and the back of the bunny. With the finer brushstrokes, I maintain even, regulated breaths.

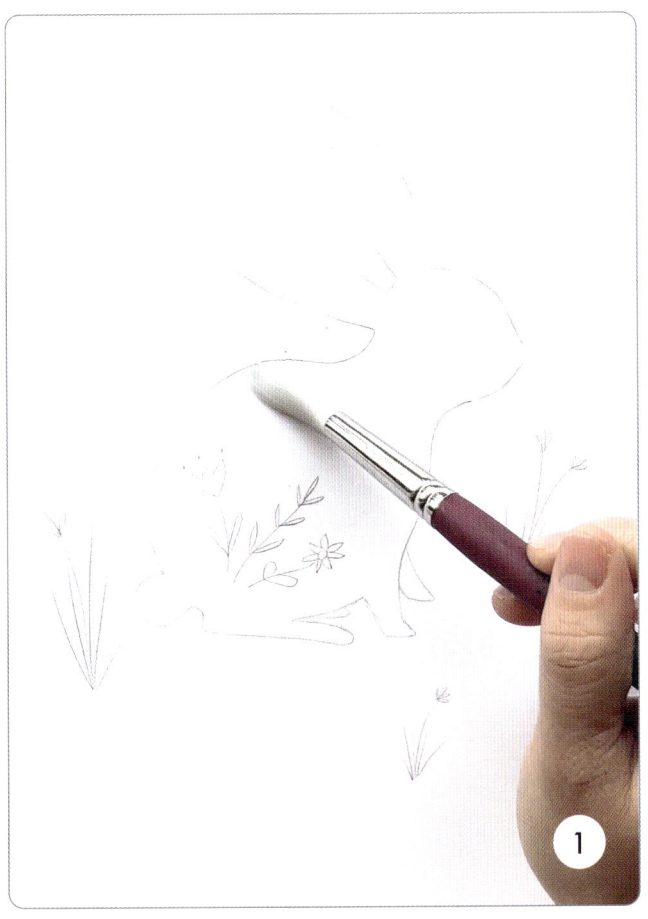

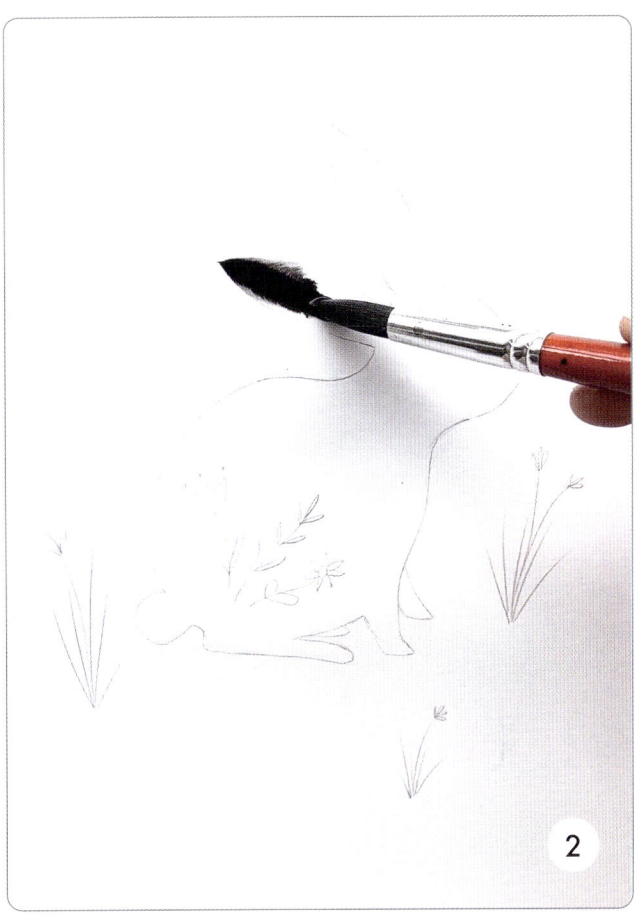

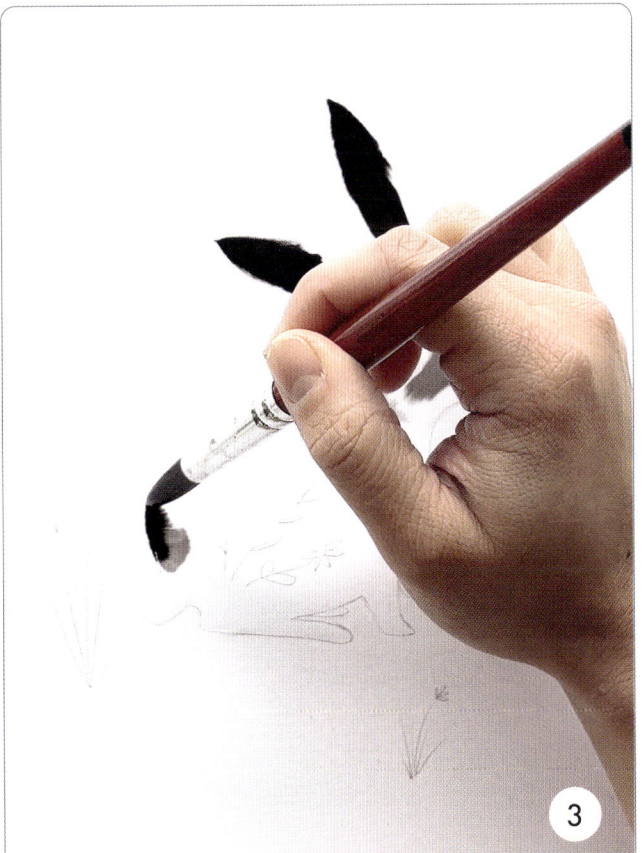

1 Trace the outline of the bunny on your page very lightly using your pencil. Dip your water brush into the water, and remove any excess by wiping it on the rim of the jar. Paint the whole bunny with water. Leave the flowers and grass around the bunny dry.

2 Dip your number 12 ink brush into the ink, and remove the excess by wiping the brush on the rim of the jar. Place the tip of the brush at the top of the bunny's ear. Press the brush down on the page as you pull it toward the bunny's head; this will give you a broader brushstroke. Repeat with the other ear. The ink from the ears will move into the face of the bunny. Don't touch it—we want this to happen.

3 Place the tip of your brush just above the bunny's tail. Pull the brush up the curve of the bunny's back along the pencil outline.

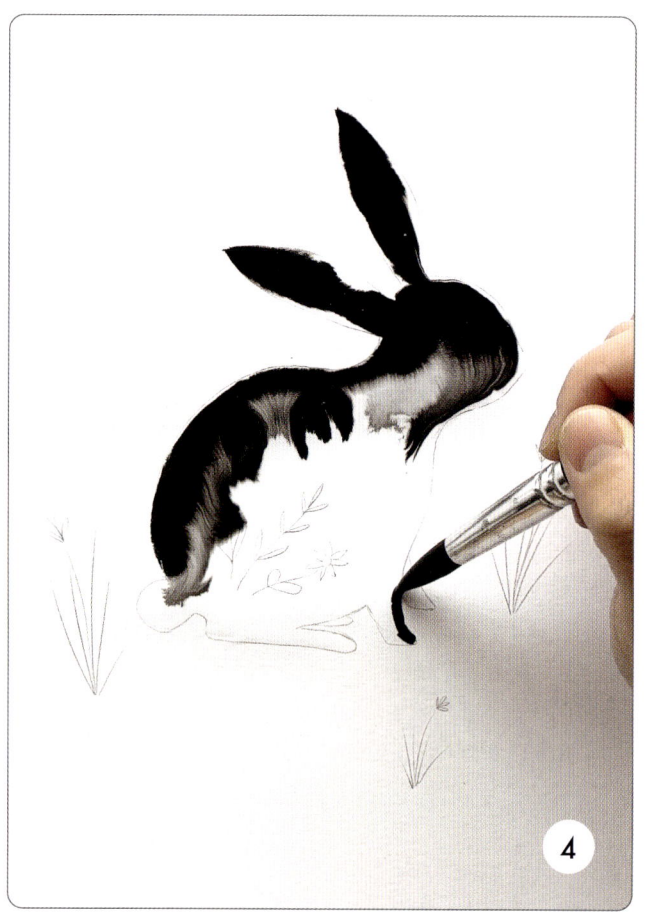

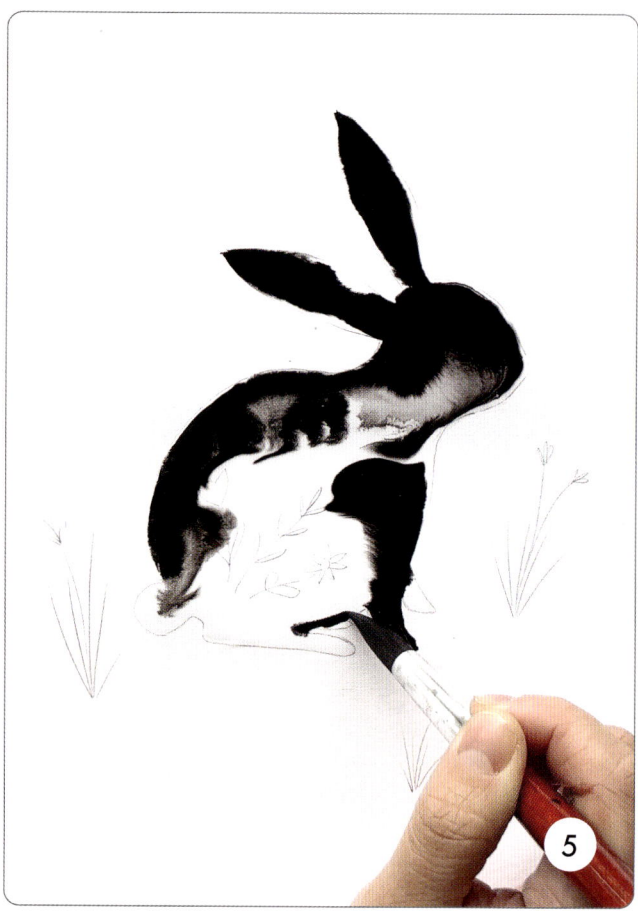

4 Place the tip of the brush on the bunny's front paw, and bring the brush up along the pencil line to meet the ink under the bunny's chin. Repeat this with the second front paw.

5 Pull the tip of the brush along the bunny's underbelly from the back paw to the front.

6 Using the tip of the brush, lightly paint a fine line to complete the back paw. Allow the ink to move into the bunny's tail.

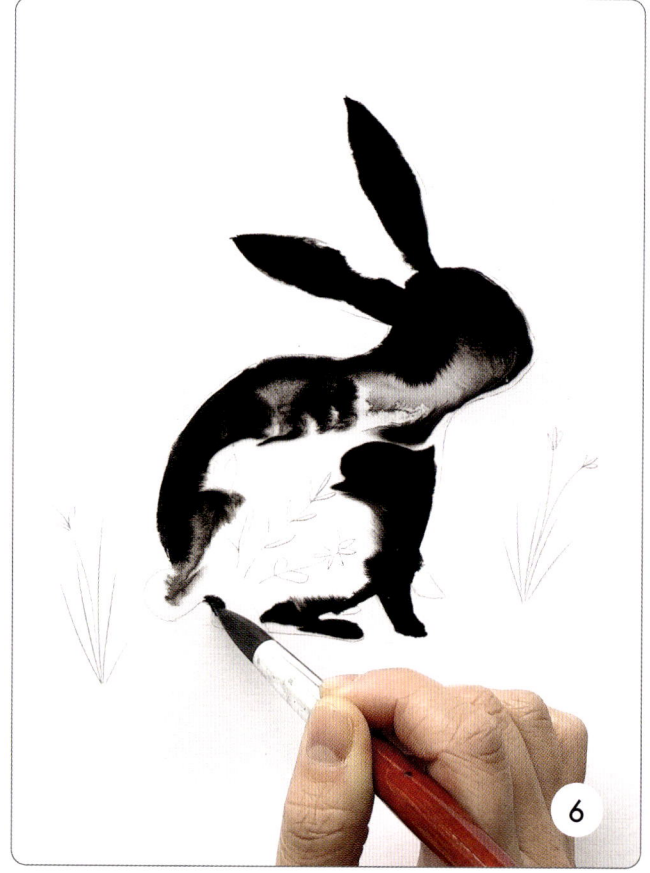

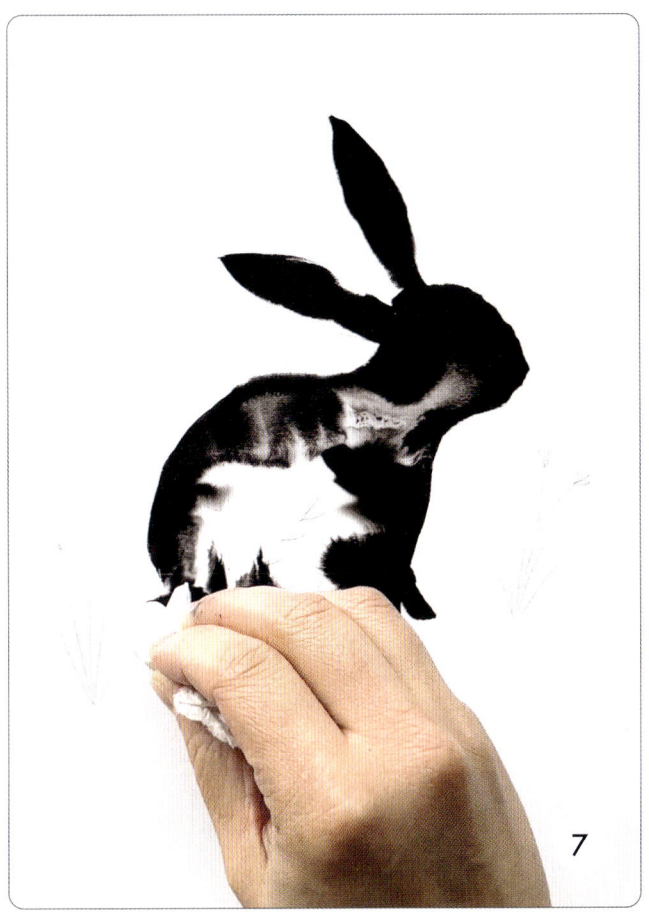

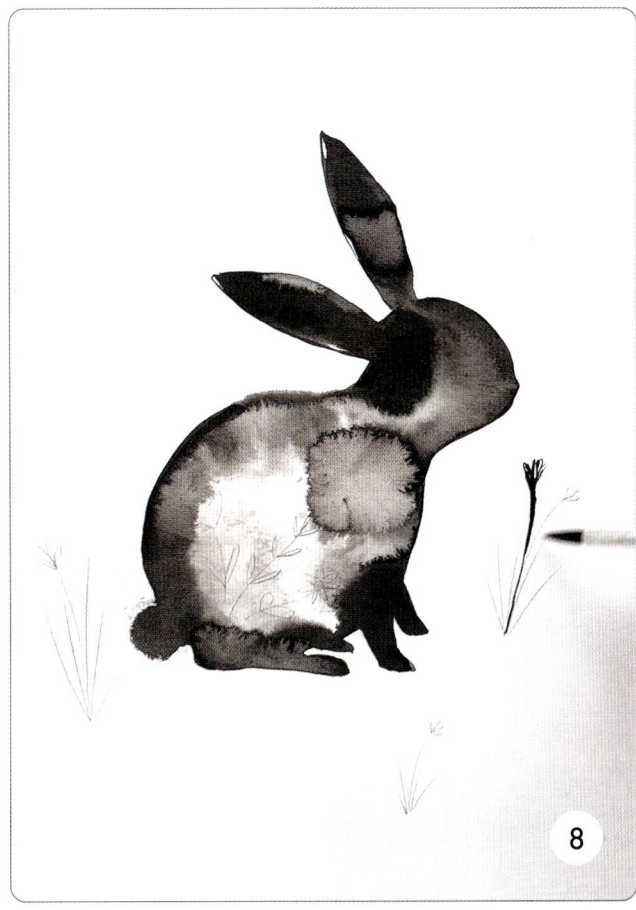

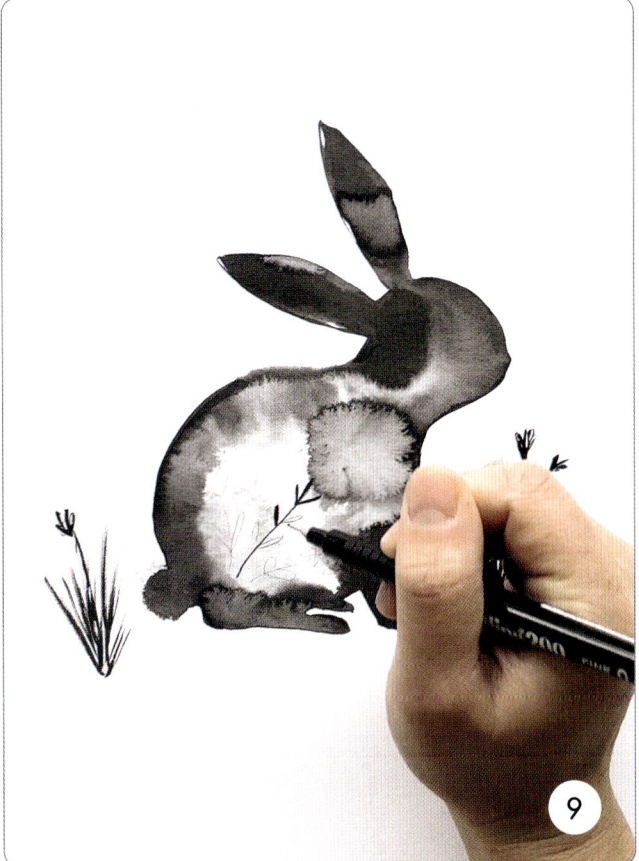

7 Bunch up a small piece of paper towel into a loose ball. Gently dab at the bunny's tail, removing small amounts of ink and water at a time. The rough, absorbent paper will give a textured, fluffy look to the bunny's tail. Allow the bunny to dry thoroughly.

8 While you wait for the bunny to dry, use your number 6 ink brush to paint in the fine lines of the grasses and flowers. Be sure to use a light hand and the very tip of the brush.

9 When the bunny is completely dry (I recommend waiting overnight, just to be sure!), use a fineliner pen to draw the floral patterns onto the bunny's body.

FOX SPIRIT

The fox is my animal guide, my kindred spirit from the wild. There are so many interpretations and symbolic associations with the fox. In Western culture, foxes are depicted as cunning, sly, and greedy. In Japanese culture, however, they are magical, powerful shapeshifters. While they are not all good, the benevolent ones are beautiful, celestial protectors who sometimes serve as guardian spirits. According to folklore, they are particularly fond of aburaage, a type of tofu that I also really enjoy!

GROUNDING

Find a comfortable sitting position, and close your eyes. Take a moment to daydream. What sort of animal guide do you have? Think of the specifics: What color are its eyes? How big is it? What is its favorite food? What does its voice sound like? Let your imagination run wild.

BREATH

The fox is quite a small piece and uses only the fine number 6 ink brush. I find that keeping an even, regulated breathing pattern helps with this one. Sometimes with fine brushstrokes, you can forget to breathe (which is very different from intentionally holding your breath!)—don't forget to breathe when painting this little fox. It's important that you breathe life into her.

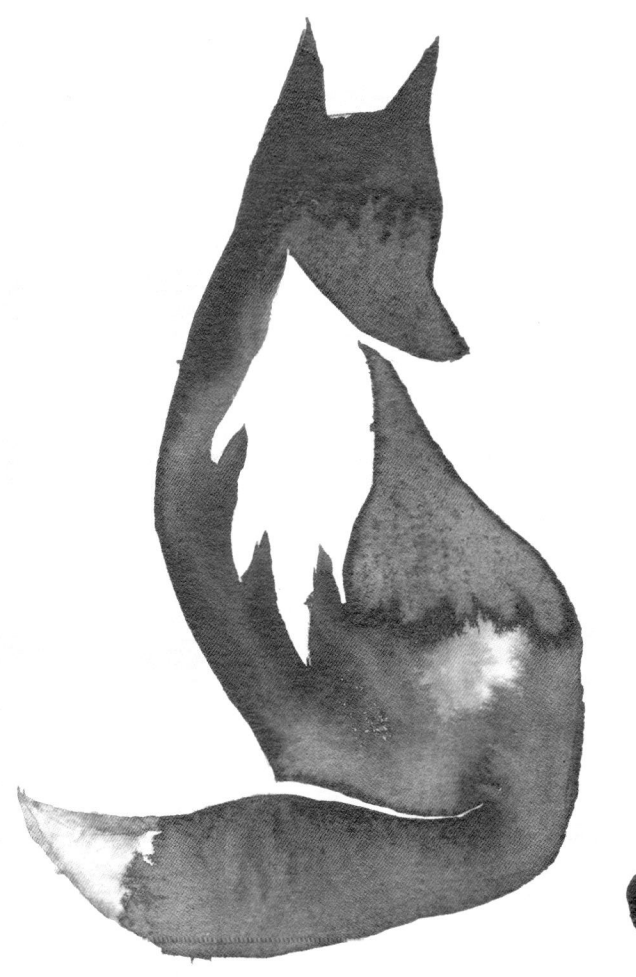

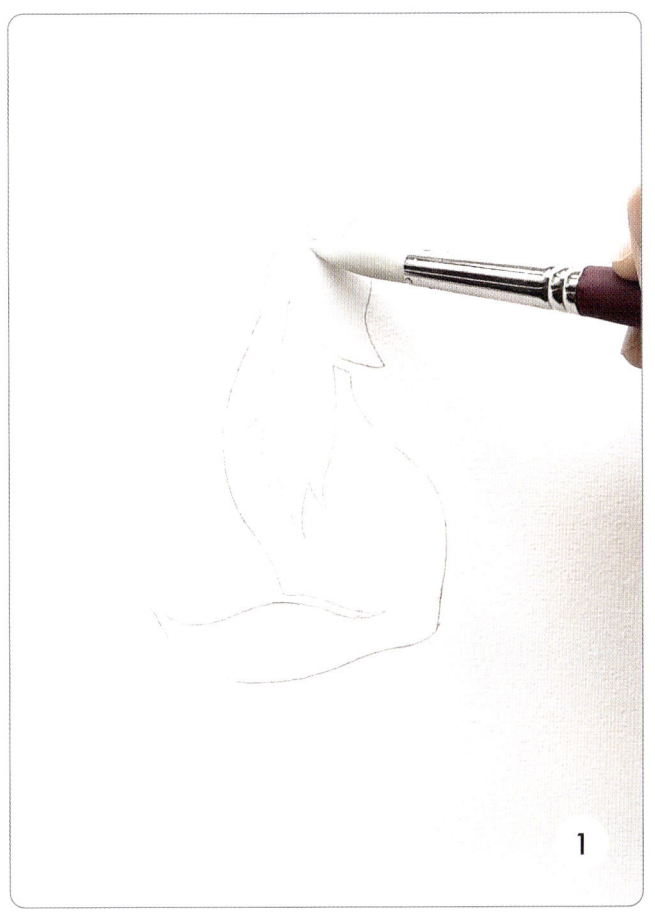

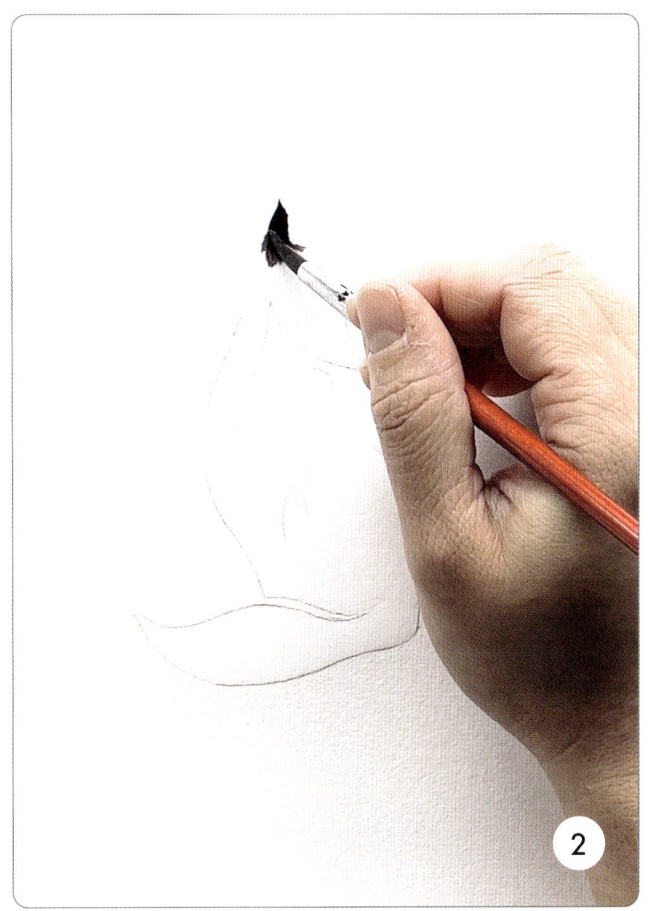

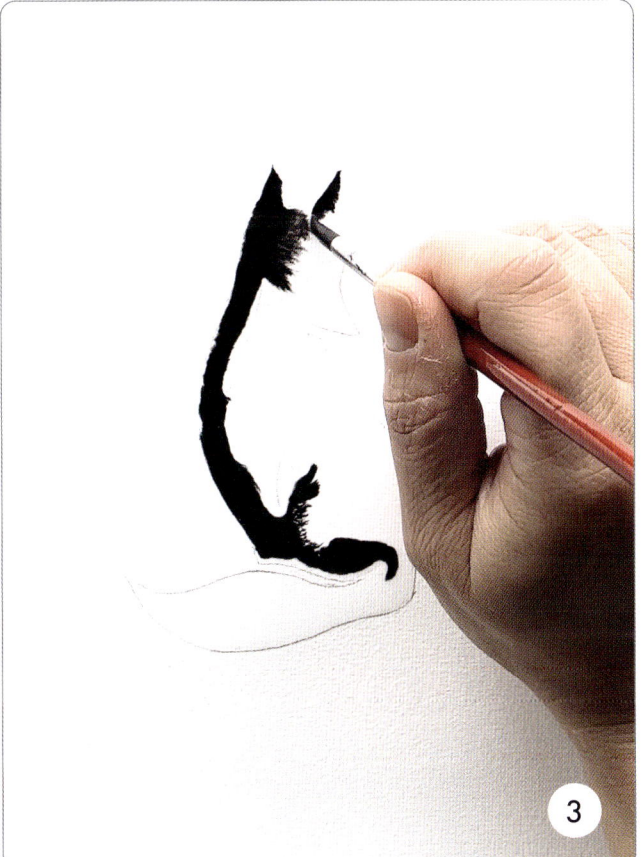

1 Trace the outline of the fox on your page very lightly using your pencil. Dip your water brush into the water, and remove any excess by wiping it on the rim of the jar. Paint water onto just the body of the fox, leaving the chest dry. Paint the entire tail.

2 Dip your number 6 ink brush into the ink, and remove any excess by wiping it on the rim of the jar. Place the tip of the paintbrush on the tip of the ear. Pull the brush down along the edge of the fox's body, following the pencil outline all the way to where the body stops, just before the tail.

3 Place the number 6 ink brush on the tip of the other ear, and pull the brush down to the tip of the nose. Pause, holding the brush at the nose for a moment. The ink will merge with the water and fill the rest of the fox's face.

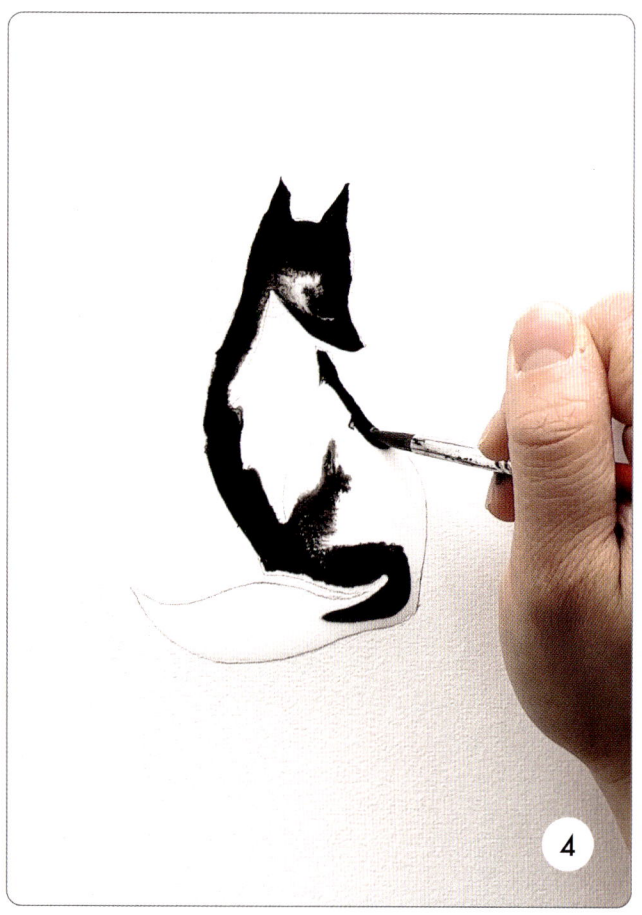

4 Reload the brush with ink, and place it on the edge of the fox's body below the nose. Pull the brush down, following the pencil line until you reach the fox's tail. The ink will start to move into the fox's tail.

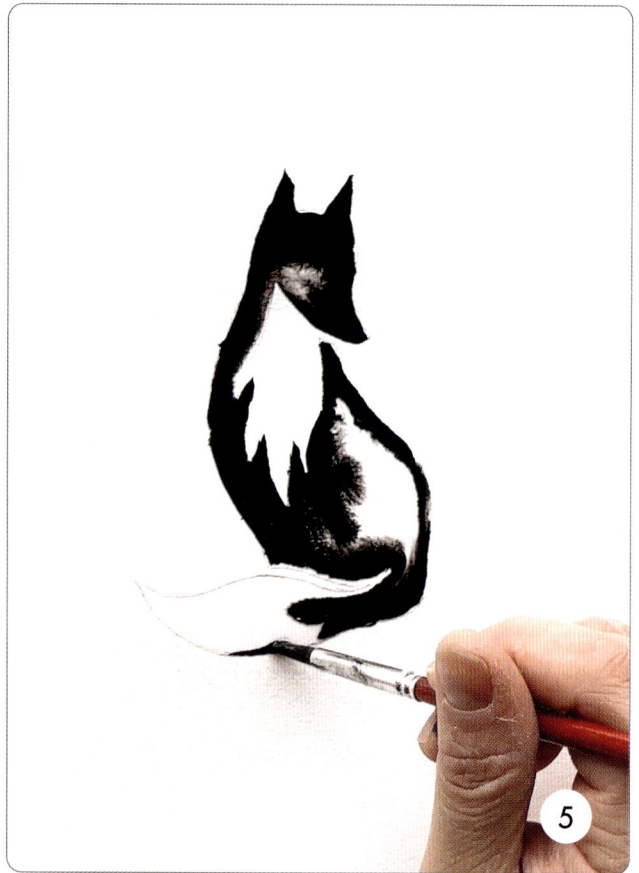

5 Using the very tip of the brush, paint an ink outline over the pencil that marks out the tip of the tail.

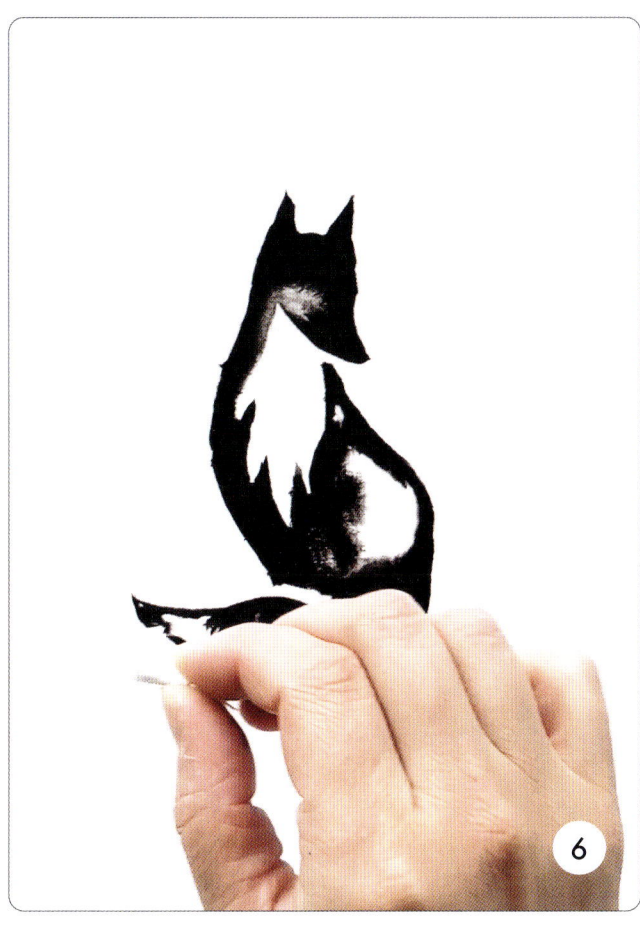

6 Roll up a small piece of paper towel, and dab it over the tip of the fox's tail, removing excess ink. This will give the end of her tail a slightly fluffy look.

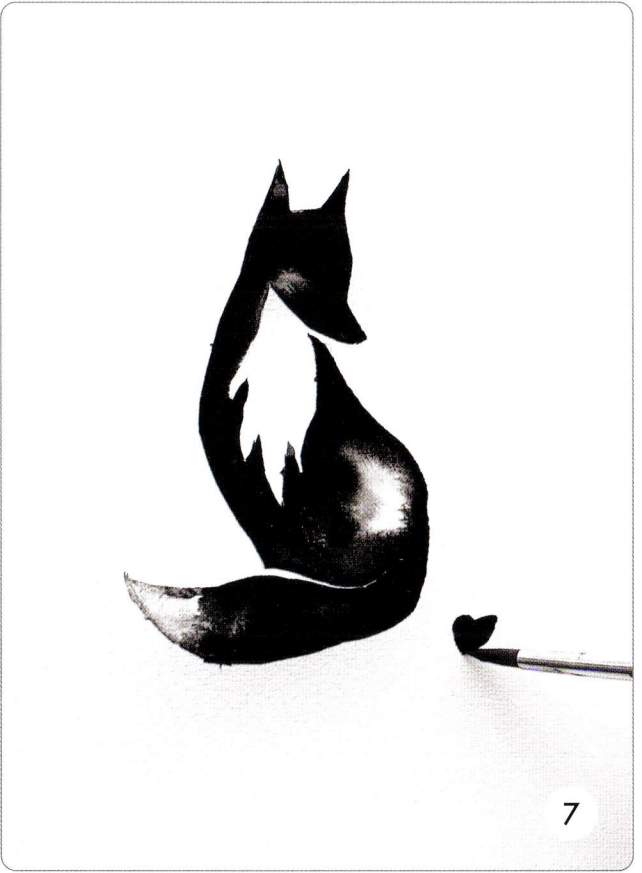

7 Use the tip of the brush to go over any untidy lines and clean up any details on the fox. Finish by painting a little heart next to the fox using straight black ink. I think it looks a bit like a heart-shaped period.

ORCA

The orca is one of the most consistent requests I get to paint on social media, and it's not surprising given how magnificent these animals are. They are particularly striking with the calligraphy ink, giving the areas of black on the body such an alluring texture. Which is your favorite whale? I don't think I can decide.

GROUNDING

Position yourself looking out a window or door to the outside world. Make sure you can see at least five different things that are not moving. Focus on one of these things, and inhale through your nose. Hold your breath for a count of three, and then exhale for a count of five. Repeat this with at least five things you can see outside.

BREATH

I love the simplicity of painting this orca—there are barely any actual brushstrokes in it! It is all about being patient, watching the ink react with the water, and breathing. When I place my brush and hold it still to the page (rather than pulling it through a stroke), I find counting and breathing an effective way to be patient, watch, and wait. The grounding breathing exercise is good practice for this and will get you in the rhythm of holding still, focusing, and exhaling.

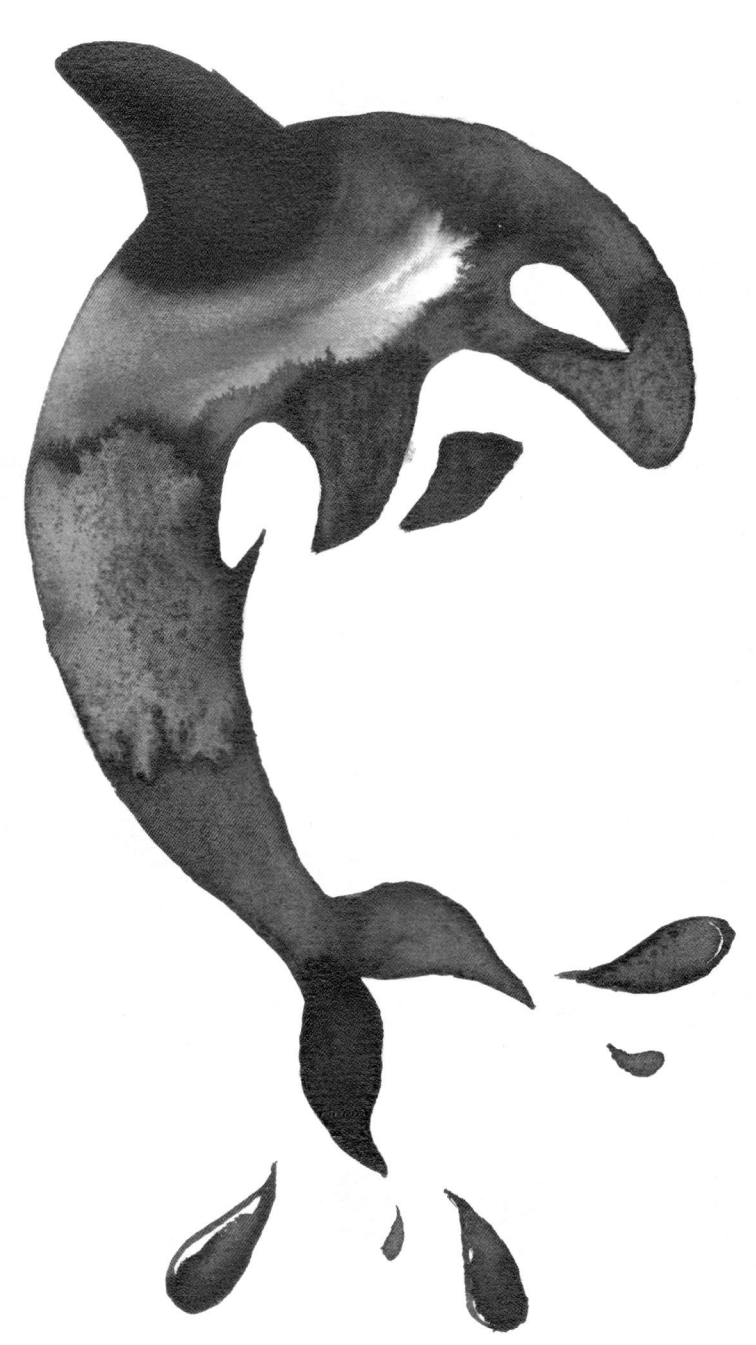

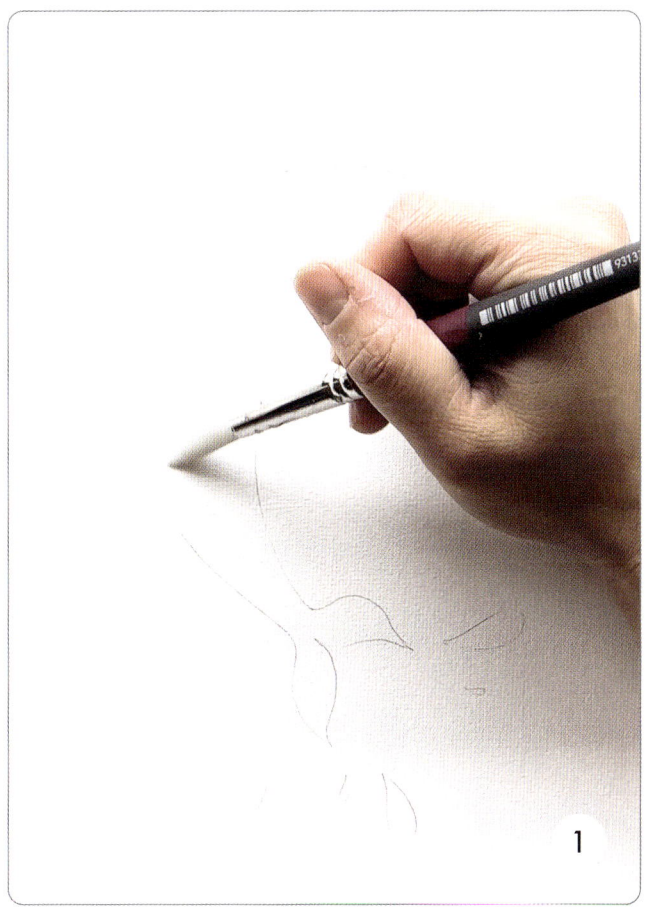

1

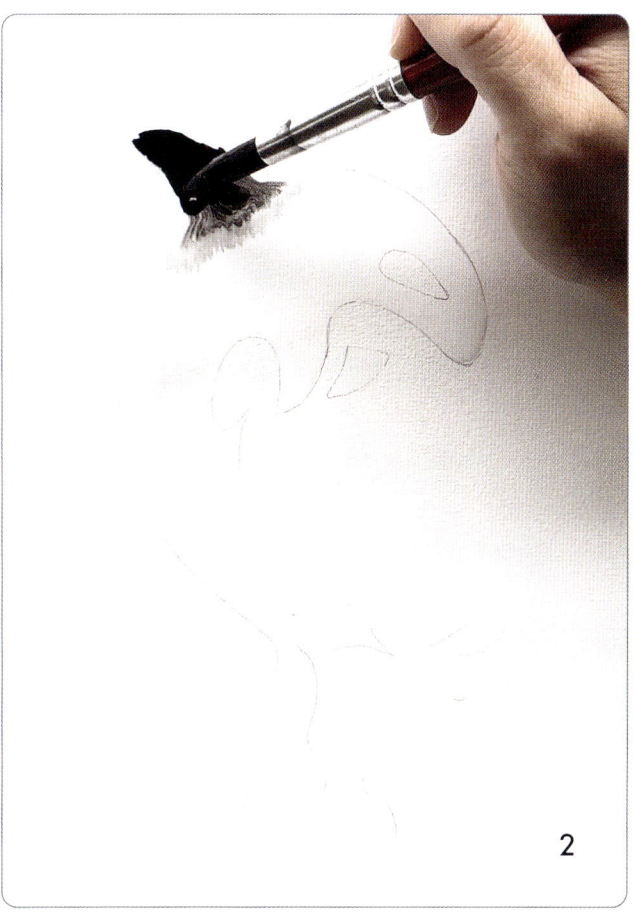

2

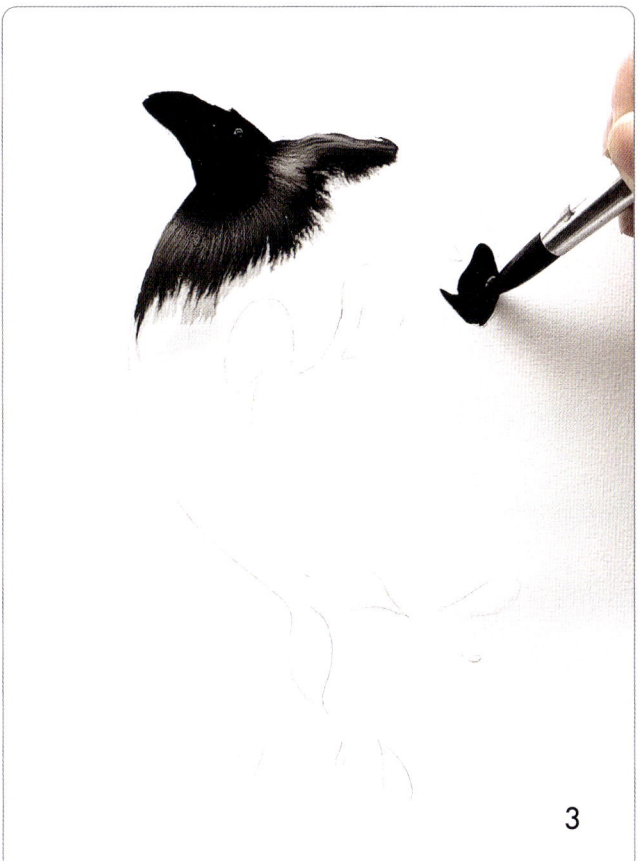

3

1 Trace the outline of the whale on your page very lightly using your pencil. Dip your water brush into the water, and remove any excess by wiping it on the rim of the jar. Paint water onto just the body of the orca and the water splashes. Be sure to leave the eye dry.

2 Dip your number 12 ink brush into the ink, and remove excess ink by wiping the brush on the rim of the jar. Place the tip of the brush on the tip of the orca's dorsal fin. Pull the brush down through the water a little, but stop before you reach the body. Hold the brush there for a few counts, and watch the water bleed into the body of the orca.

3 Reload the brush with ink, and place the tip of the brush on the nose of the orca. Hold it on the wet surface for a few counts, and watch the ink spill into the face and neck of the orca.

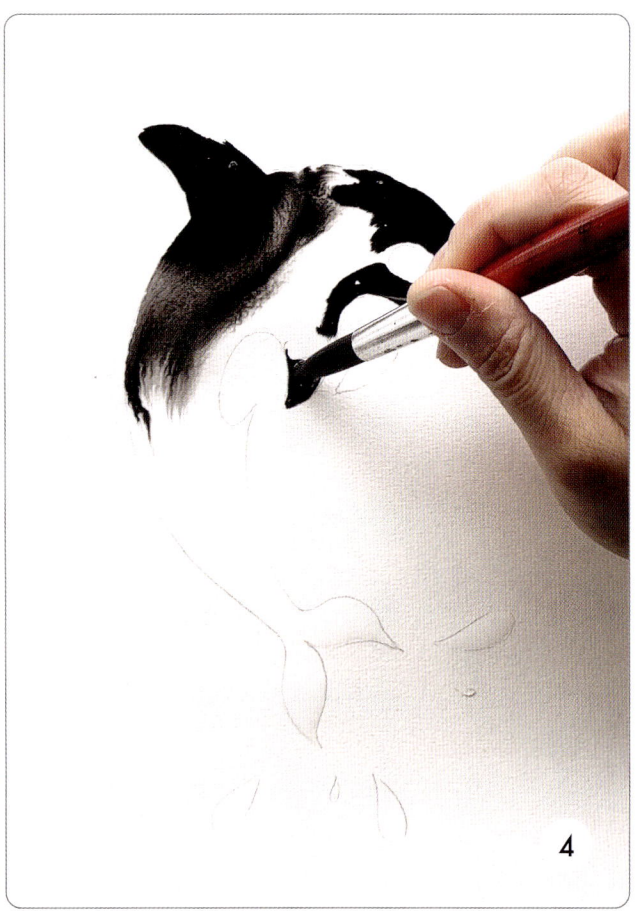

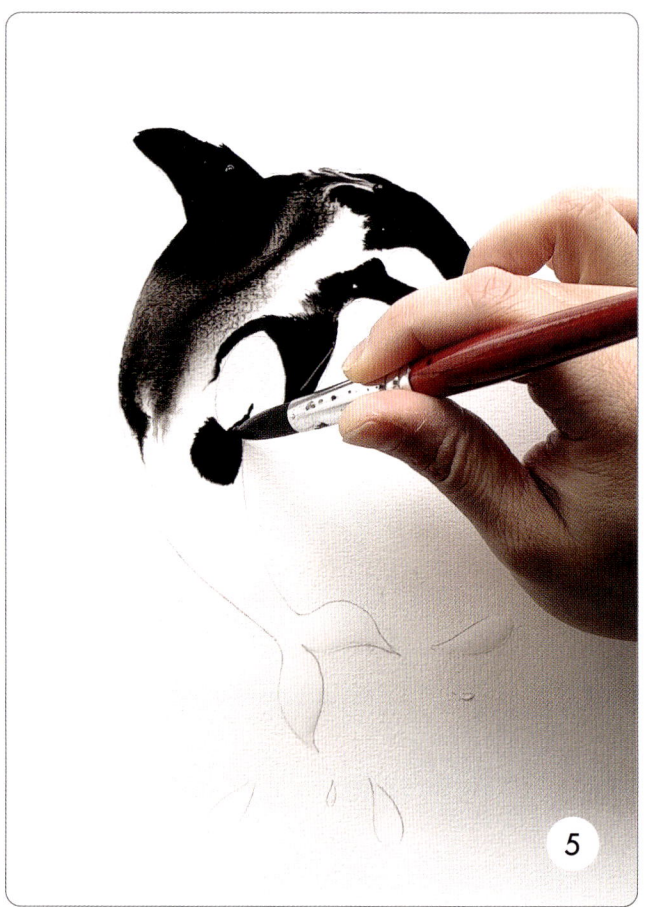

4 Reload your brush with ink, and hold it to the tip of the fin that connects to the body. Watch the ink move into the wet areas and merge with the ink areas. You will notice the body slowly filling up with ink.

5 Reload your brush with ink, and hold it to the tip on the belly below the fin. Watch the ink spread into the tail of the orca.

6 Reload your brush with ink, and place it on the tip of the tail flipper. Pull the brush up toward the tail, and stop when you reach the base of the tail. Hold the brush here, and watch the ink move into the blank wet areas. Repeat this with the other tail fin. Most of your orca should be fairly ink-filled by now. If there are a couple of white patches, don't worry—they usually fill as the ink dries.

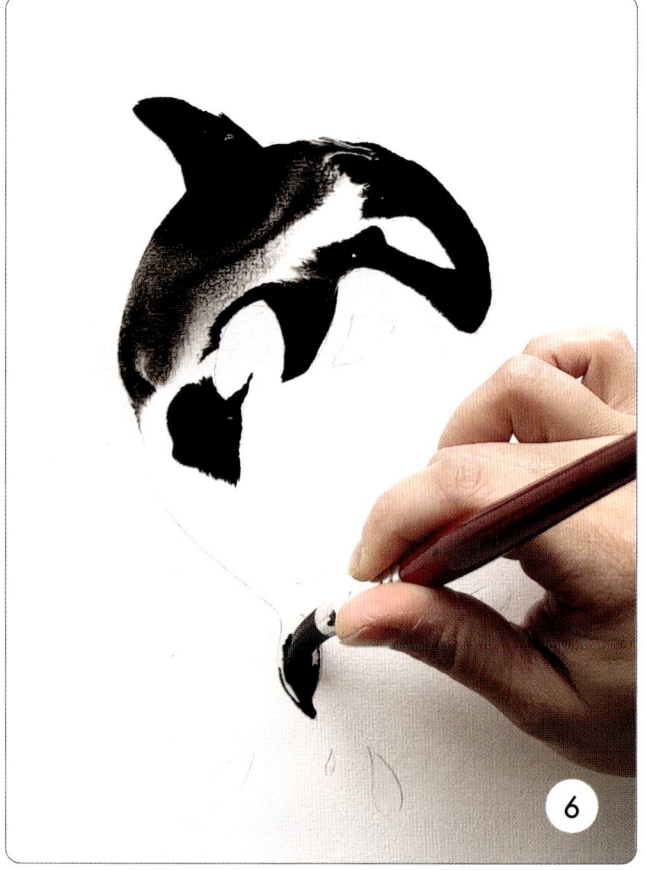

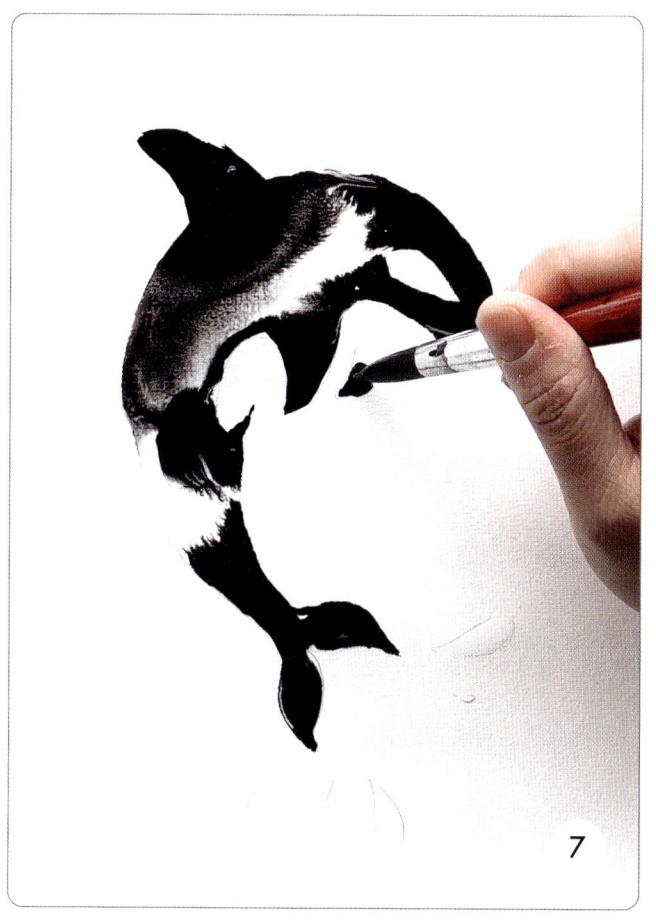

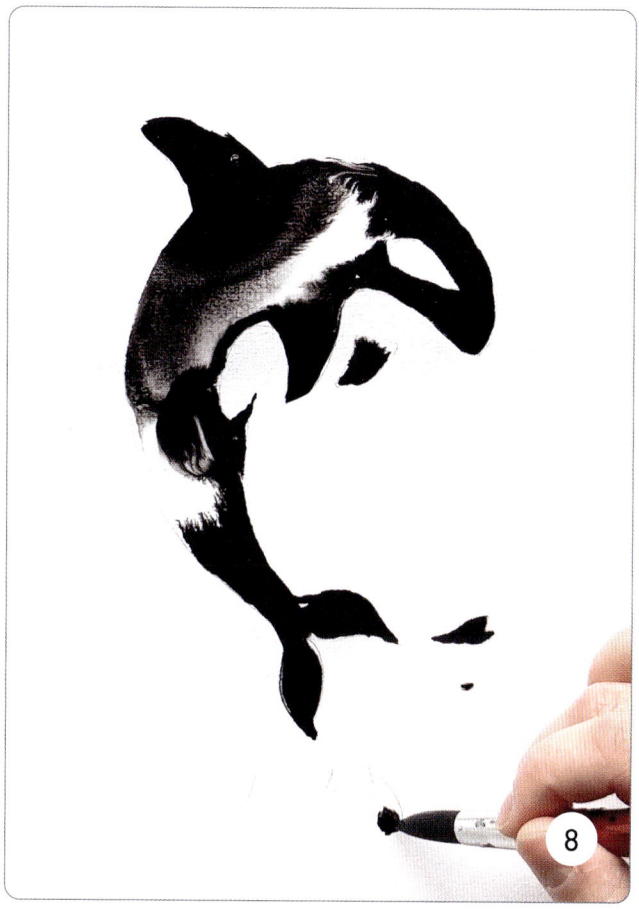

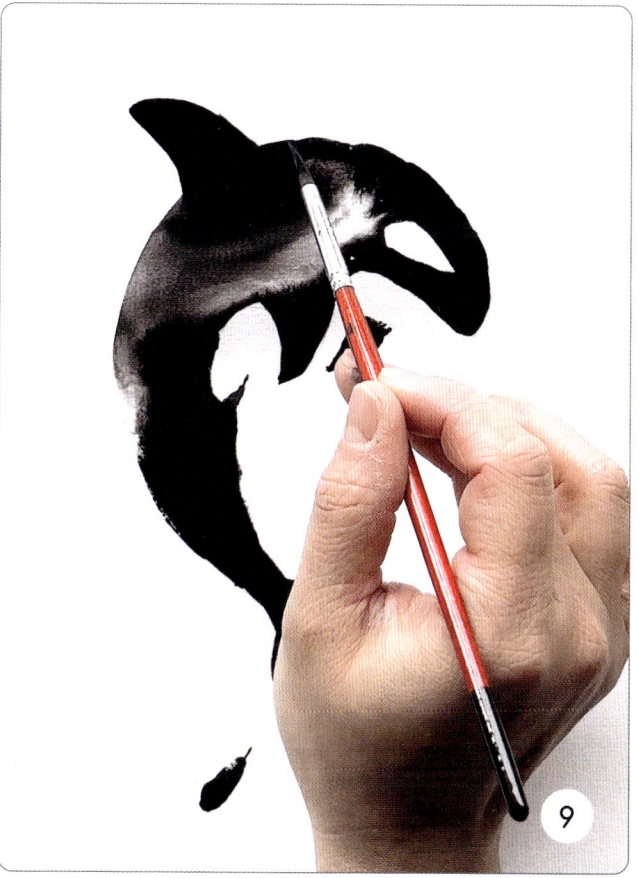

7 Reload your brush, and hold the tip to the wet area of the other fin. Watch the ink fill this smaller wet space. The negative space will create the white underside of the orca's belly without you needing to paint anything.

8 Hold the tip of the brush to each of the water splashes so they fill with ink. Then leave the painting to dry a little.

9 When the painting has dried slightly (it doesn't need to be completely dry), dip the number 6 ink brush in the ink, and remove any excess by wiping it on the rim of the jar. Tidy up any edges that need cleaner lines using the very tip of the brush. I find it sometimes helps to rotate the page around to get the right angle.

RAY

This ray is the piece that went viral on TikTok and ultimately projected these inky mediations into the big wide world. It has had so many comments, criticisms, suggestions, and shares—it's by far the biggest conversation starter I've ever had anything to do with. When I painted it, I didn't think much of it, as I was just playing with the combination of wet and dry ink. But here it is now in a book, ready to be replicated again and again. The infinite ray.

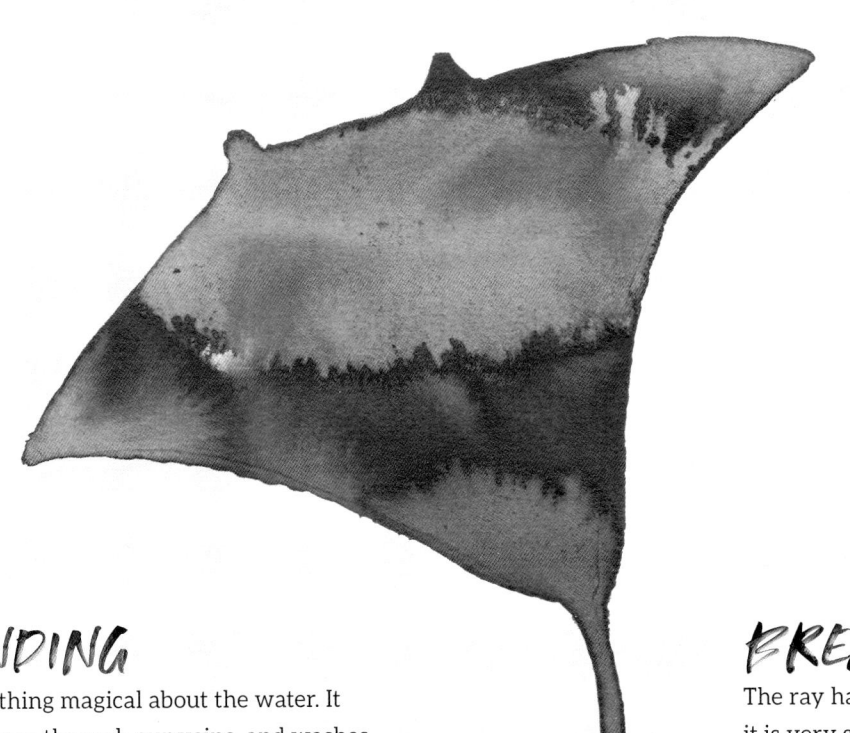

GROUNDING

There is something magical about the water. It gives life, courses through our veins, and washes everything away. Before sitting down to paint this project, take some time to run water through your hands. This can be as simple as turning the tap on and letting the water run through your fingers. What does it feel like? How does it catch the light? How does it move? How does it sound? Send your thoughts way out to everything that water touches, that is made from water, or that moves through water. Then bring your thoughts back here, to right now, to the water flowing over your fingers.

BREATH

The ray has only five brushstrokes—it is very specific and intentional. I breathe out as I paint the first brushstroke, the tail that bleeds in the body. Then I don't breathe again until it is finished. I don't specifically hold my breath, but I keep it sustained. When I have finished the last brush touch, I breathe again slowly, watching the ink move and make the picture by itself.

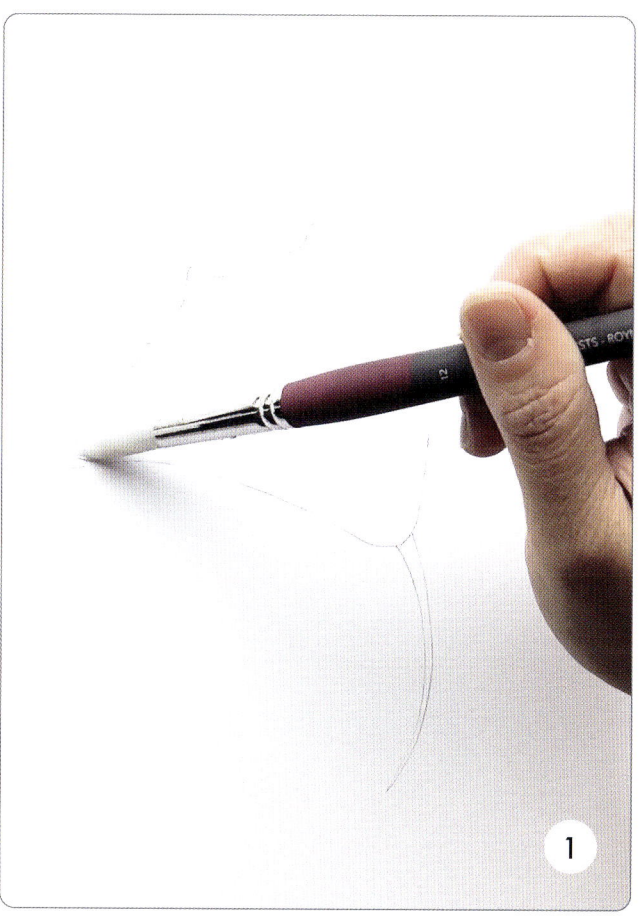

1 Trace the outline of the ray on your page very lightly using your pencil. Dip your water brush into the water, and remove any excess by wiping it on the rim of the jar. Paint water onto the body of the ray. Leave the tail dry.

2 Dip your number 12 ink brush into the ink, and remove excess ink by wiping the brush on the rim of the jar. Place the very tip of the brush at the tip of the tail, and pull the brush toward the body of the ray, painting about one-third of the way into the wet area.

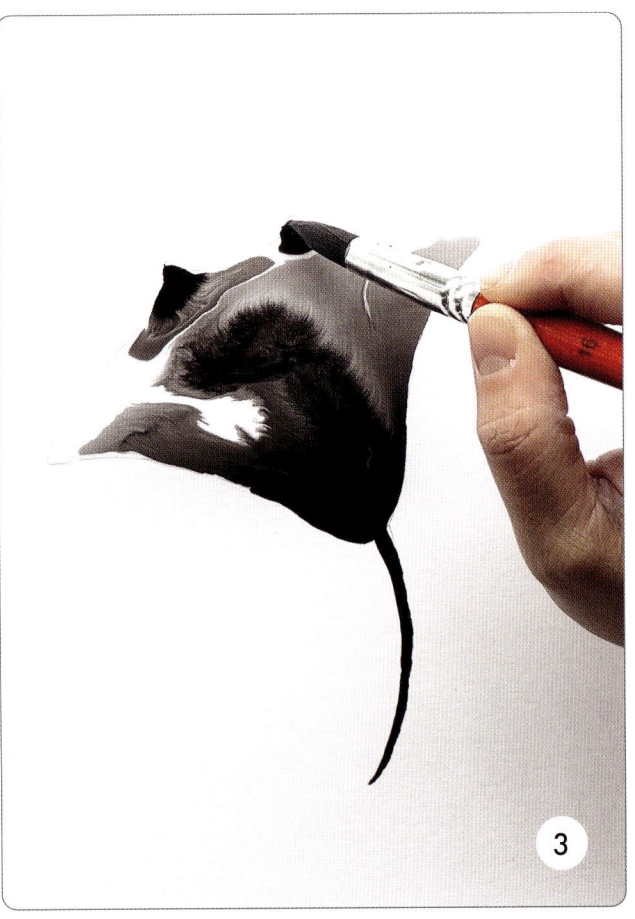

3 Still using the tip of the brush, paint a dot onto each of the eyes.

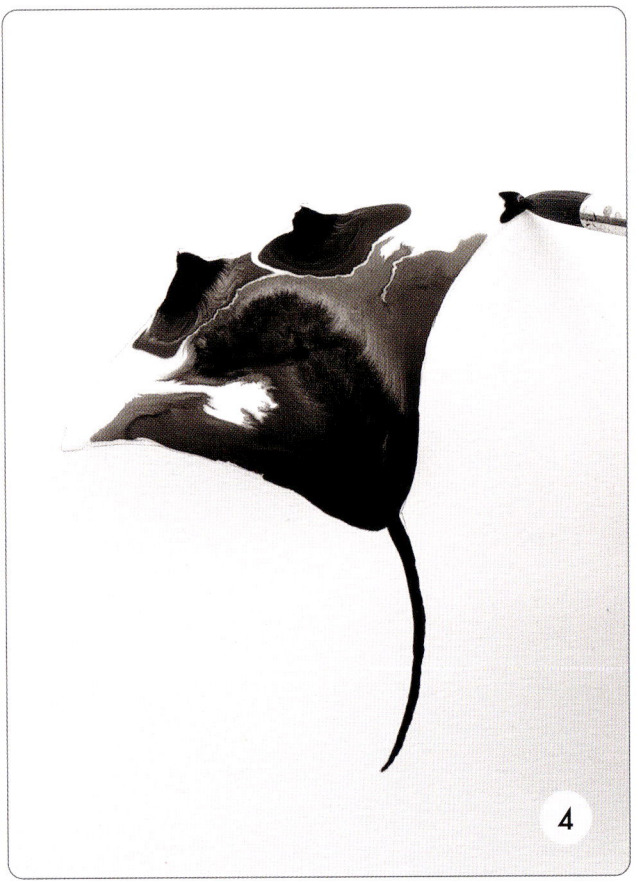

 Using the tip of the brush, paint one dot onto the tip of one of the wings. Watch the ink spread into the wet body of the ray.

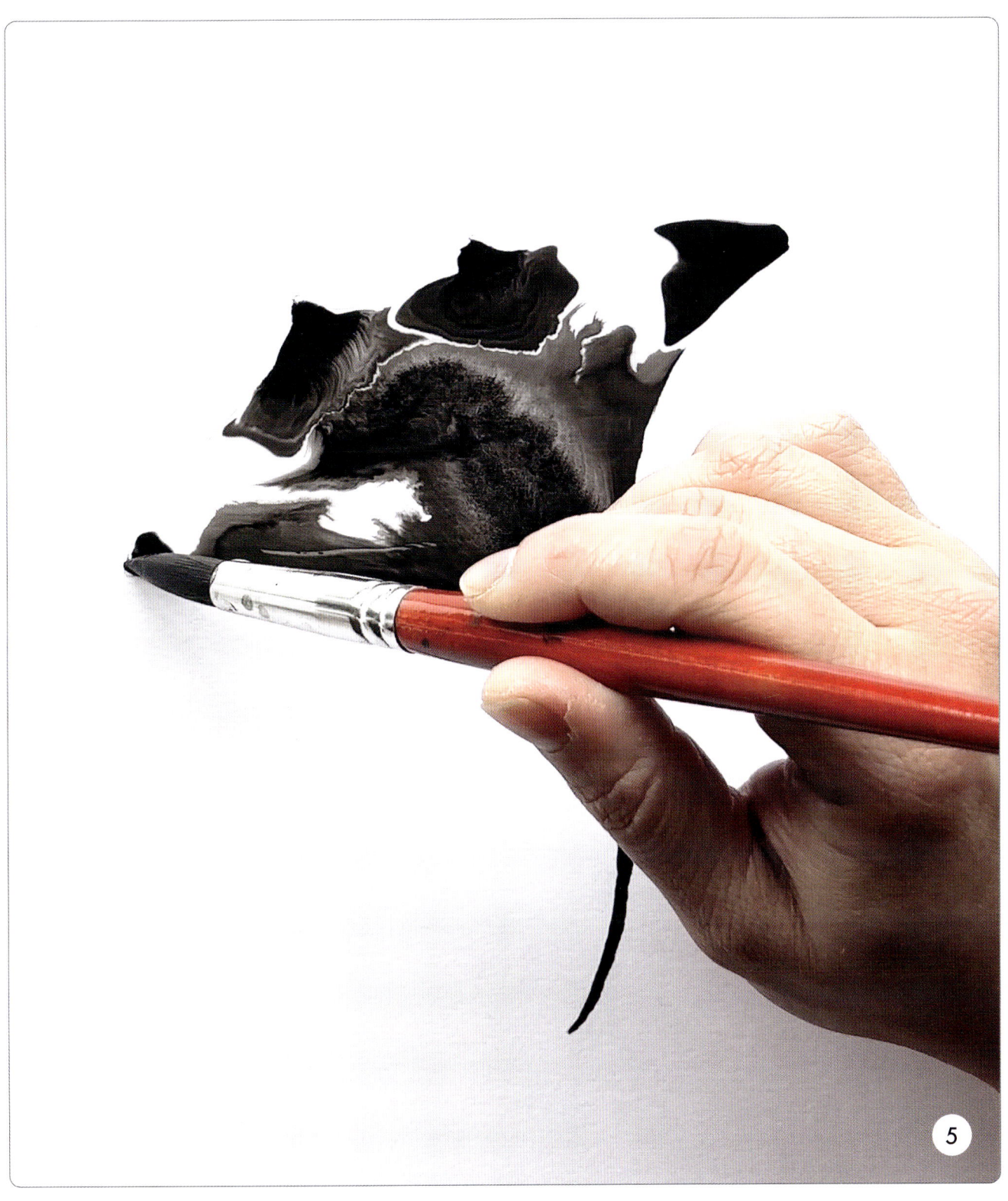

5 Repeat step 4 with the other wing. Watch how the ink and water react. Don't try to control it; let it flow and see what happens. Why not paint a few and see how they all change?

CHONKY NARWHAL

I was asked to share some of my bloopers on socials, and one of them was a particularly chonky whale that people seemed to really love. When I was painting this narwhal, he turned out a little chonky too, and I think he's quite cute. It's a good reminder that not everything has to be sleek and elegant; this chonky narwhal is feeling fine and loving himself!

GROUNDING

Rest your elbows on the table, and hold your hands up in front of your face. Push your fingertips against each other, and apply pressure, counting slowly to five. As you apply pressure and count, breathe in deeply through your nose. When you release the pressure, release your breath through your mouth. Repeat this five times before you begin.

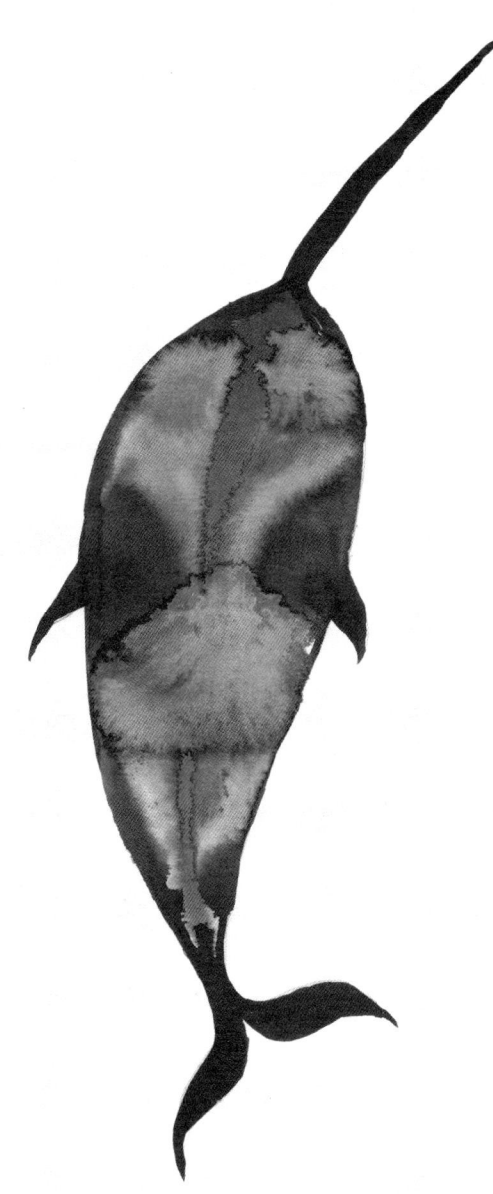

BREATH

The trickiest part of the narwhal is getting a fine and steady line for his horn, then continuing the line all the way through the body. It is one long, steady, sweeping action. I find it helpful to take a deep breath before I begin and then release it very slowly as I paint the line. Sometimes it helps to release the breath using a *shhhh* sound. It makes the release more even, and this passes through into your line work.

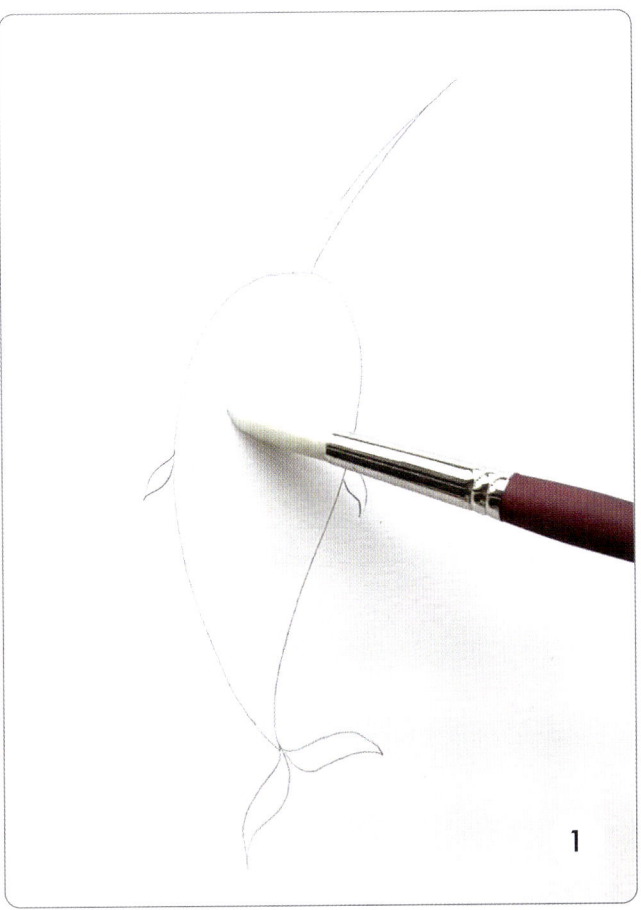

1 Trace the outline of the narwhal on your page very lightly using your pencil. Dip your water brush into the water, and remove any excess by wiping it on the rim of the jar. Paint water onto the main body of the narwhal, leaving the fins, horn, and tail flippers dry.

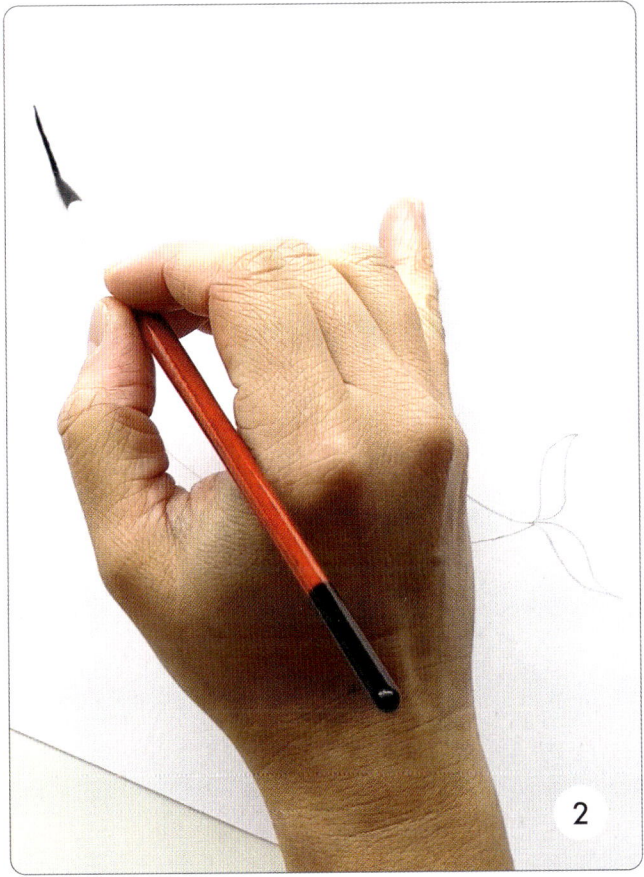

2 Dip your number 6 ink brush in the ink, and remove the excess by wiping it on the rim of the jar. Place the tip of the brush at the tip of the narwhal's horn. Slowly pull the brush down toward the body. When you hit the water, keep pulling the brush down, all the way to the tip of the tail where the fins meet. I find it helps my brush balance if I stick out my pinky finger and rest it on the page.

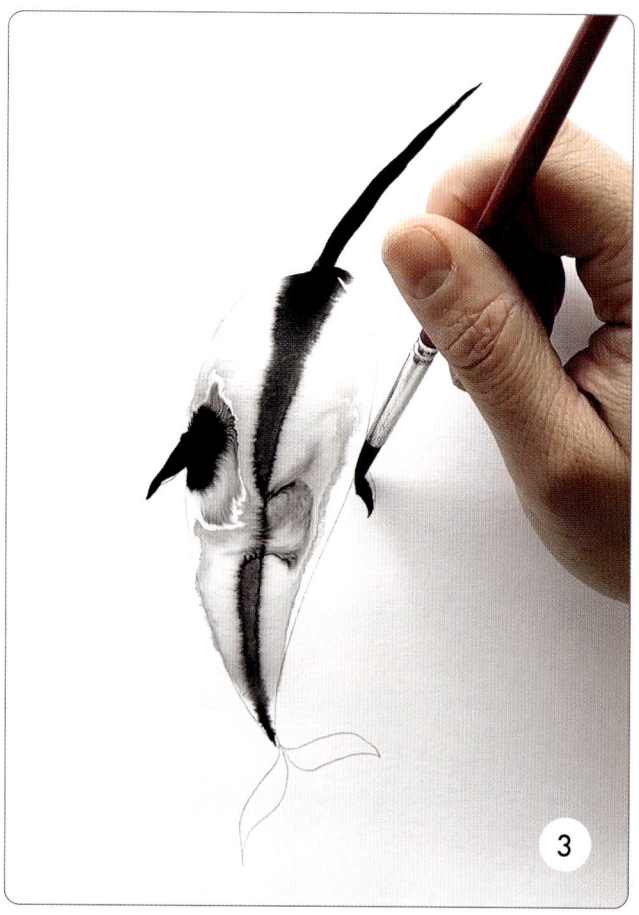

3 You may need to dry your brush off on a paper towel and reload it with ink after it has pulled through the wet body. Place the tip of the number 6 ink brush at the tip of the fin, and pull the brush toward the body until you hit the water. Lift the brush, and repeat with the other fin.

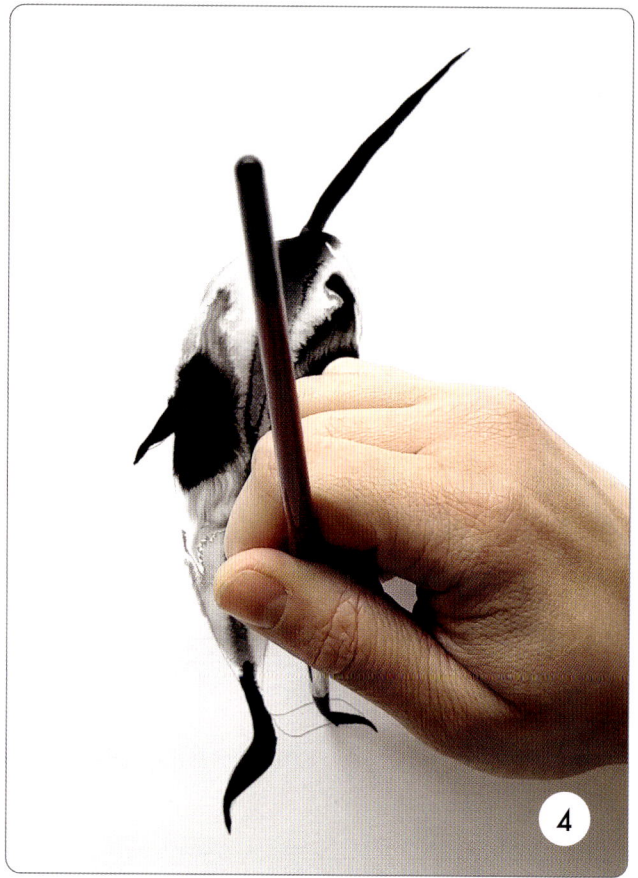

4 Place the tip of the number 6 ink brush at the tip of the tail fin, and pull it toward the wet body of the narwhal. Lift the brush when you hit the water, and repeat with the other fin.

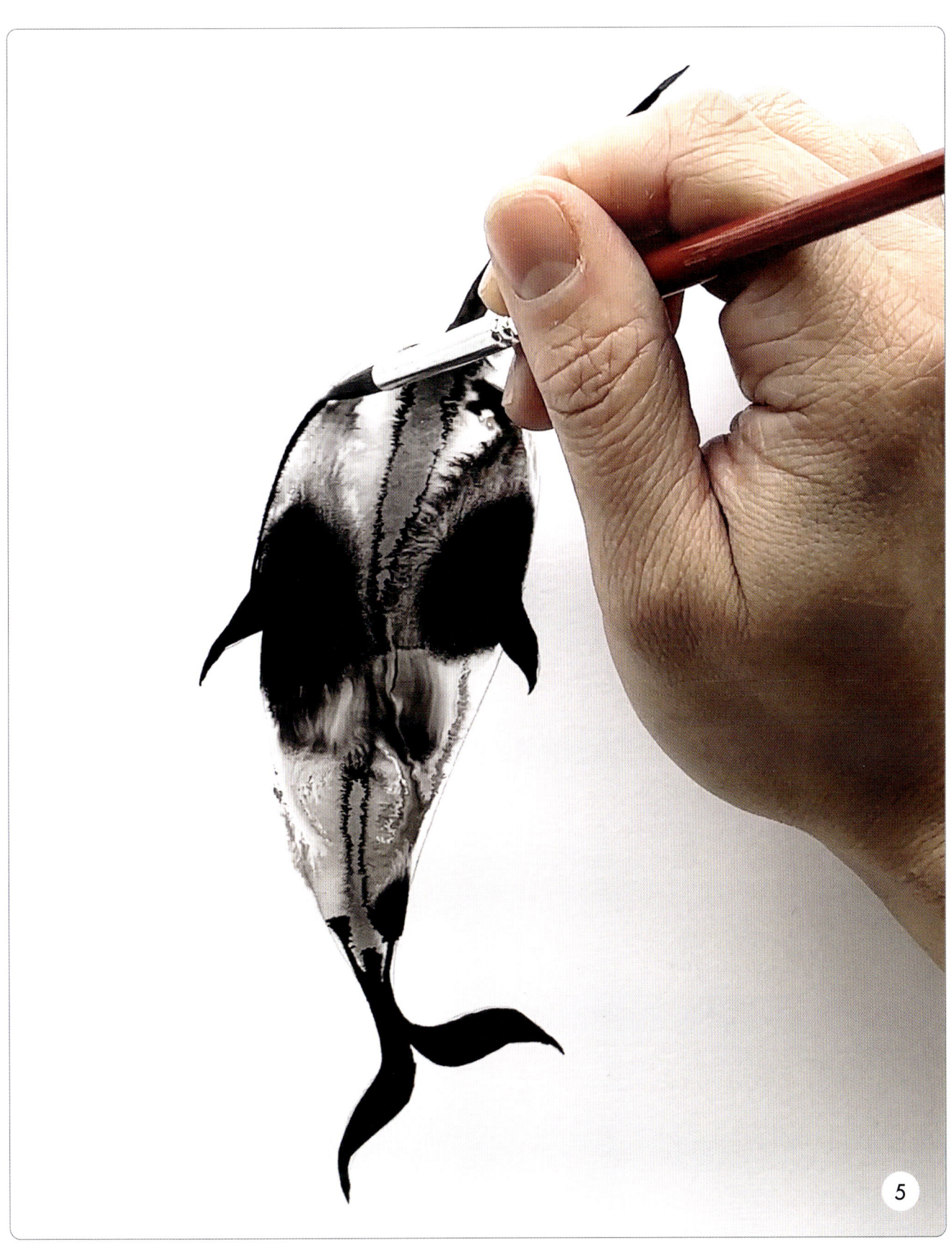

5 Dry off your brush, and reload it with ink, but not too much. Touch up the edges of the narwhal using just the tip of the brush to paint fine lines.

LUMINESCENCE

Jellyfish are probably the most magical sea creatures I've ever seen. They can produce their own light in the depths of the ocean, shimmering out like glowing aliens. I could watch them for hours, gently billowing along, almost like they are dancing . . .

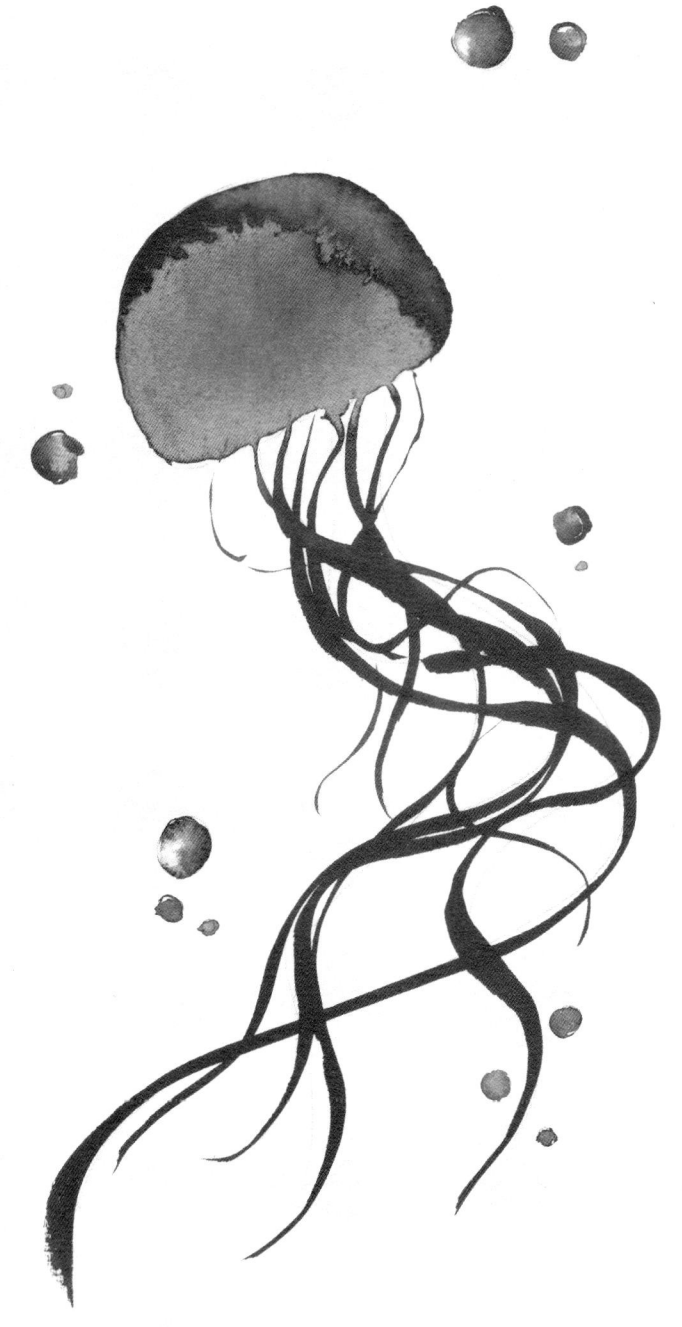

GROUNDING

Close your eyes, and find a calm, even breathing rhythm. As you continue breathing, gently move your body as if it were fluid—roll your neck from side to side, and move your arms, your legs, your shoulders. Feel your breath move smoothly through each of the areas of your body as you move them. Continue breathing and moving until your whole body feels loose and fluid.

BREATH

The main lines of the jellyfish are the tentacles, and I find it useful to lead with the breath when painting them. I breathe in through my nose and then slowly out through my mouth, allowing the brush to swirl wherever feels natural. Remember the pencil lines are just guidelines; you will create more fluid lines if you are concentrating on breathing rather than painting exactly over the pencil sketch.

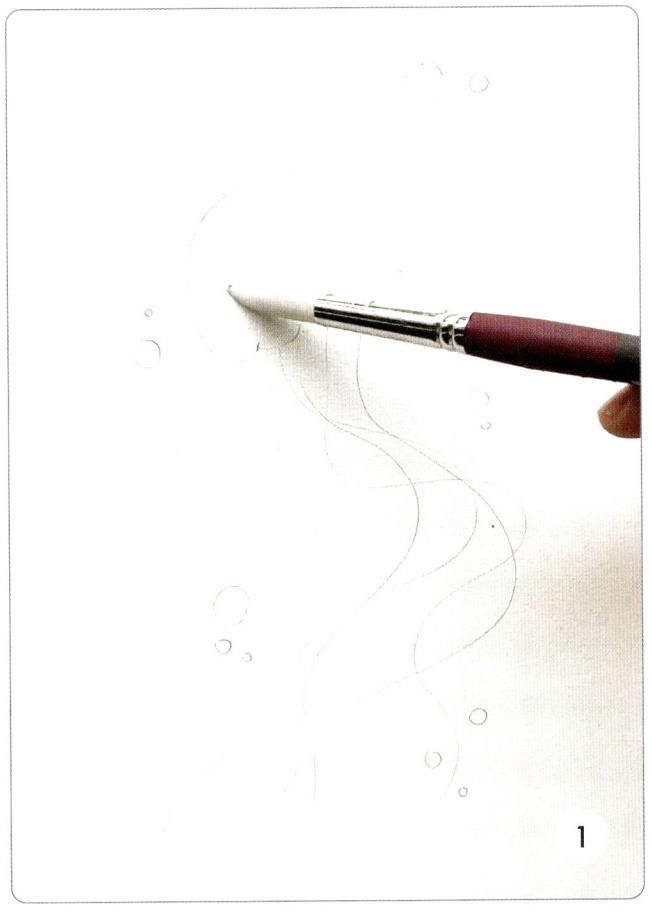

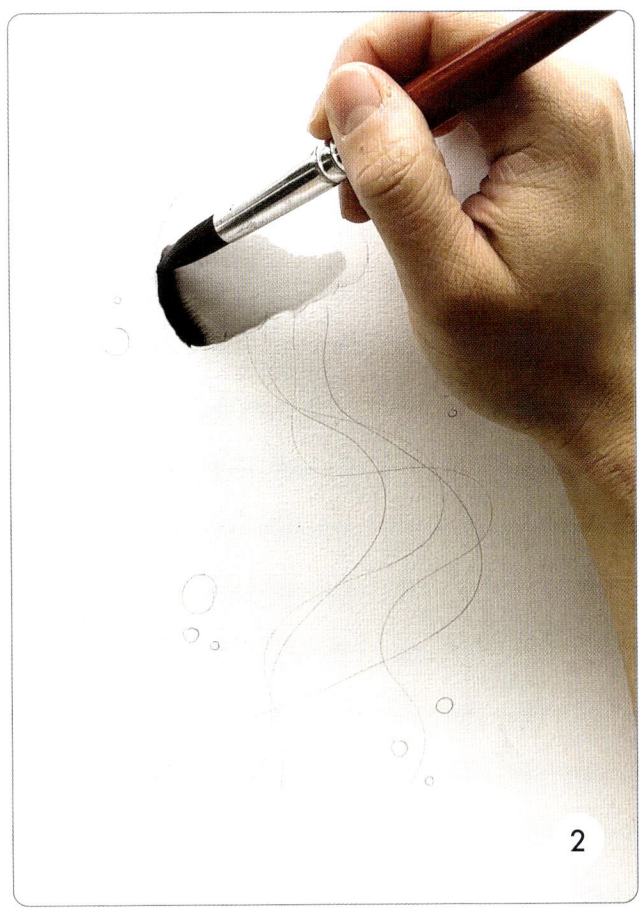

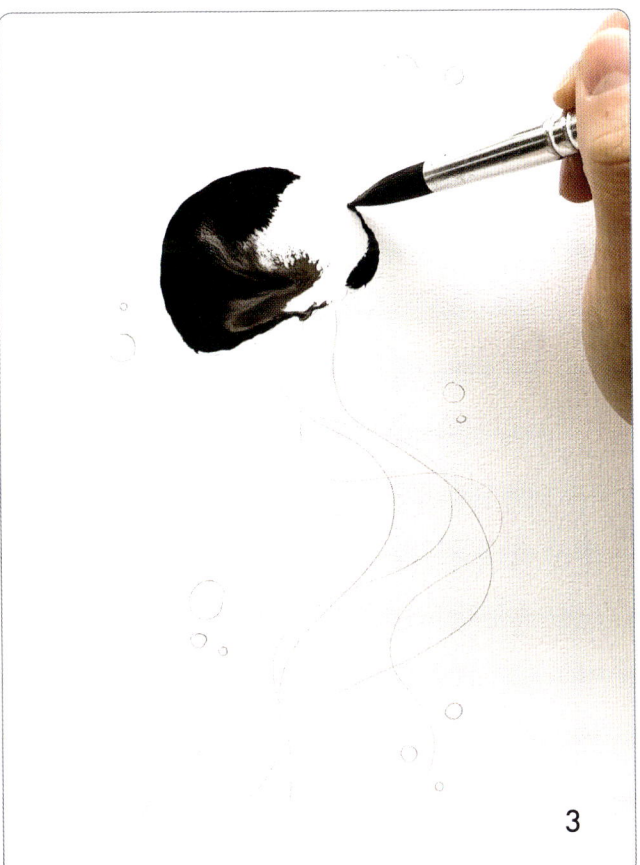

1 Trace the outline of the jellyfish on your page very lightly using your pencil. Dip your water brush into the water, and remove the excess by wiping it on the rim of the jar. Paint water onto the body of the jellyfish. Leave the tentacles and bubbles dry.

2 Dip your number 12 ink brush into the ink, and remove excess ink by wiping the brush on the rim of the jar. Place the tip of the brush on the tip edge of the jellyfish body. I start on the left and pull my hand around the edge of the water to the right, stopping about two-thirds of the way around. If you are left-handed, you might find it easier to do the opposite.

3 Without reloading the brush, place the tip of the brush on the right side of the jellyfish body, and pull the brush up to meet the ink that you've already painted. Leave the jellyfish body now. For best results, don't touch it too much.

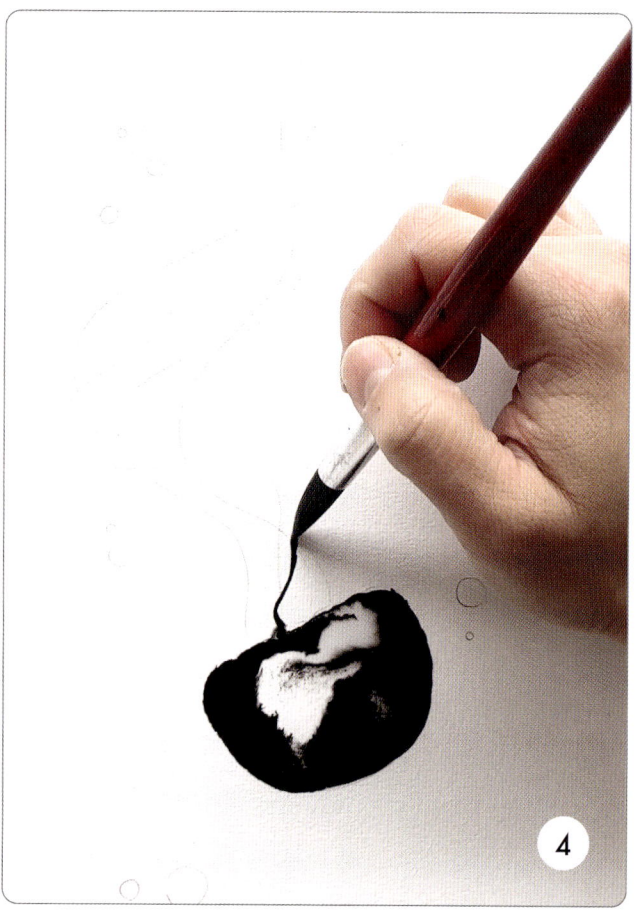

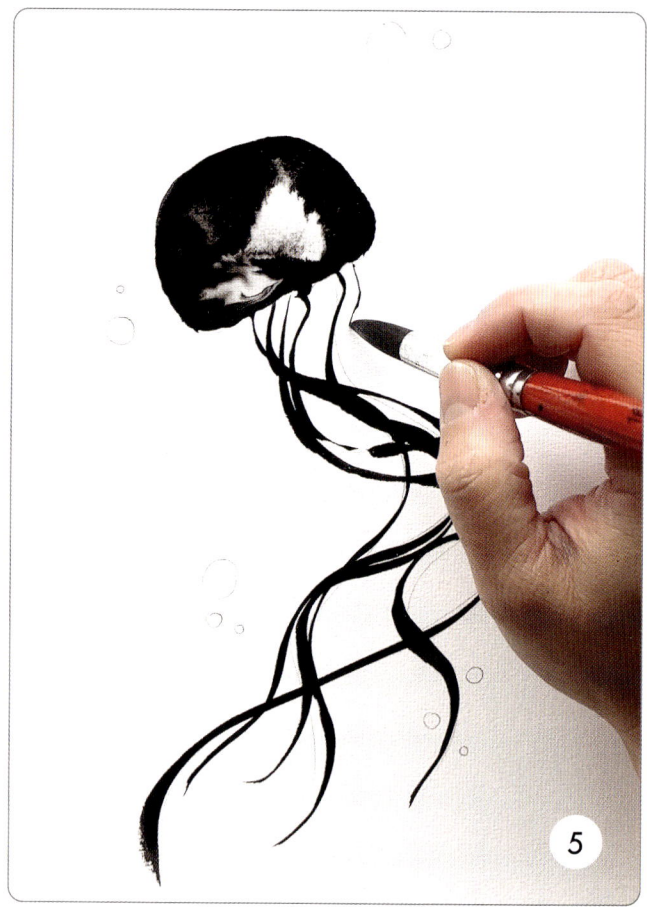

4 Reload your brush with ink. I like to use the number 12 ink brush for this one, as I feel like it has better flow, but if you are struggling to get a fine line, you can use the number 6 ink brush. When painting the tentacles, I find it easier to rotate the jellyfish upside down. Place the tip of your brush where the tentacles meet the body. Keep your elbow loose and your hand relaxed. Drag the brush along, painting swirly tentacles.

5 Once you have a few tentacles painted, rotate the jellyfish right-side-up, and add any extra tentacles that you think it needs. Remember that the pencil lines are just a guide. You can rub them out when the ink is dry or leave them, as they look like very fine tentacles.

6 Using your water brush, paint water onto each of the bubbles.

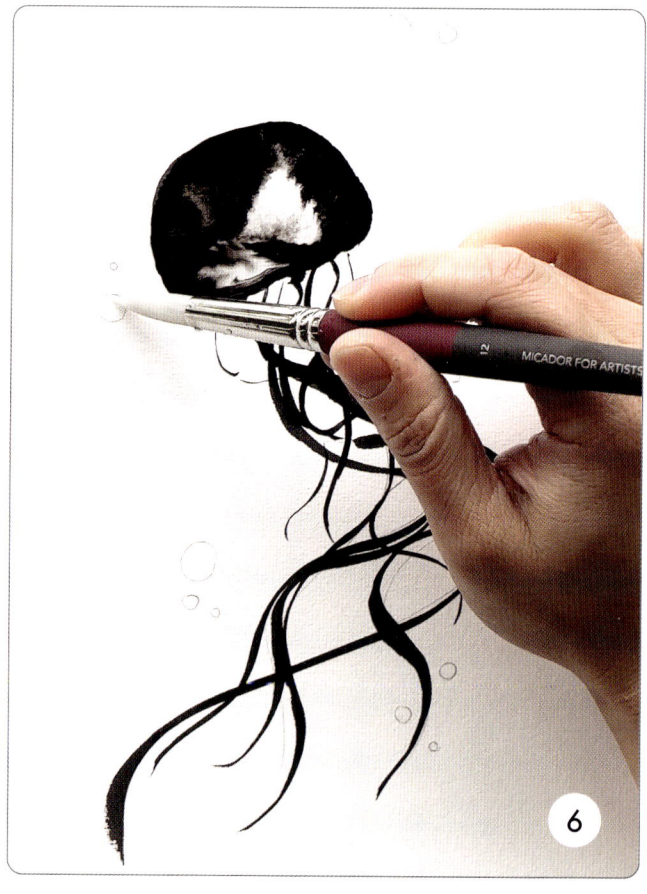

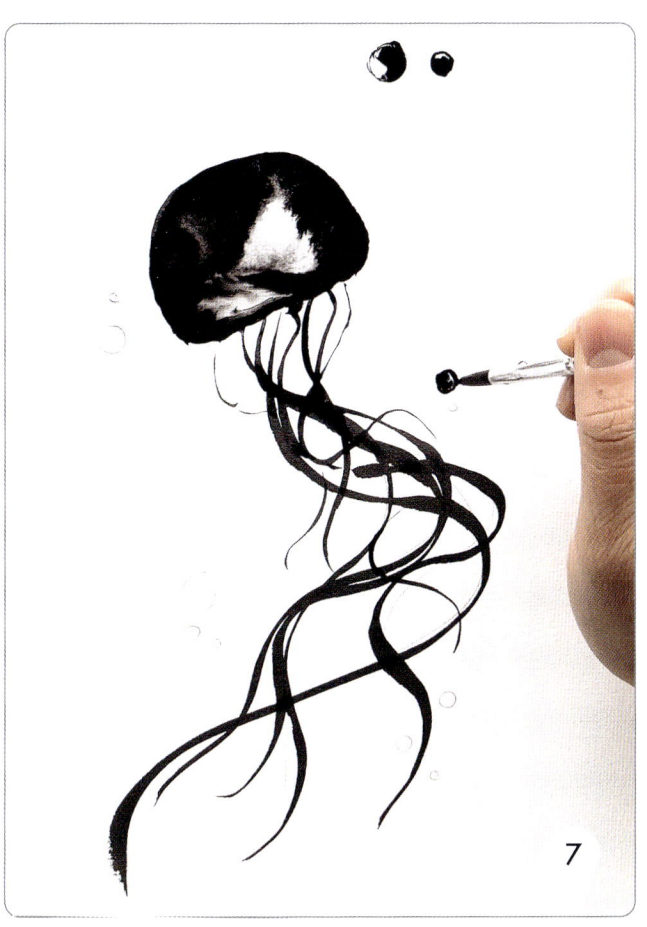

7 Dip your number 6 ink brush into the ink, and gently touch it to each of the bubbles so the water and ink merge together.

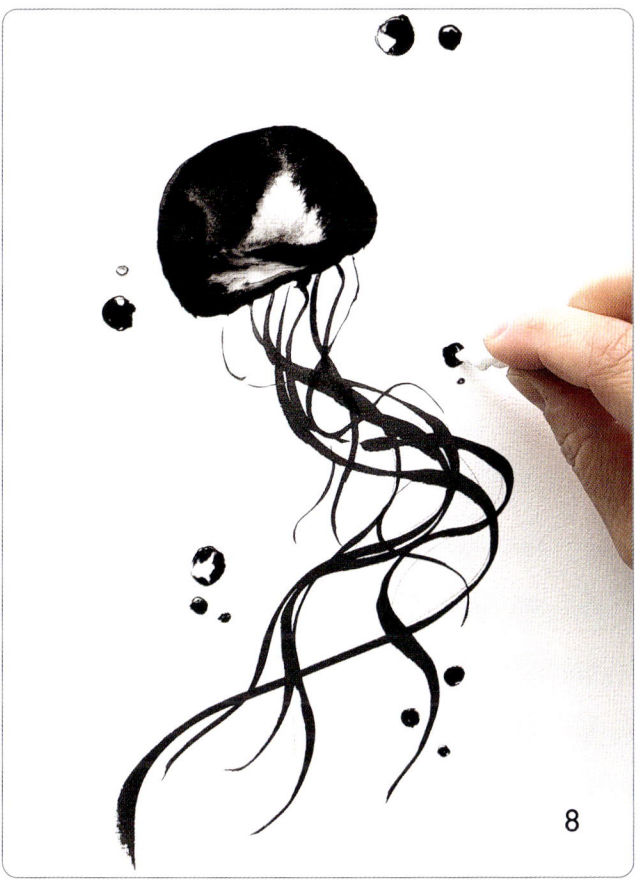

8 Use a small piece of paper towel to remove excess ink in the bubbles. Dab it gently on the surface of the inky water, and the bubbles will dry light and translucent.

RELEASE THE KRAKEN

In the deepest parts of the ocean live creatures that we can only imagine.
Giant, monstrous, and inky black . . .

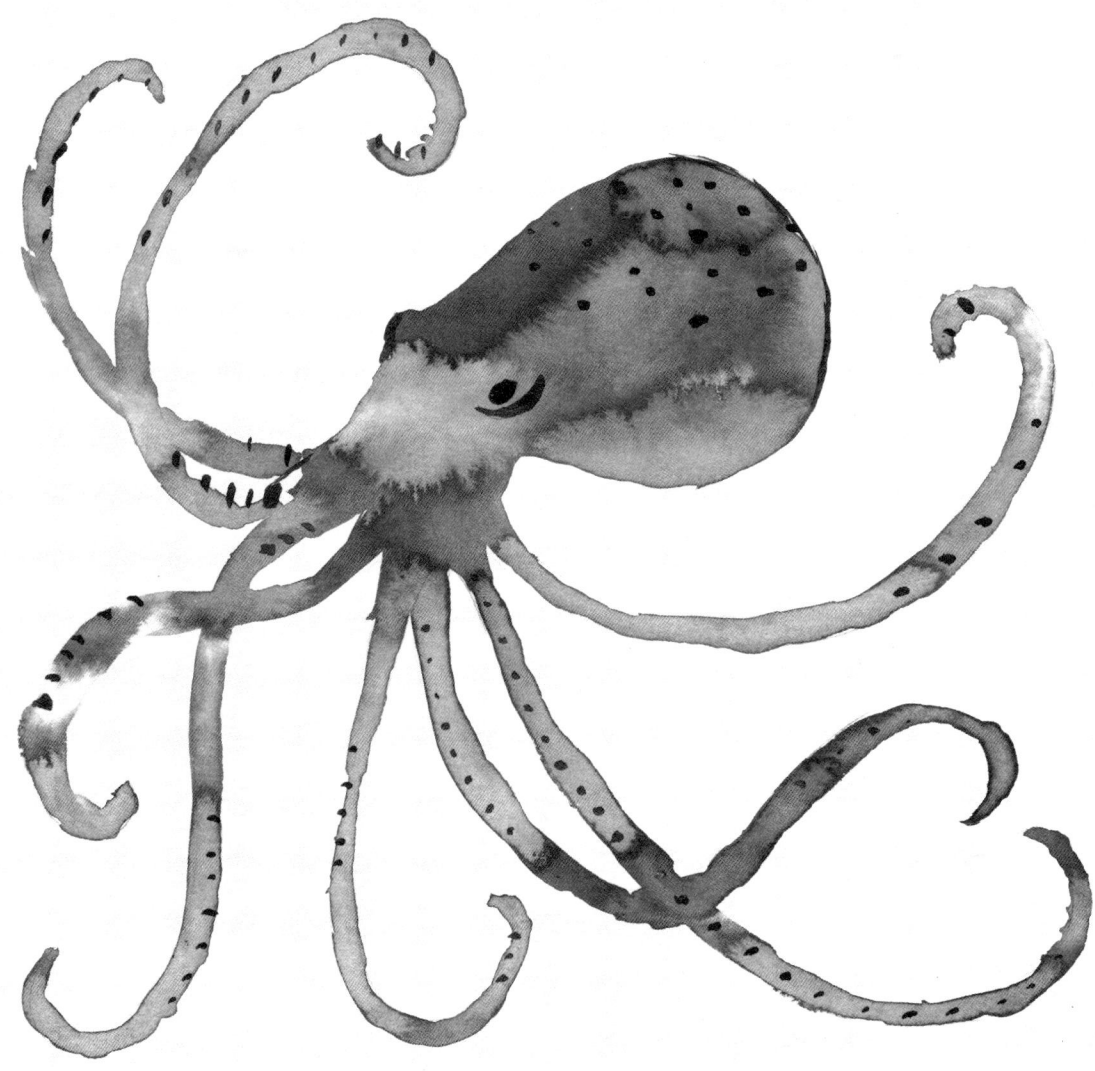

GROUNDING

Turn off the lights, and draw the curtains. Close your
eyes, and feel the darkness around you. Breathe evenly
and deeply, feeling the objects you know around you,
your chair, and the ground underneath you. You'd be
surprised how much you can see in the dark.

BREATH

The trickiest part of this octopus is painting the water on.
You need a steady hand to paint within the lines of each
arm. I sometimes find it easier to hold my breath for this.
You may want to only paint one arm at a time, both to
avoid holding your breath for too long and also to avoid
the water drying before you are ready to paint!

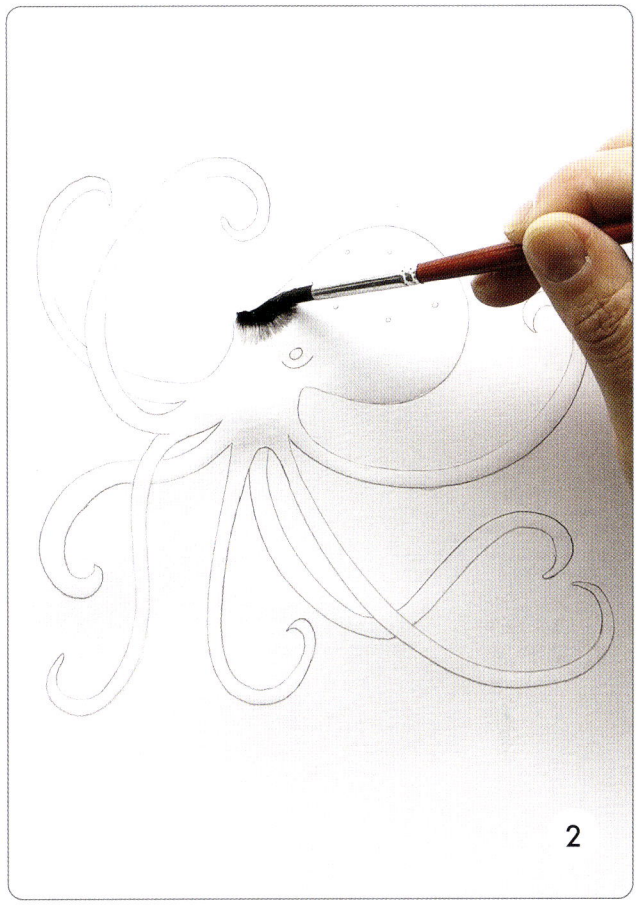

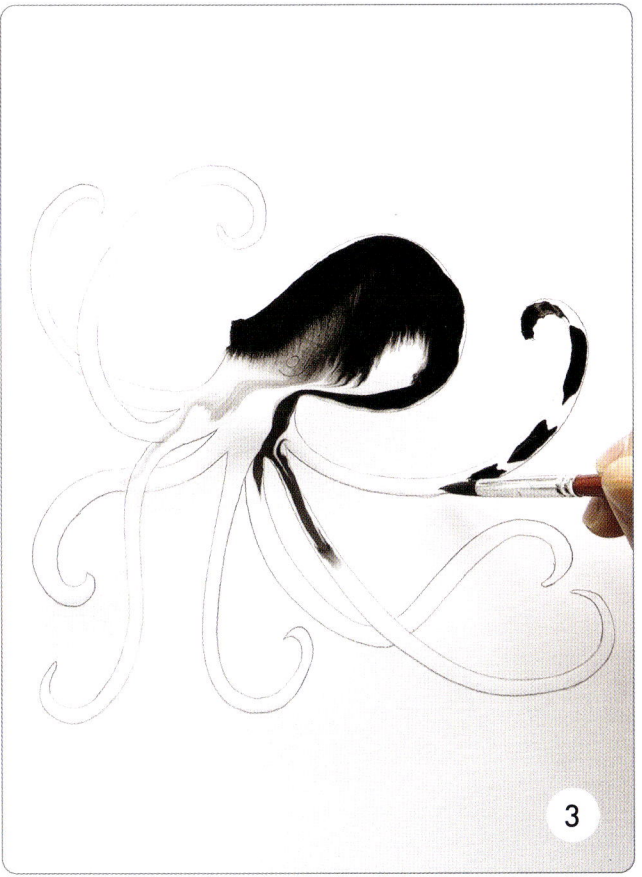

1 Trace the outline of the octopus on your page very lightly using your pencil. Dip your water brush into the water, and remove any excess by wiping it on the rim of the jar. Paint the body and arms of the octopus with water. You can do just a few arms at a time if you are worried about them drying up too quickly.

2 Dip the number 6 ink brush into the ink, and remove the excess by wiping the brush on the rim of the jar. Place the tip of the brush on the outer eye of the octopus, and follow the line right around the head to the other side. The ink will start to move into the arms that are wet.

3 Paint small dots of ink at intermittent points along each arm.

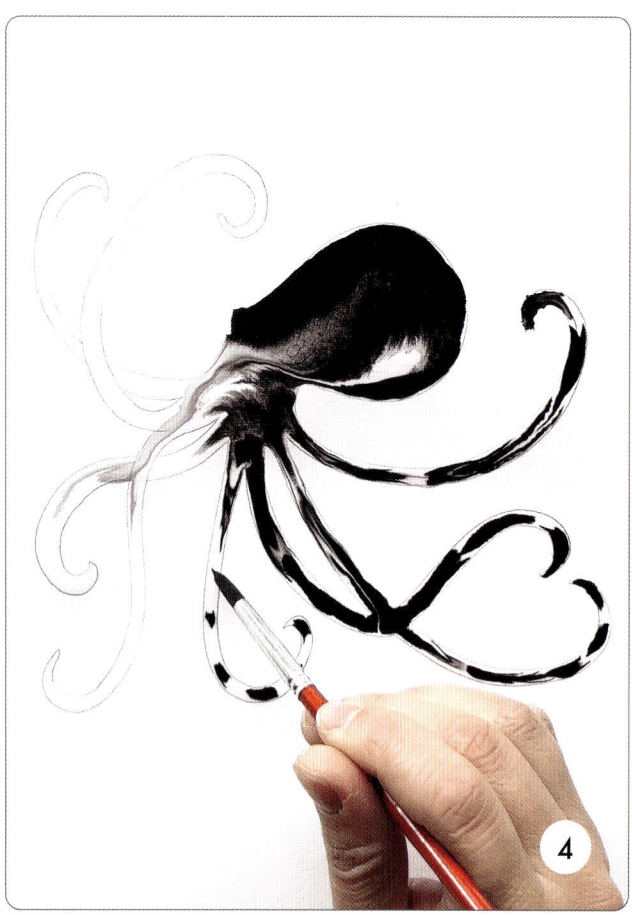

4 The ink will move and merge into the water, and the dots will lose definition, but this will help create the watery, inky texture of the octopus. Once each arm is inked, leave it to dry completely (I like to leave it overnight just to be safe).

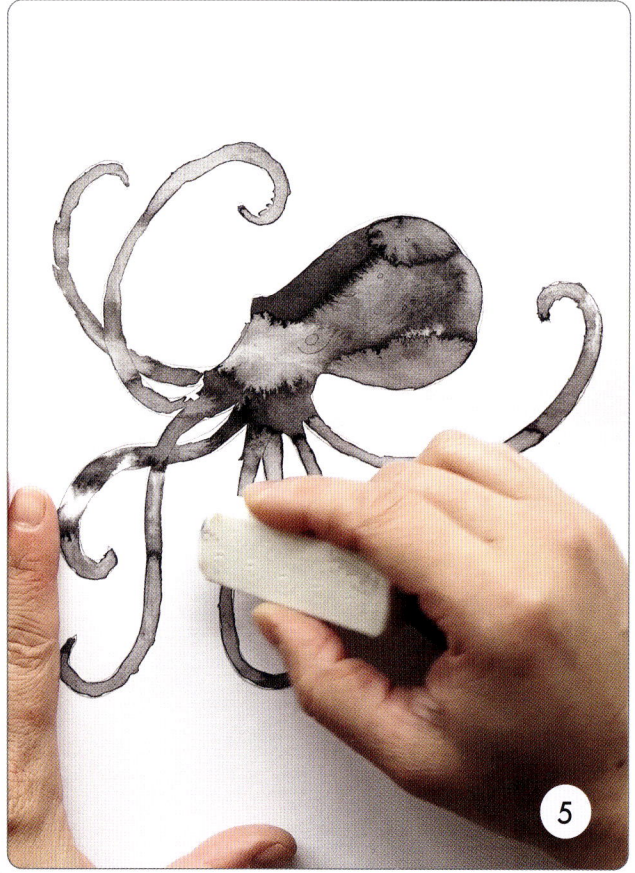

5 Taking an eraser, gently rub out any pencil lines that haven't been covered up with ink.

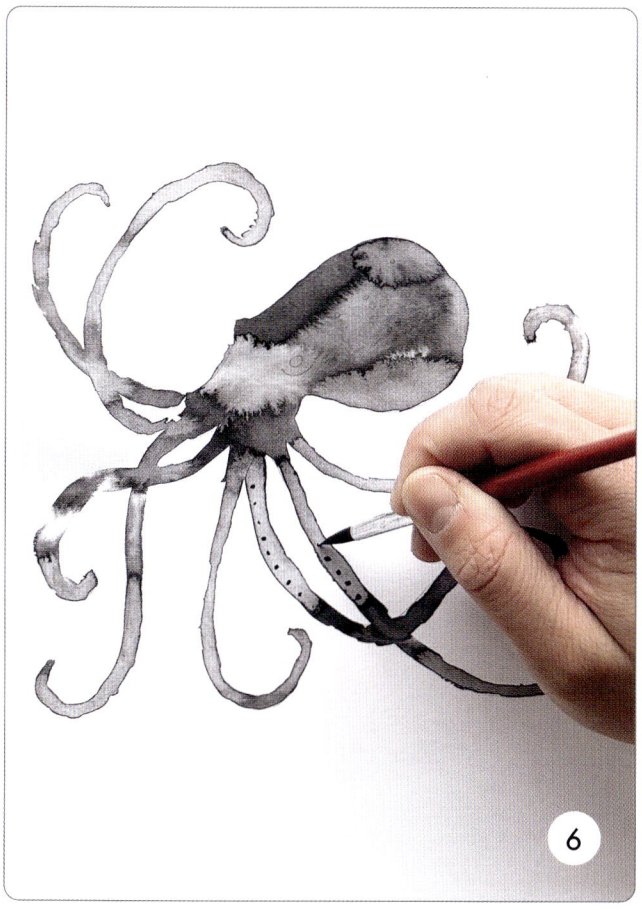

6 Dip the number 6 ink brush into the ink, and remove any excess by wiping the brush on the rim of the jar. Paint delicate dots intermittently along the legs to create tentacles and texture.

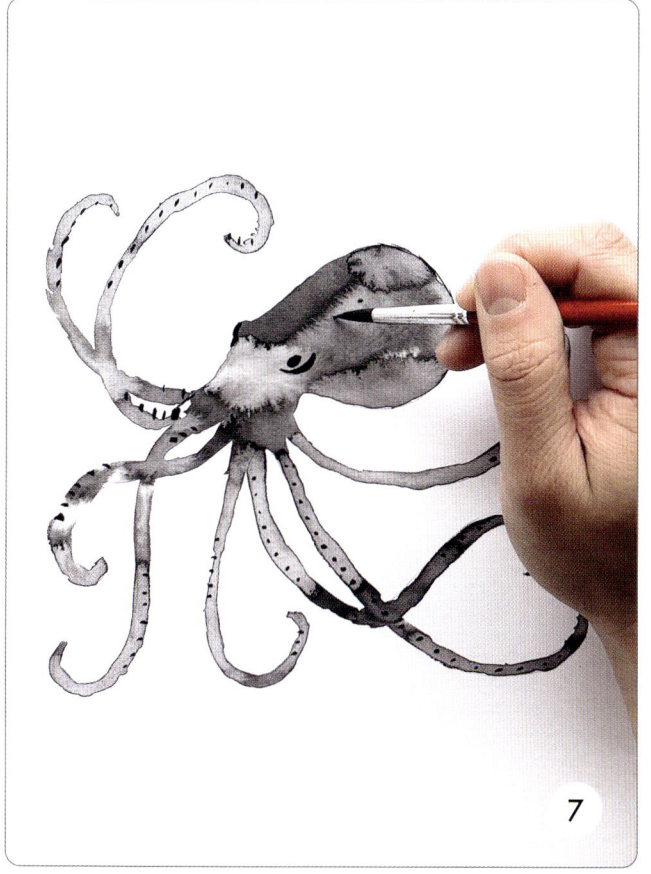

7 Using the tip of the brush, paint in the detail of the eye and the spots on the octopus's head. (You should still be able to see these pencil markings through the ink.)

MAMA & BABY WHALE

Whales are magnificent beasts, and one of my favorite inky sea creatures to paint. Here we have a mama and baby whale. The way the ink moves makes it seem like there is an ocean painted into their bodies. Or is it the night sky? Perhaps it is the whole universe.

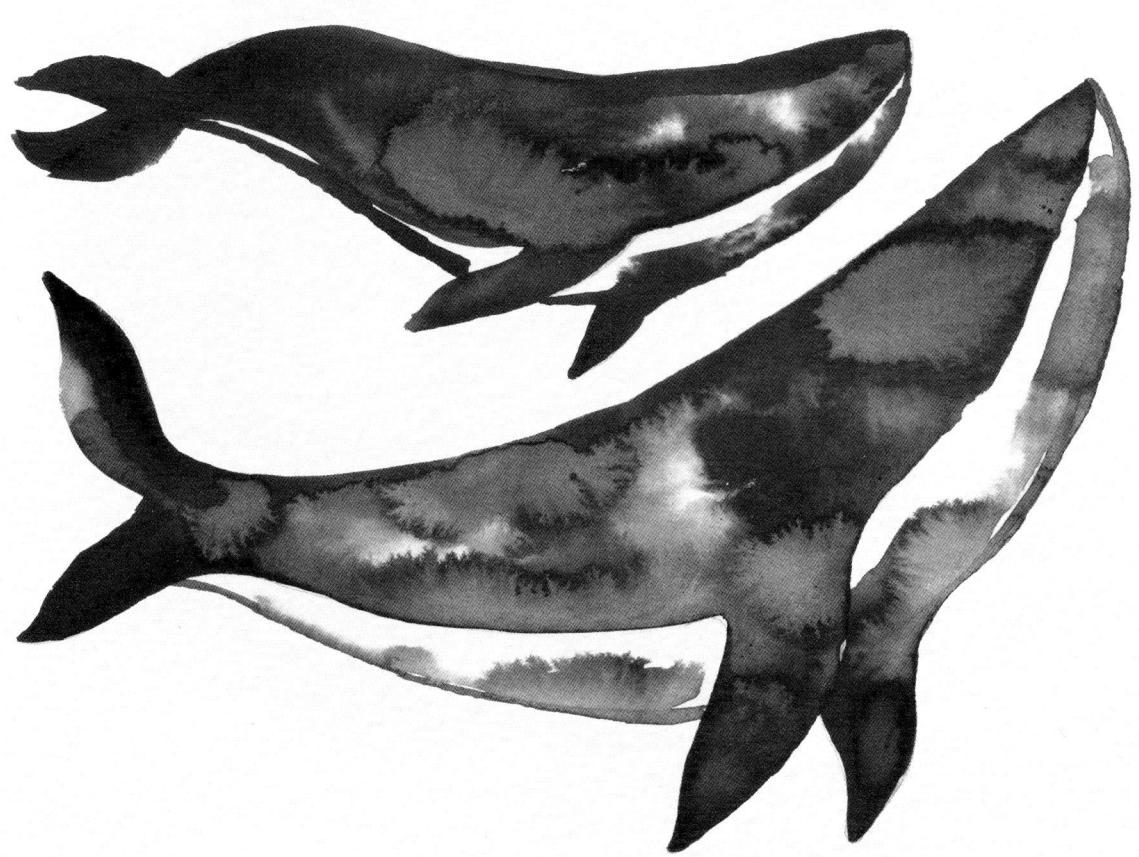

GROUNDING

Begin by taking a moment to pause and ground yourself. Take a deep breath in through your nose, hold your breath for a count of three, and exhale slowly through your mouth. Repeat this three times. Each time you exhale, feel your feet plant firmly into the ground, and focus your eyes on the page in front of you.

BREATH

Remember to inhale when your brush is poised, ready to paint, and exhale slowly as you place the brush on the paper and paint your line. In this project, there are a number of long brushstrokes that run along the body of the whale, and I find it best to exhale slowly and evenly through my nose while painting these lines. When I lift my brush, I inhale again.

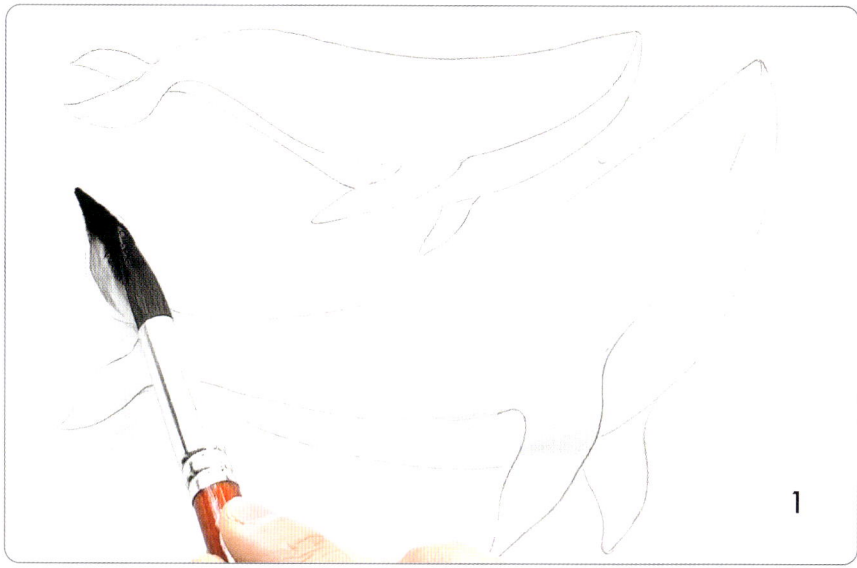

1 Trace the outline of the whales on your page very lightly using your pencil. Dip the water brush into your clean water so it is well soaked. Remove excess water by wiping the brush along the rim of your water jar. Paint water inside the outlines of the mama whale's back. Dip the number 12 ink brush into your ink, and remove any excess by wiping the brush on the rim of the jar. Focus on the tip of the mama whale's tail. Place the tip of your brush on the tip of the tail, and pull your brush along the upper outline of the back.

2 Take time to see how the ink moves before painting your next brushstroke. As the ink movement slows (remember, you can't wait too long or the water on the page will dry out!), move the tip of your ink brush to the tip of the mama whale's flipper, and gently pull the paintbrush up toward the body. You can do this in one single stroke or multiple.

3 Place the tip of the brush on the tip of the mama whale's tail that hasn't been painted yet. Pull the brush lightly along toward the fin.

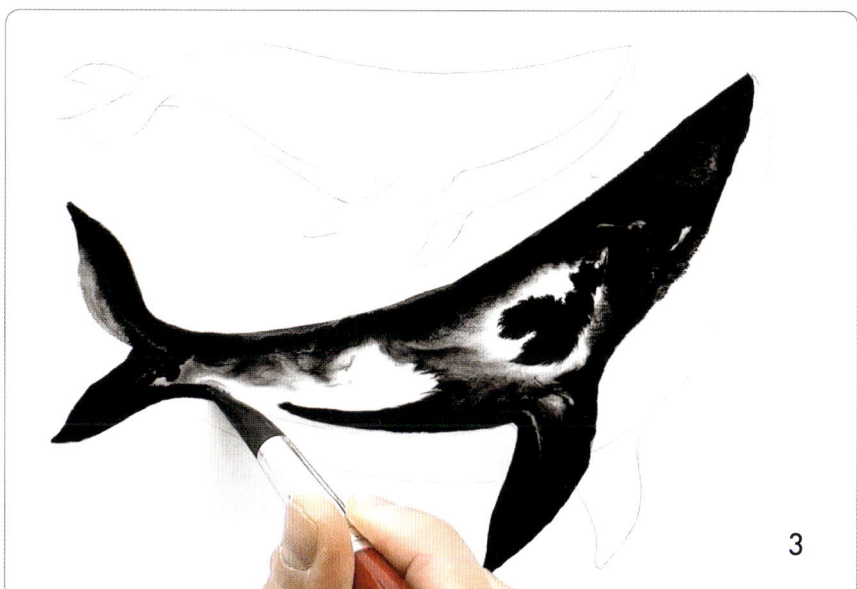

4 Leaving the mama whale to dry a little, wet your water brush again, and fill in the baby whale's back area. Dip your number 12 ink brush into the ink again, wipe any excess off on the rim of the jar, and place the tip of the brush on the tip of the baby's tail, pulling the brush along the upper outline of its back. Move the tip of your brush to the tip of the baby whale's flipper, and pull the brush back toward the body. Observe how the ink and water swirl around.

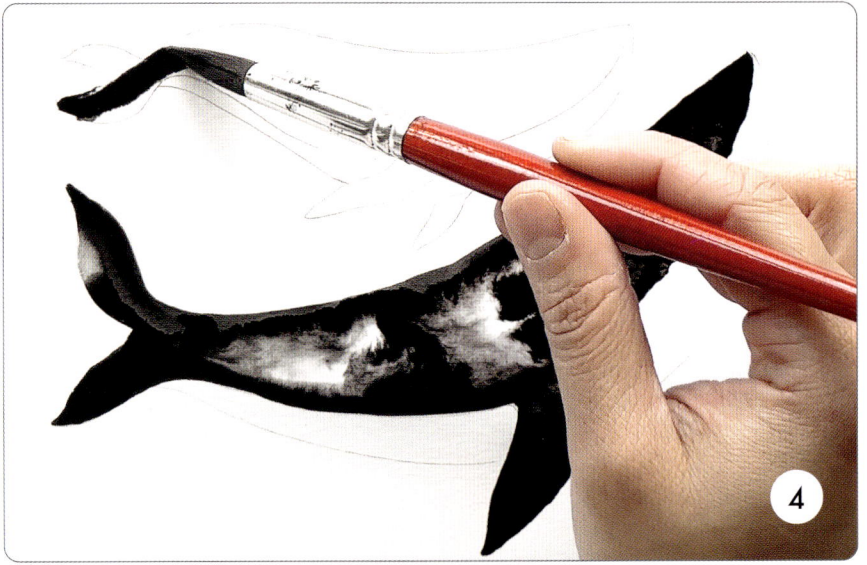

5 Place your brush back on the tip of the baby's tail. Pull the brush along, filling in the fin so it connects with the back.

6 Allow your whales to dry a little; we don't want the edges of the inked areas to be wet. Take your water brush, and wet it once more. Fill in the belly of both whales with water.

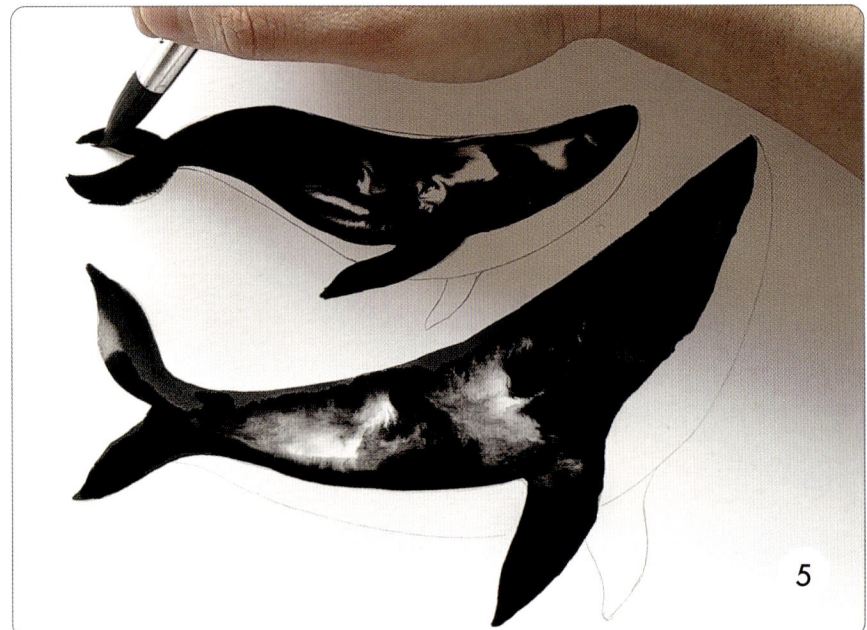

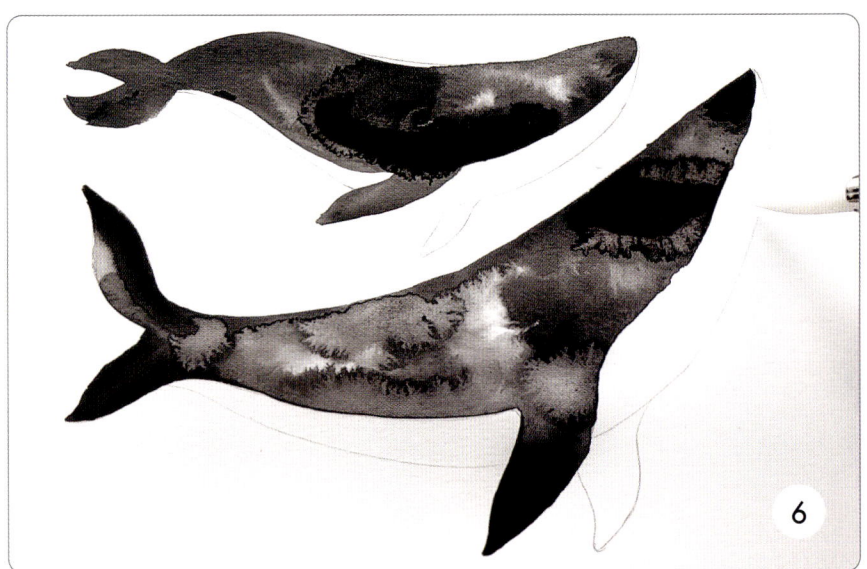

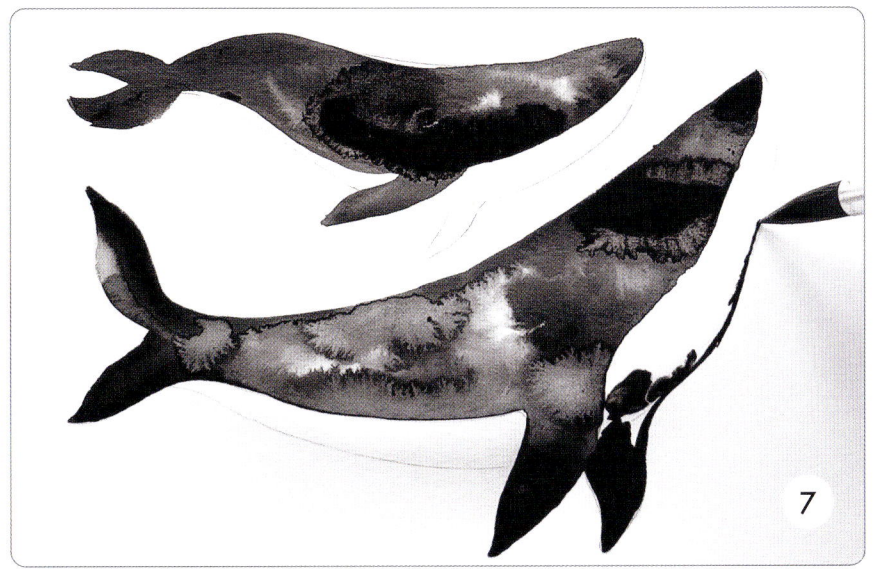

7 Dip your number 12 ink brush back into the ink, and place the tip of the brush at the tip of the mama whale's unpainted fin. Slowly pull the brush along the pencil outline up toward the mouth. Lift your brush nice and high, using just the point so you get a very fine line.

8 Still holding your brush high, using just the tip, paint a very fine line along the lower belly of the mama whale, from tail to fin.

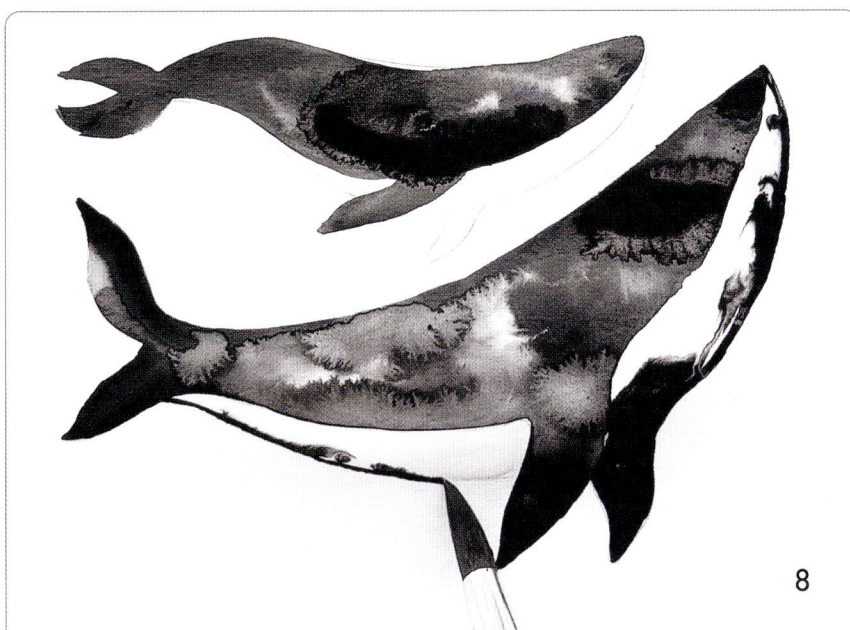

9 Now it's Baby Whale's turn. Dip your brush back into the ink, and place the tip of the brush at the tip of the baby's unpainted fin. Pull the brush along the pencil outline up toward the mouth. Use just the point of your brush so you get a very fine line. Without redipping your brush in the ink, paint a very fine line using just the tip of the brush along the lower belly of the baby whale. Add any finishing touches to both mama and baby. You may want to neaten up some of the lines around the edges so they are nice and crisp.

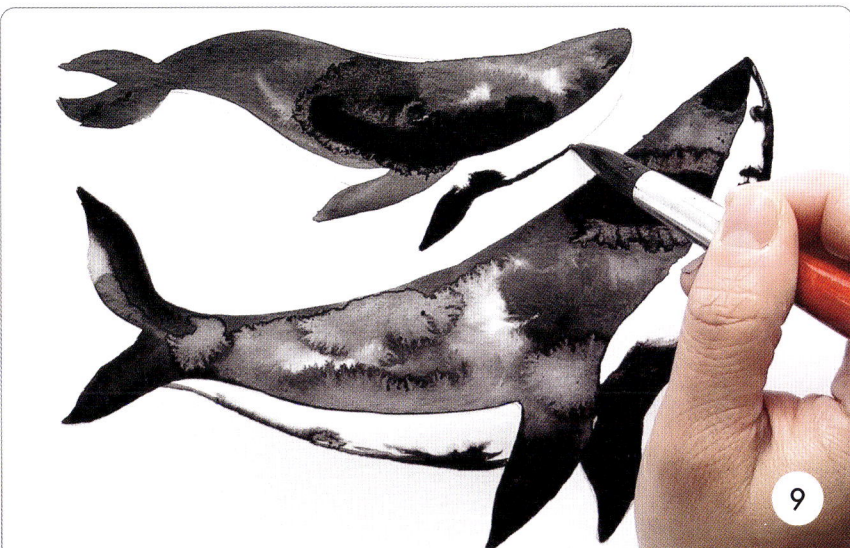

WATER DUET

Fish are one of the most commonly requested paintings on my social media, and there are so many amazing fish to choose from. I really enjoy spending time looking at beautiful photos of fish, trying to work out how to best capture their movement in ink. I find that fish always look more alive when they are wet. Once the ink dries, it is almost like it leaves watery ghosts of the fish behind.

GROUNDING

In this project, you will be painting quite a few circular motions that have the best results when you use a light touch. Before you begin, rub your hands firmly together. Feel the sensation of your hands against each other. Then rotate your wrists independently, making small circles with your hands as fists. Finally, bring your hands together in a clap, and then shake them freely. You might notice the palms of your hands are tingly and more sensitive. I find this helps paint flowing, light lines.

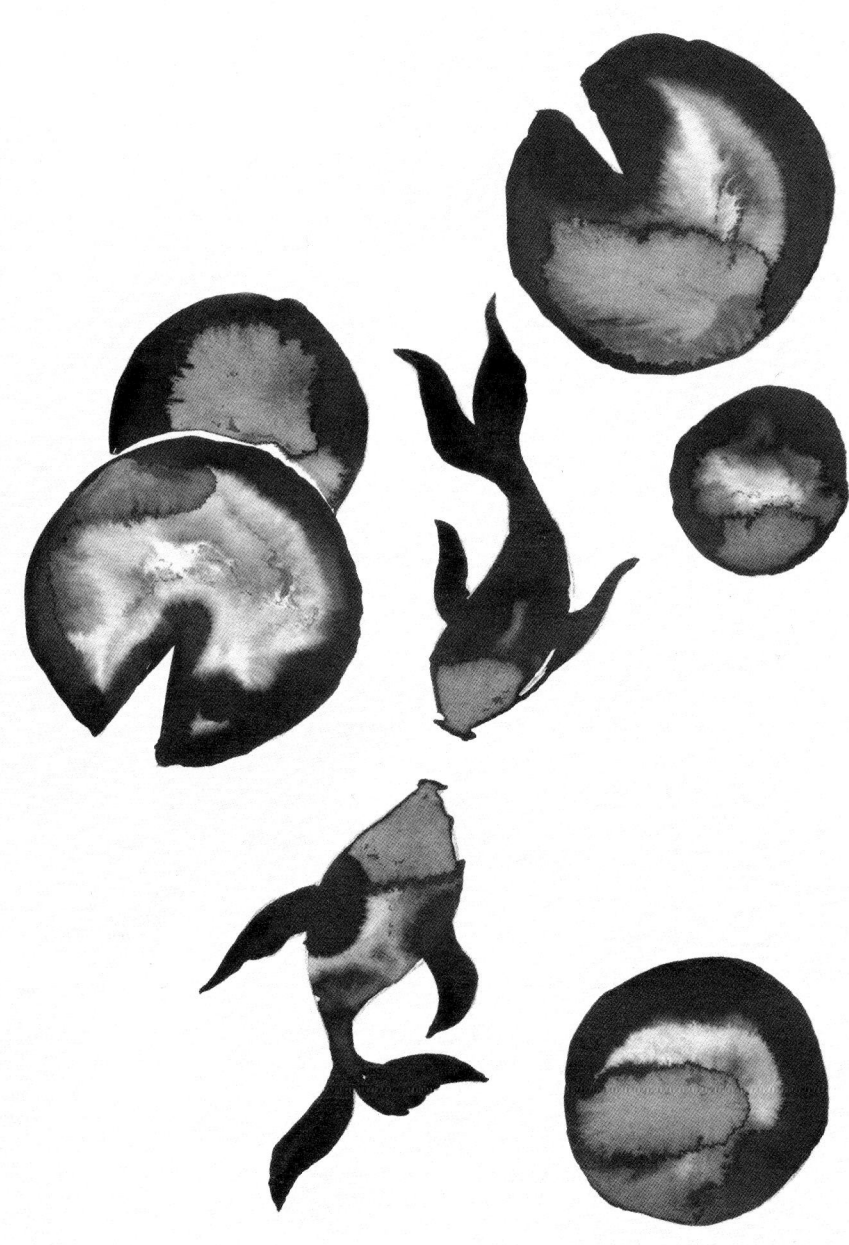

BREATH

In this project, we are using less ink and allowing the water to do the work. Remember to inhale when your brush is poised, ready to paint, and exhale slowly as you place the brush on the paper and paint your line. When you have lifted the brush, continue to breathe deeply while you watch the ink and water react. Try to slow your breathing as the ink's movement through the water slows.

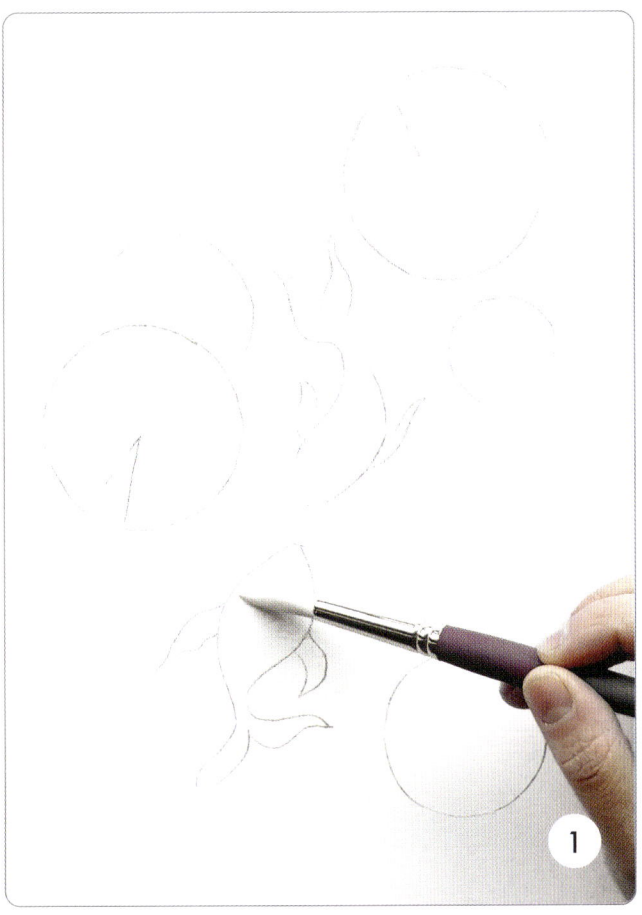

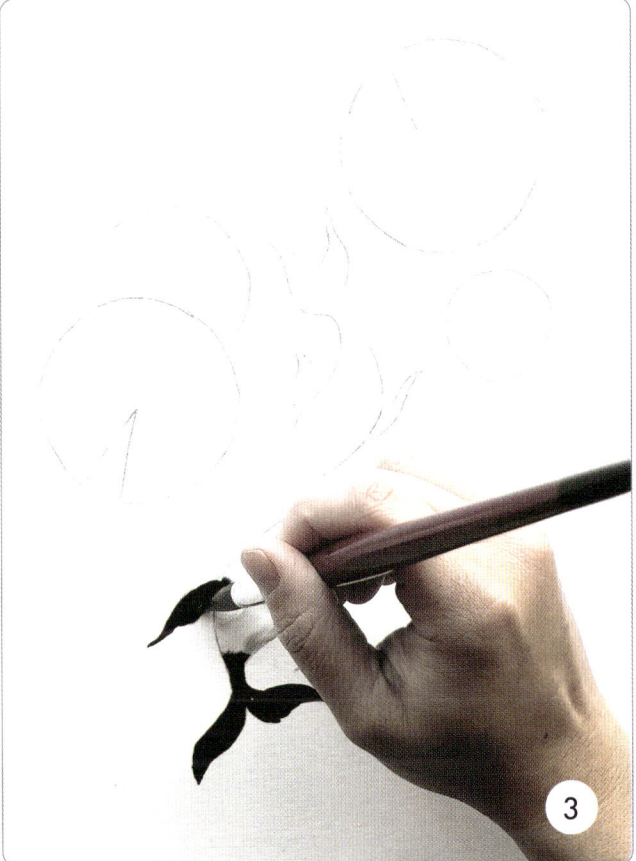

1 Trace the outline of the fish on your page very lightly using your pencil. Dip the water brush into your clean water so it is well soaked. Remove excess water by wiping the brush along the rim of your water jar. Paint water inside the body of the lower fish. Do not paint any water on the fins or tail.

2 Dip the number 12 ink brush into your ink, and remove excess ink by wiping the brush on the rim of the jar. Place the tip of the brush on the tip of the fish's tail. Pull the brush up to meet the water in the body. Lift the brush when you touch the edge of the water—the ink will start to move into the body of the fish on its own. Repeat with the second tip of the fish's tail.

3 Place the tip of your brush on the tip of the fish's fin. Pull the brush toward the body, and let it meet the water. Lift the brush when you get to the water's edge. The ink will bleed into the water. Repeat with the other fin. Take a moment, and wait for the ink to stop moving through the water.

4 Using the very tip of your brush, paint along the tiny mouth line of the fish. This ink will also move into the watery body area.

5 Using your water brush, paint clean water into the body of the other fish. Do not paint any water on the fins or tail.

6 Dip the number 12 ink brush into your ink, and remove the excess ink by wiping the brush on the rim of the jar. Place the tip of the brush on the tip of the fish's tail. Pull the brush up to touch the water in the body, and then lift your brush. Repeat with the second tip of the fish's tail.

7 Just as you did with your first fish, place the tip of your brush on the tip of the fish's fin, and brush toward the body until it touches the water. Repeat with the other fin.

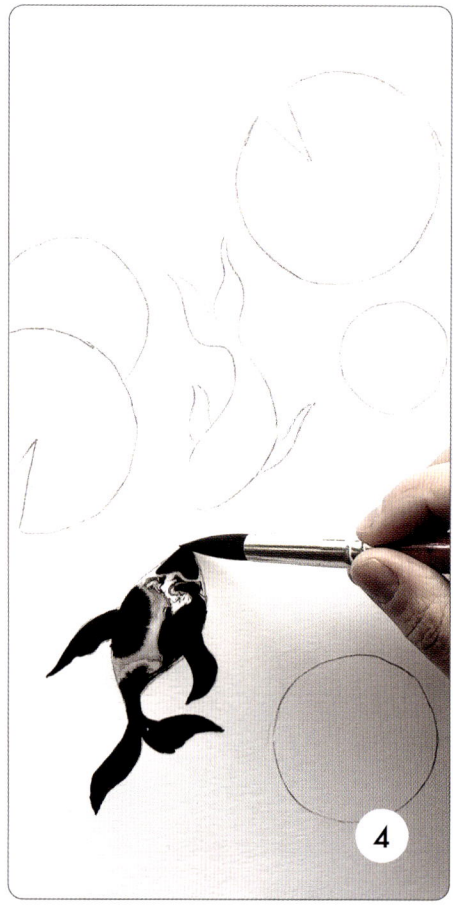

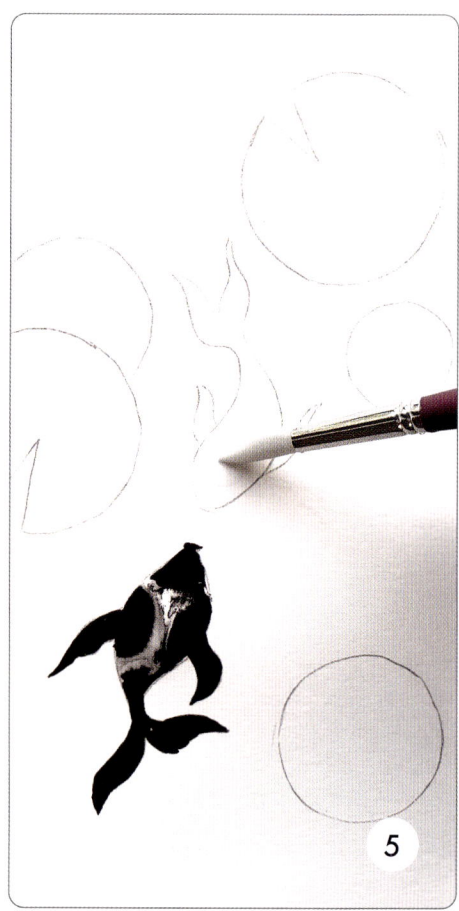

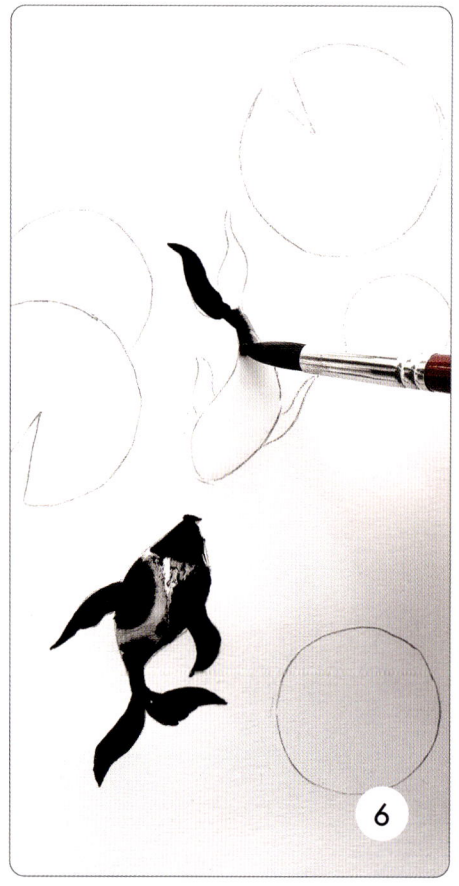

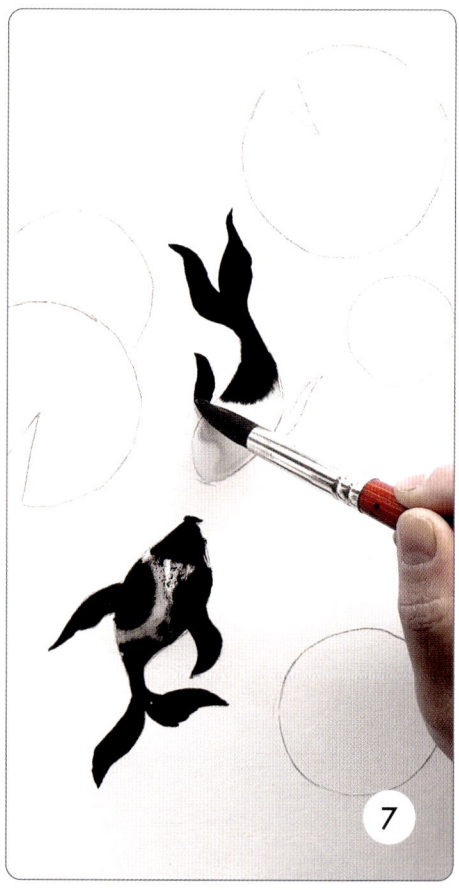

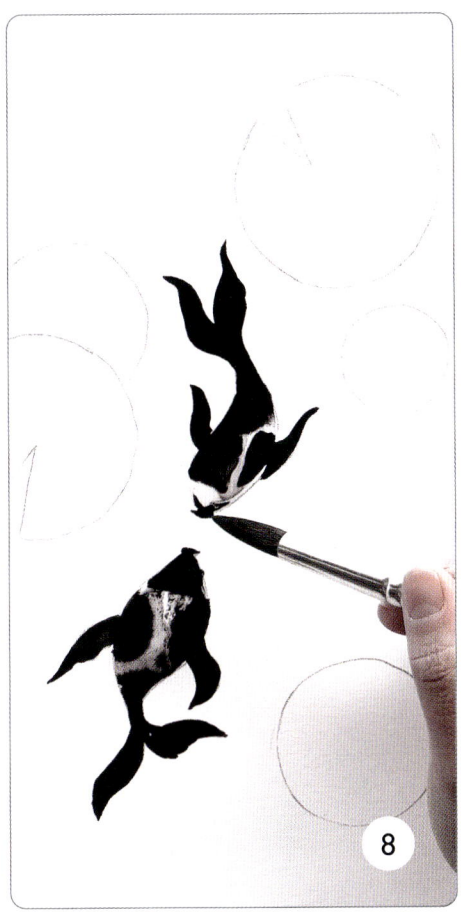

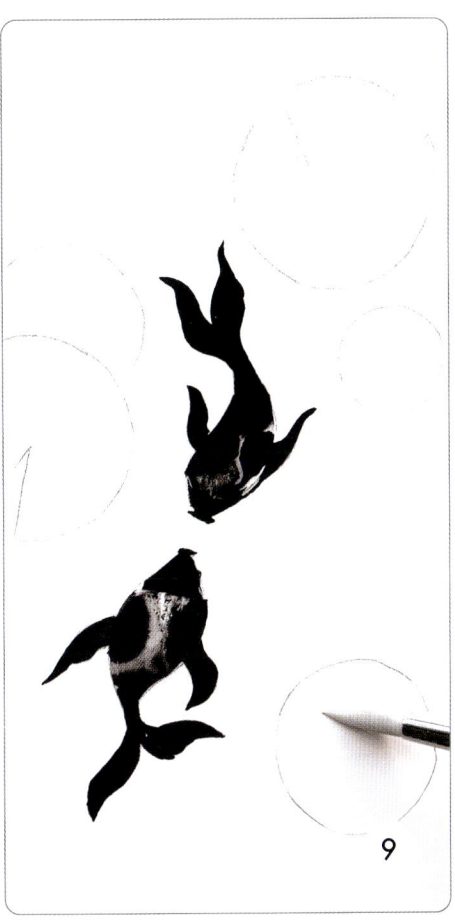

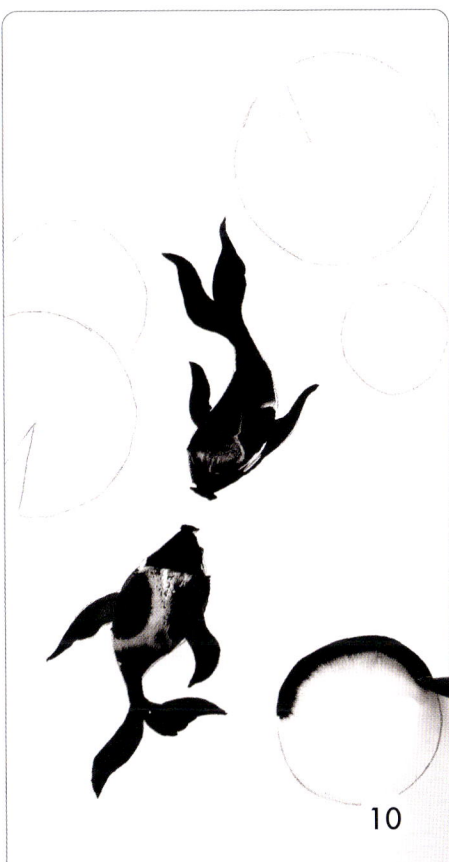

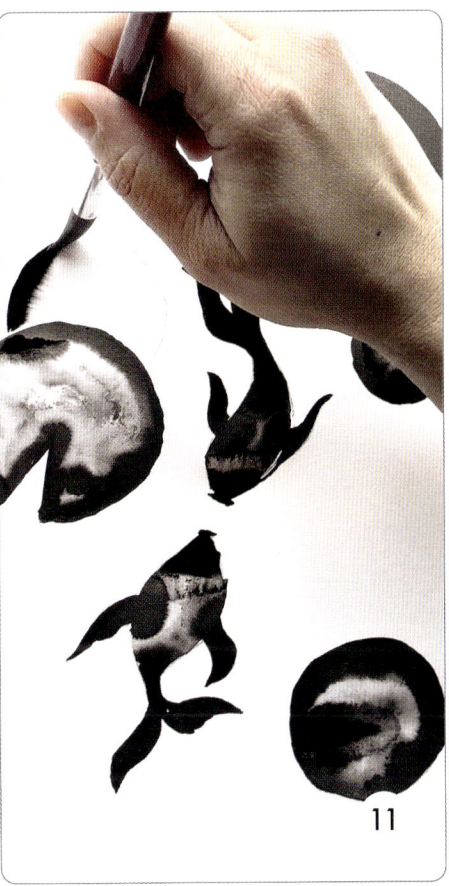

8 Using the very tip of your brush, paint along the mouth line of the second fish.

9 Using your water brush and clean water, paint the lily pads. Depending on how fast you paint, you can paint the water on multiple lily pads at once, and then add ink. If you don't feel confident working fast enough to get the ink on each lily pad before the water dries, you can do one at a time. (Note: You will need to paint the lily pads that overlap separately so they have time to dry; otherwise, they will bleed into each other.)

10 Dip your number 12 ink brush into the ink, and wipe away any excess on the rim of the jar. Paint along the lily pad with the tip of the brush, only just touching the edge of the water. Drag the paintbrush around the whole edge of the lily pad. See how the water catches the ink and fills the middle.

11 Repeat this with each lily pad. Make sure the edge of your overlapping lily pad is dry before painting the second one. I also like to leave a thin, dry gap between the two so there is a little bit more definition and the ink doesn't spread right up to the edge.

TAKING FLIGHT

Swallows just love to fly. They are incredibly agile and spend most of their time on the wing. I love how tiny but determined they are, and I think if I were a bird, I would want to spend as much time playfully flying about as they do. Scan the QR code to watch me paint this project!

GROUNDING

Sit, stand, or lie down, whichever is most comfortable for you. Find a steady rhythm to your breathing, and close your eyes. Imagine you are weightless, lifting lightly from the ground and floating in the air. How do your feet feel? Your spine? Your head? Your neck? You are so light that if a breath of wind came past, it would move you gently through the air. Now feel the weight come back into your body—feel it resting on the ground, pushing against the earth, and the earth pushing back. You are completely grounded, no longer weightless. Which feeling do you prefer? (There is no right or wrong answer!)

BREATH

This project is made up of very few brushstrokes. They are fairly bold and intentional, and I find it useful to measure my breathing with brushstrokes like this: With each inhale, I poise my brush, ready to paint. With each exhale, I place my brush on the page and paint.

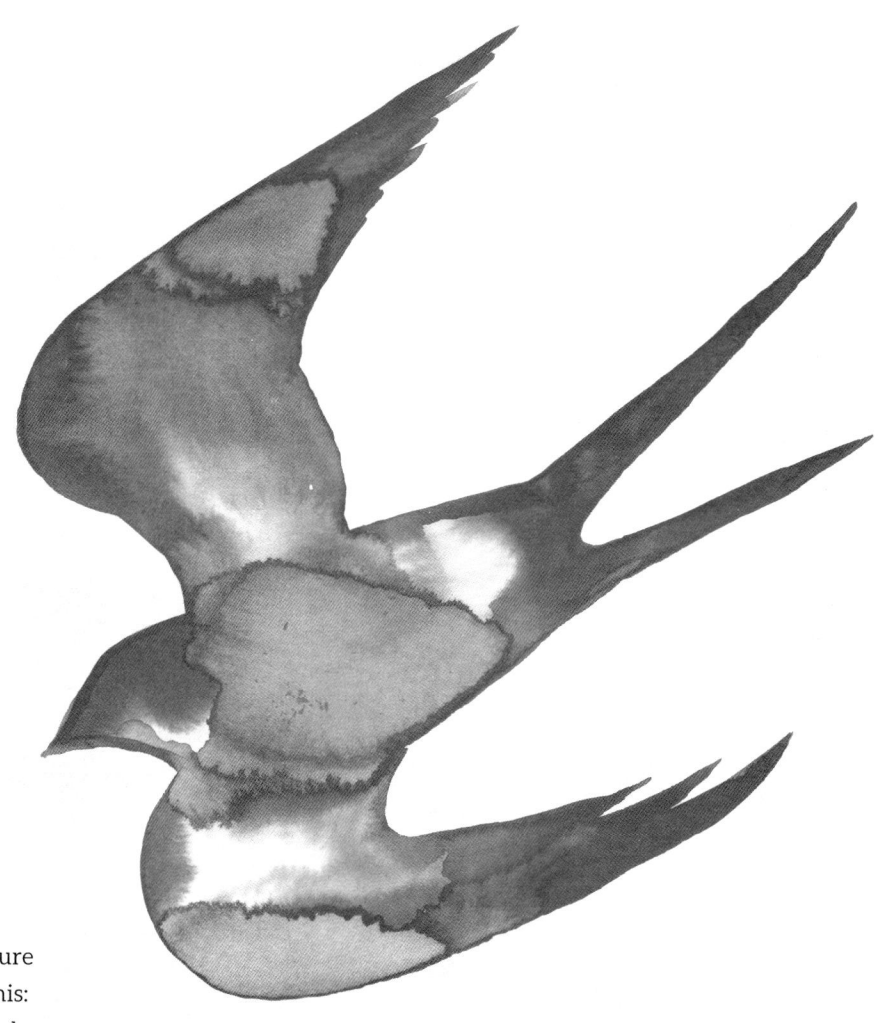

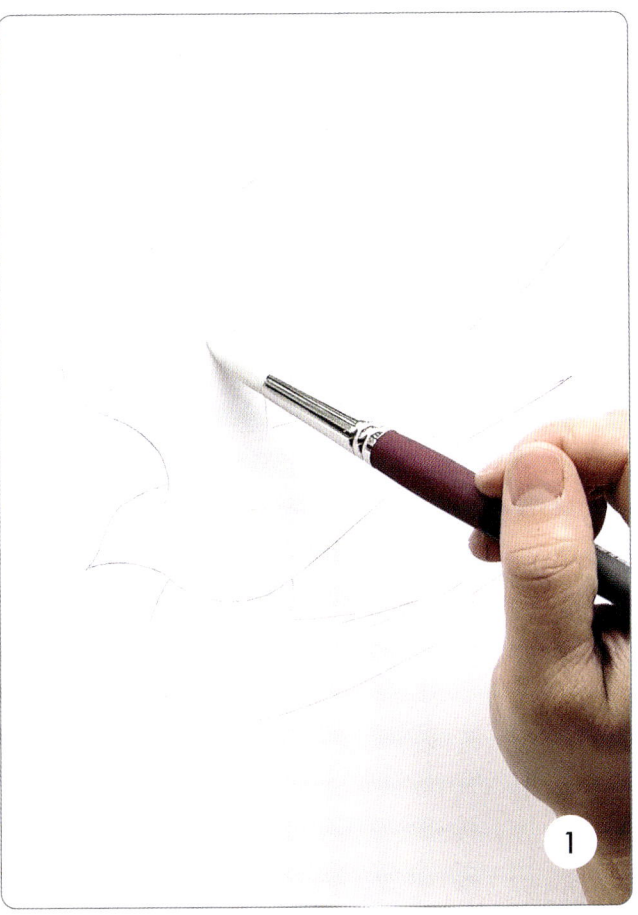

1 Trace the outline of the swallow on your page very lightly using your pencil. Dip the water brush into your clean water so it is well soaked. Remove excess water by wiping the brush along the rim of your water jar. Paint water inside the body of the swallow. Leave the very tips of the wings and tail dry.

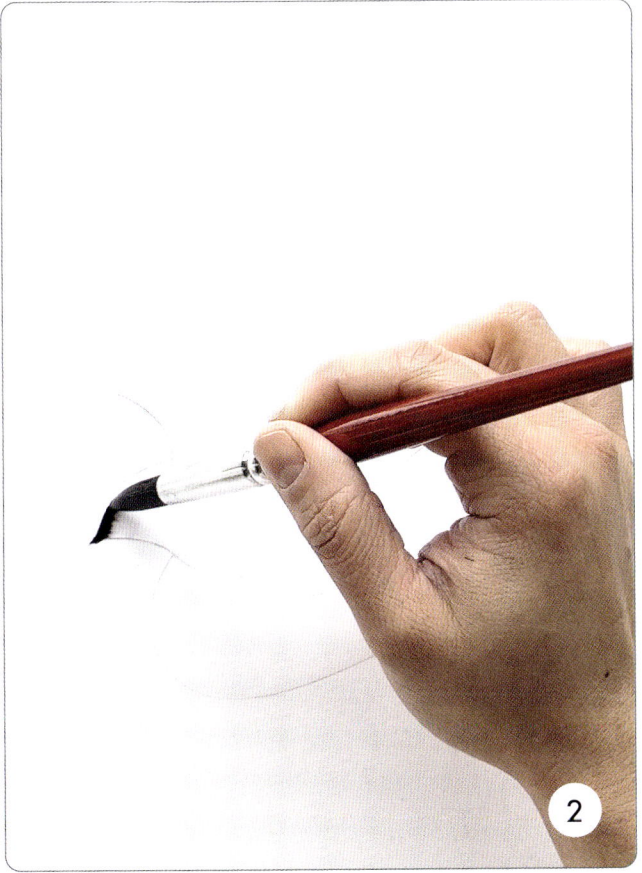

2 Dip the number 12 ink brush into your ink, and remove excess ink by wiping the brush on the rim of the jar. Place the tip of the paintbrush at the tip of the bird's beak. Pull the brush back along the edge of the water until the swallow's neck meets the wing.

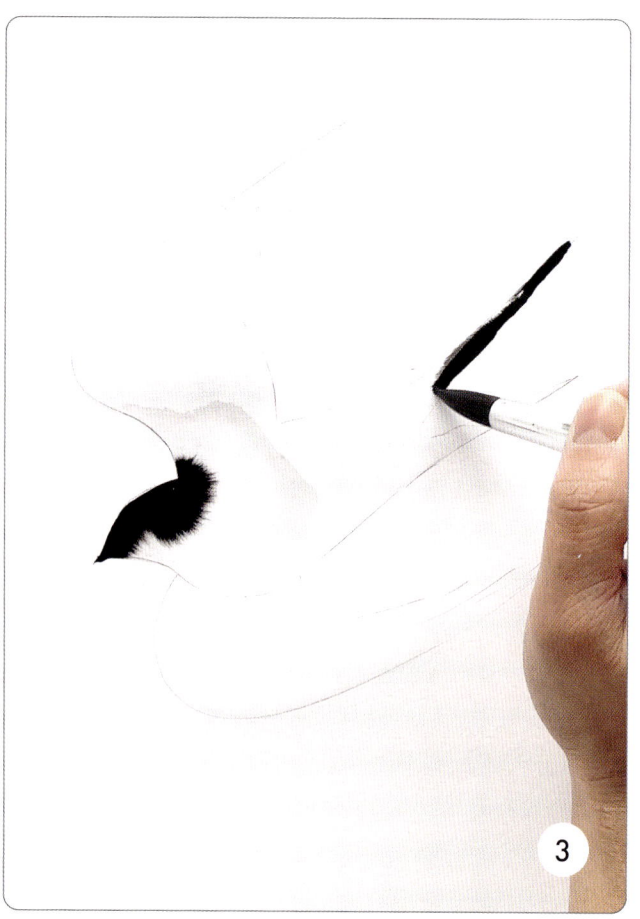

3 Place the tip of the brush on one tip of the tail, and pull the brush down toward the body until it touches the water. The ink will move into the body of the bird. Repeat this with the other tip of the tail.

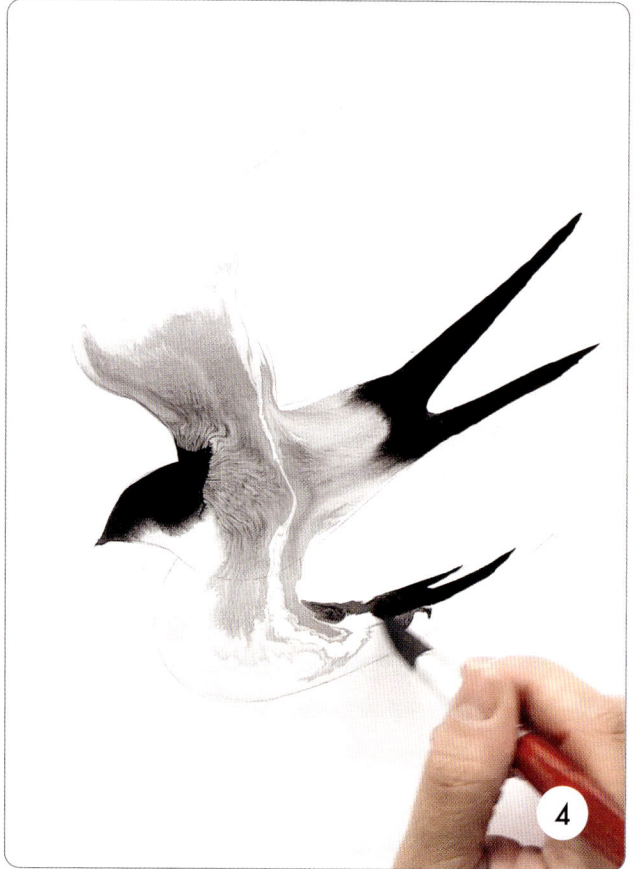

4 Reload your number 12 ink brush with ink, and place the tip of the brush at the tip of the wing feathers. Using long, sweeping brushstrokes, paint each of the wing feathers, pulling the brush toward the bird's body and into the water.

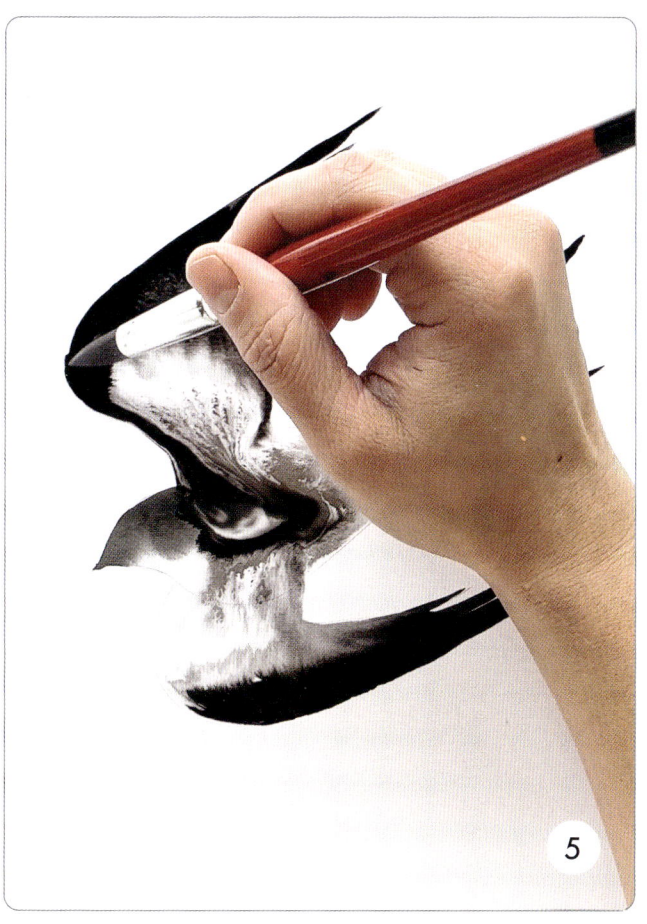

5 Touch up the edges of the wings, head, and tail using the tip of your brush.

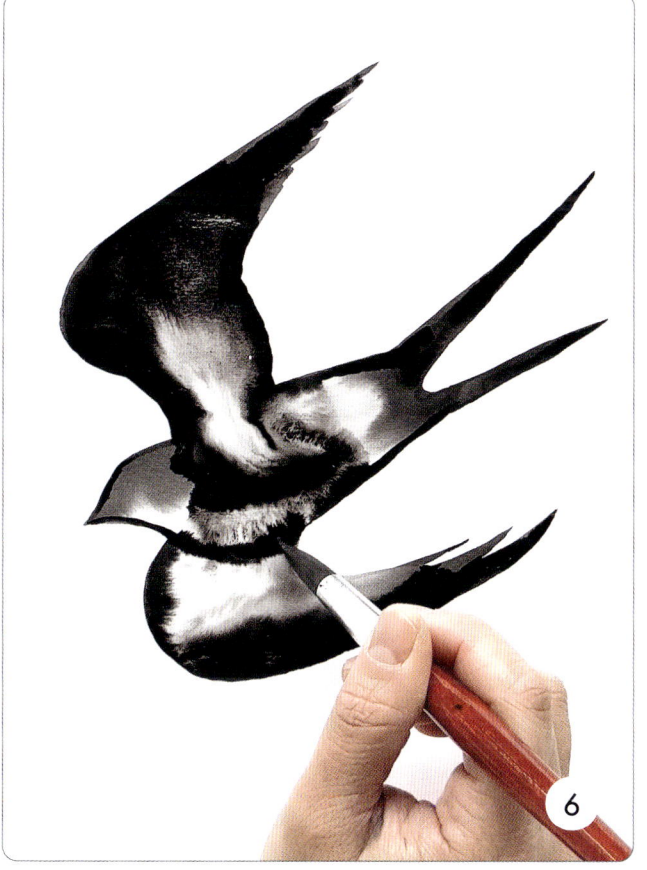

6 Once the body has dried slightly (it doesn't need to be completely dry and can still be quite damp), place the tip of the brush at the tip of the beak, and paint a fine line under the chin and chest of the bird, all the way to the tail.

RED-CROWNED CRANE

The red-crowned crane is a symbol of peace, luck, and longevity. Japanese legend says that if you fold one thousand paper cranes, you will be granted a wish. I'm not sure if you will be granted a wish if you ink one thousand paper cranes, but you will certainly become an expert at painting them!

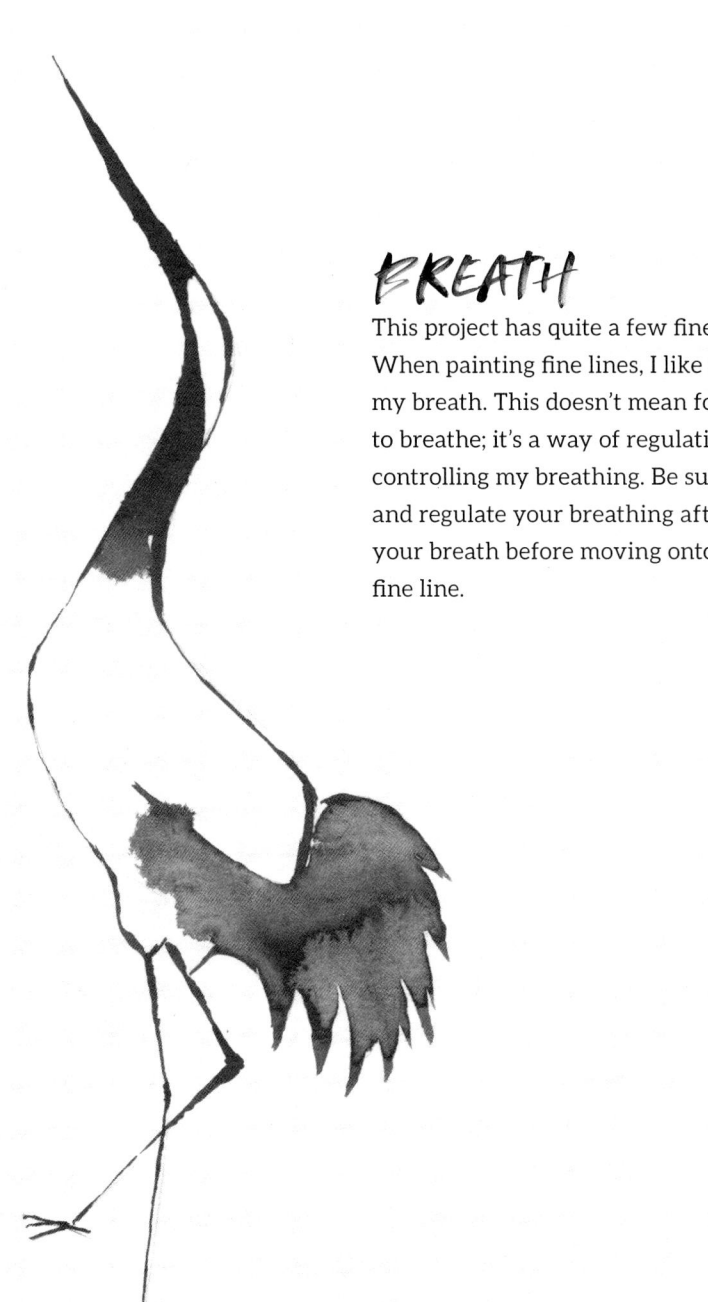

GROUNDING

Pick an object in your field of vision that interests you. Trace around the outline of the object with your eyes, remembering to breathe as you do so. Now close your eyes, and count to three. Open your eyes, and look at the page in front of you. Trace around the outline of the crane with your eyes. Think about how you will breathe with each brushstroke you place.

BREATH

This project has quite a few fine lines. When painting fine lines, I like to hold my breath. This doesn't mean forgetting to breathe; it's a way of regulating and controlling my breathing. Be sure to pause and regulate your breathing after holding your breath before moving onto the next fine line.

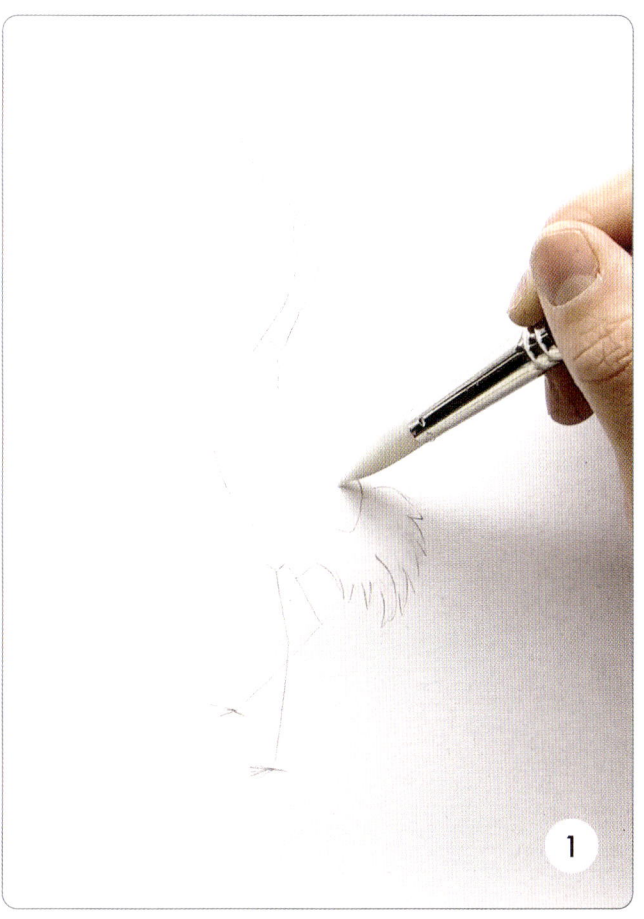

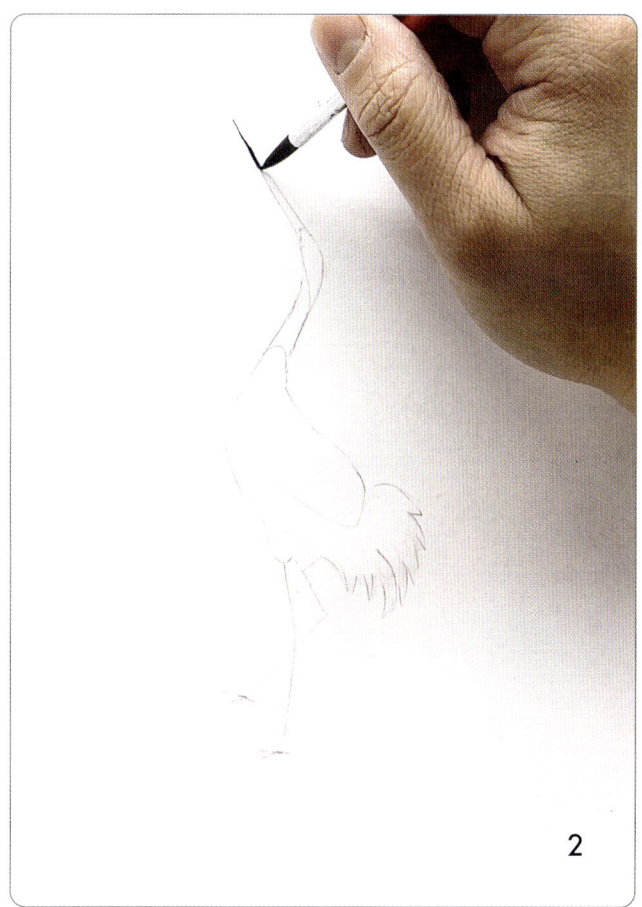

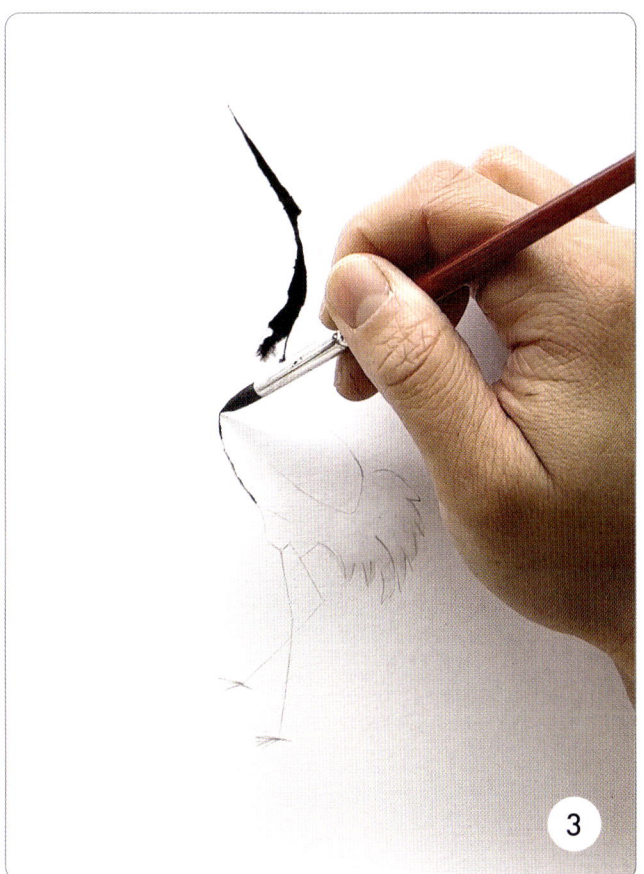

1 Trace the outline of the crane on your page very lightly using your pencil. Dip the water brush into your clean water so it is well soaked. Remove excess water by wiping the brush along the rim of your water jar. Paint water along the neck, body, and tail feathers of the crane. Leave the crown, beak, and legs dry. Using your paper towel, lightly dab excess water off the body of the crane so it is damp but not wet.

2 Dip the number 6 ink brush into your ink, and remove excess ink by wiping the brush on the rim of the jar. Place the tip of the brush to the tip of the beak. Holding your hand high above the page and painting very lightly with the brush, pull down to cover the beak and under the chin to the wet neck of the crane. The ink will move into the wet neck area as the brush touches the water.

3 Place the tip of your brush where the leg and the chest meet on the crane. Paint lightly along the pencil line so it meets the ink on the neck.

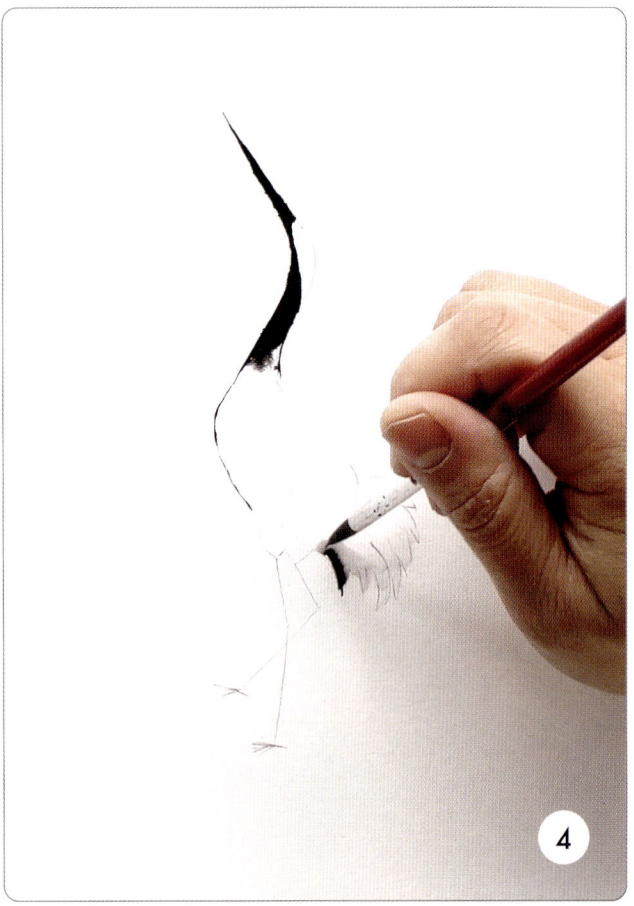

4 Reload the number 6 ink brush with ink. Place the tip of the brush on the tip of the tail feathers, and pull the brush up toward the body. Repeat this until all the tail feathers have been painted.

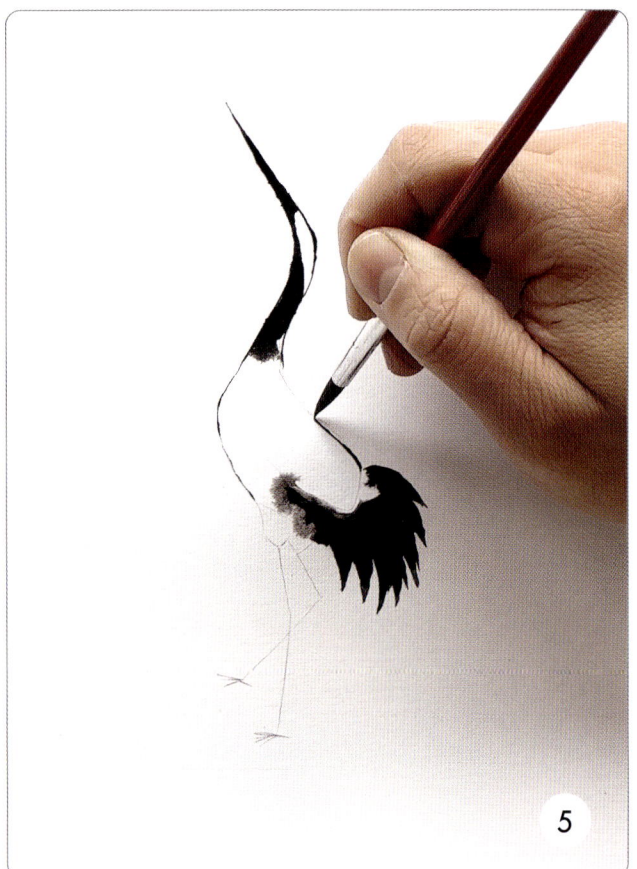

5 Use the tip of your brush to paint a fine line from the tail feathers to the neck. Keep your brushstrokes nice and light to achieve the thin lines.

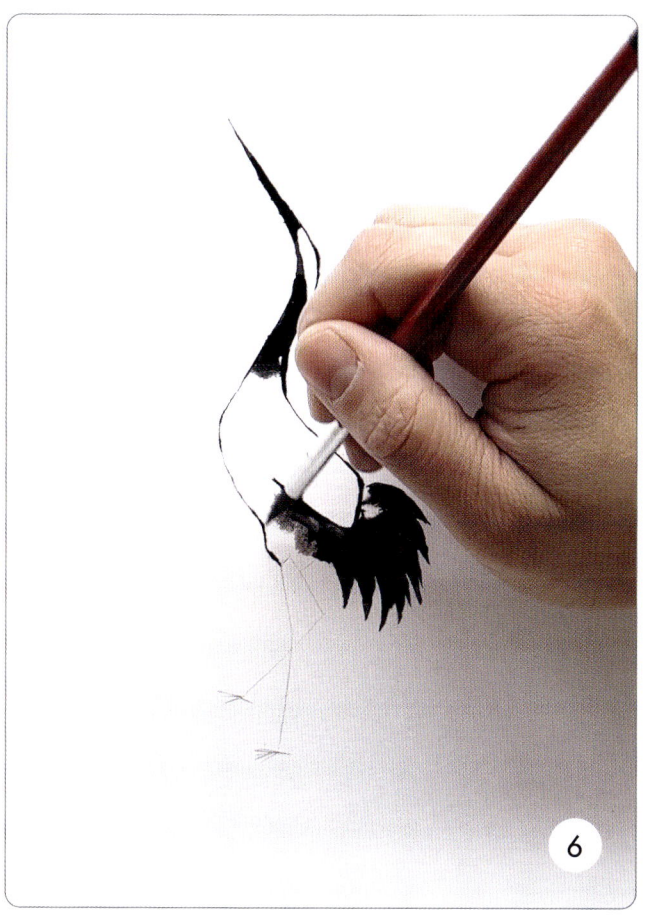

6 Use the tip of the brush to paint the fine outlines on the crane's thighs. All the pencil lines on the body of the crane should now be covered with ink.

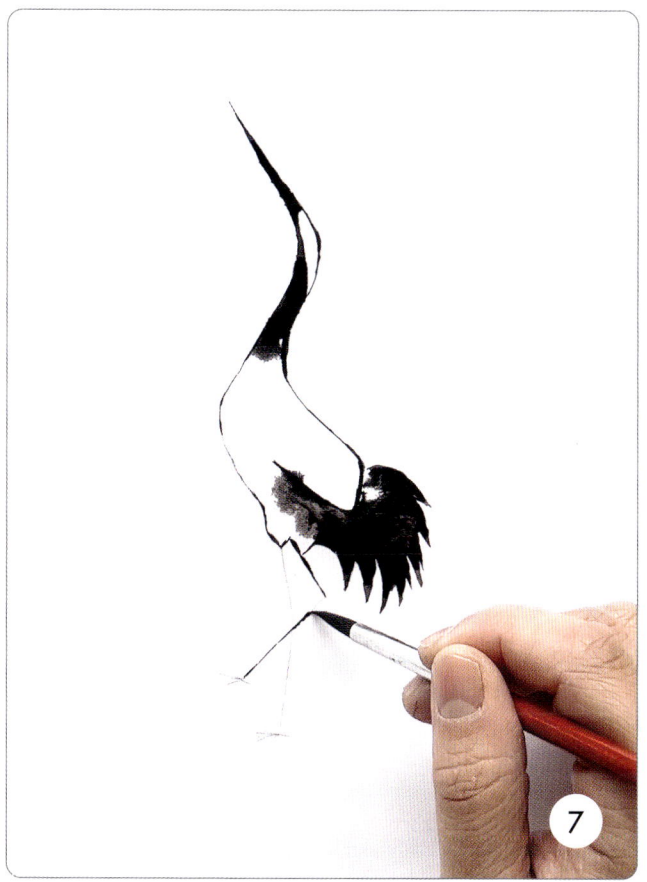

7 Use the tip of the brush to paint very fine lines over the crane's legs and feet. If you struggle to do this detail with a brush, you can do it with a fineliner pen.

PAPA & BABY PENGUIN

Did you know that male emperor penguins incubate the egg of their baby chick for around sixty-five days? Ink works beautifully for this project, capturing the elegance of the adult penguin and the fluffiness of the chick.

GROUNDING

Clench your hands into fists, hold for five counts, and then release. Inhale when you clench your fists, and exhale when you release them. Repeat this three times. Then rub your palms together; feel the warmth, and notice the sound they make. Hold your palms together for a moment before you begin.

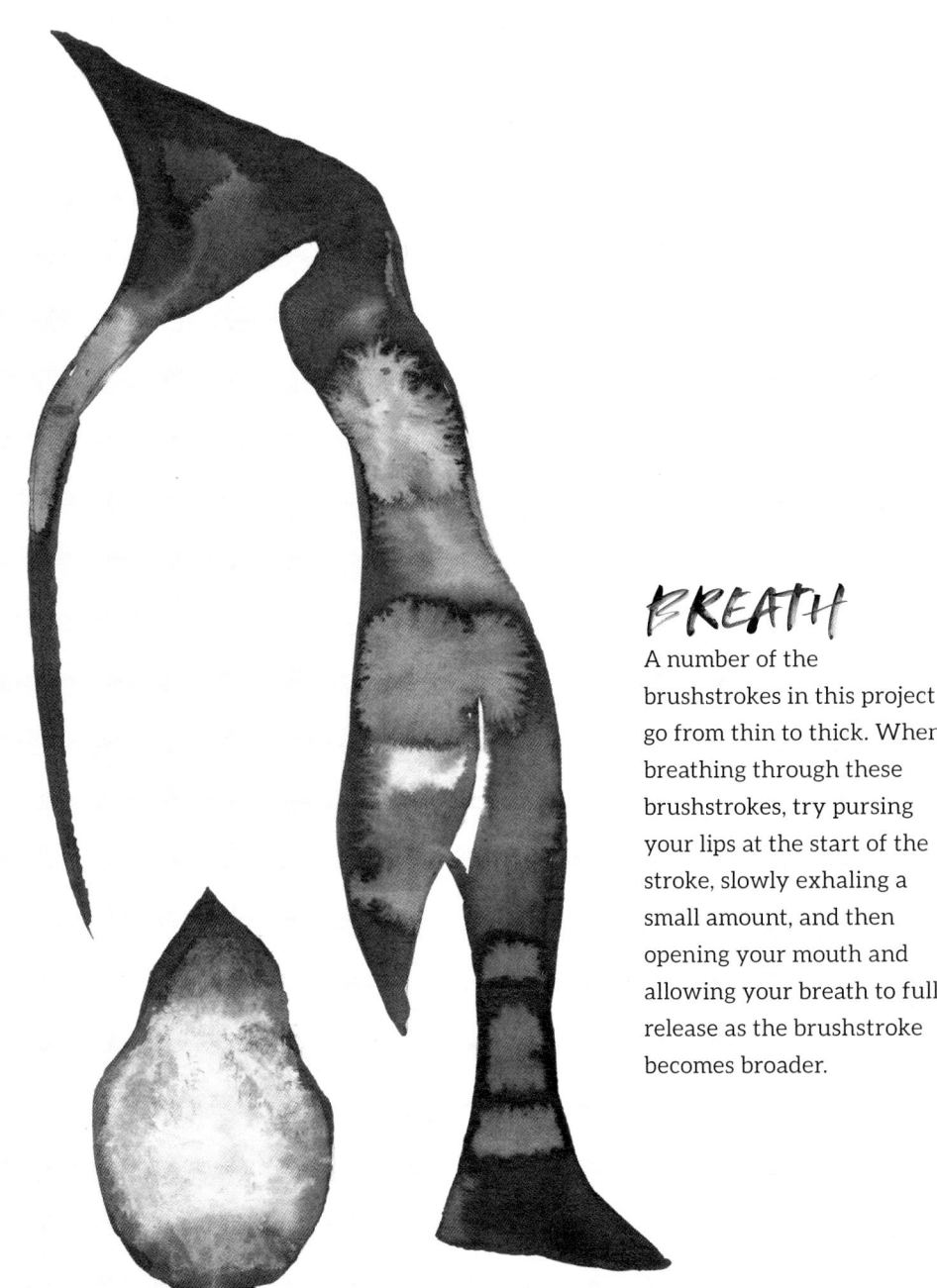

BREATH

A number of the brushstrokes in this project go from thin to thick. When breathing through these brushstrokes, try pursing your lips at the start of the stroke, slowly exhaling a small amount, and then opening your mouth and allowing your breath to fully release as the brushstroke becomes broader.

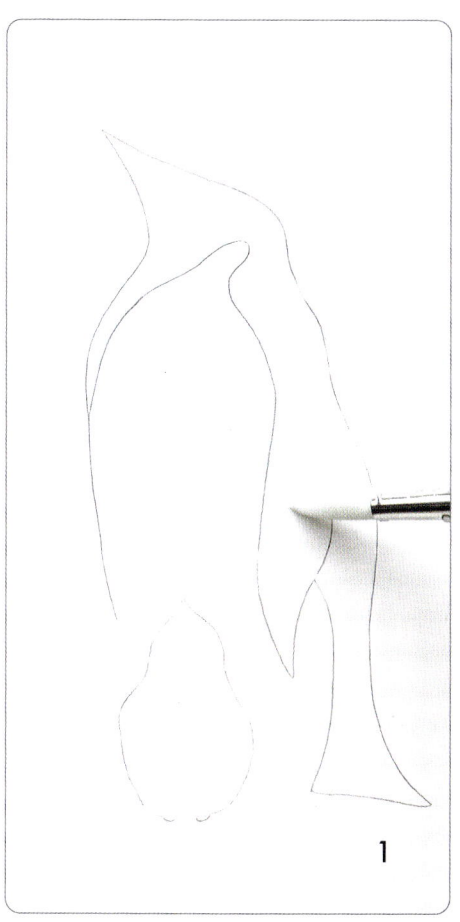

1

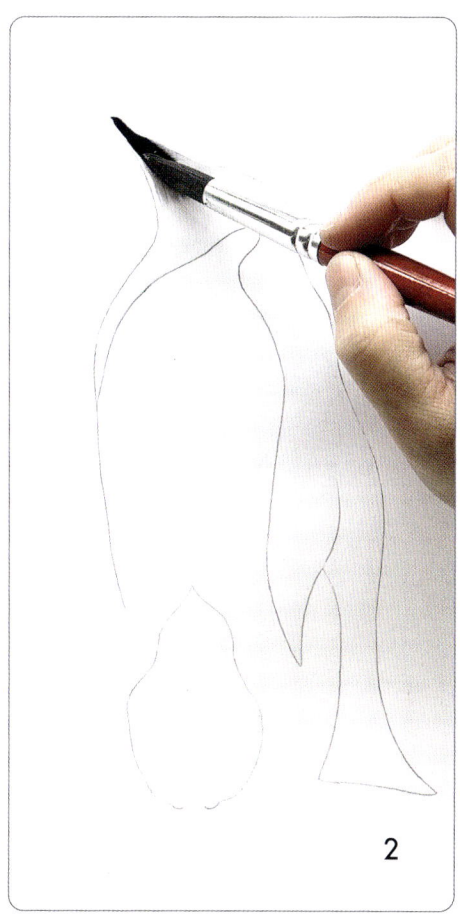

2

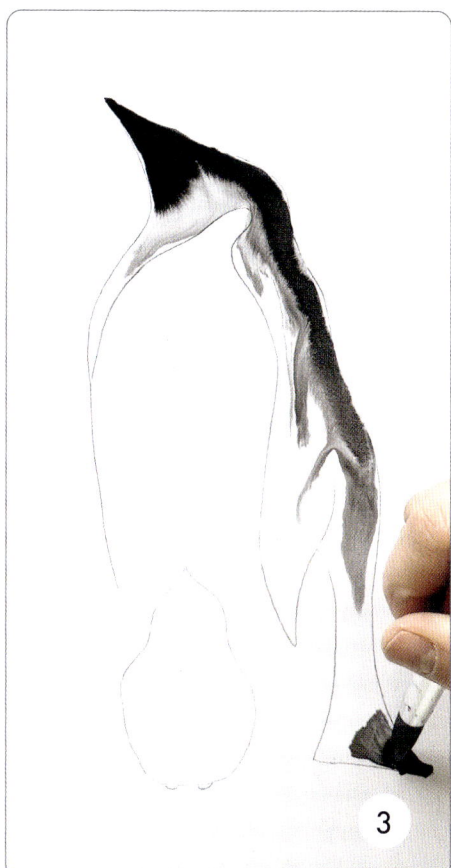

3

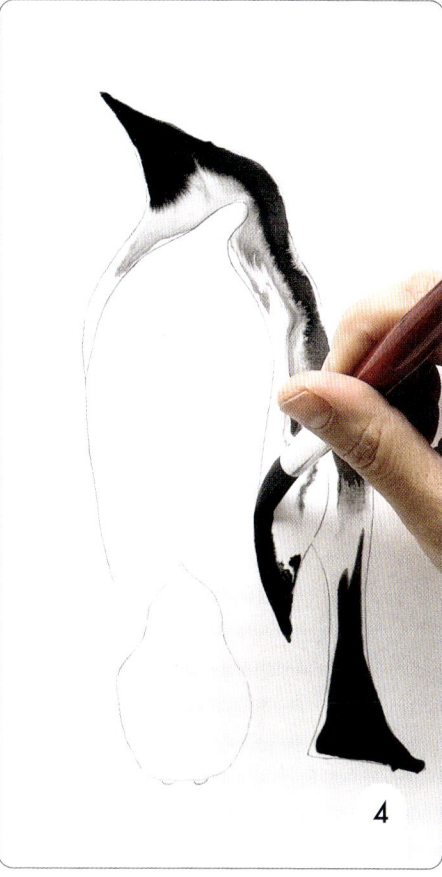

4

1 Trace the outline of the penguins on your page very lightly using your pencil. Dip the water brush into your clean water so it is well soaked. Remove excess water by wiping the brush along the rim of your water jar. Paint water inside the papa penguin, leaving a thin, dry gap between his fin and his body. Leave his belly and the baby chick dry.

2 Dip the number 12 ink brush into your ink, and remove excess ink by wiping the brush on the rim of the jar. Place the tip of the brush at the tip of the papa's beak, and pull it down along the edge of his body, following the line of his head and back. Lift the brush about three-quarters of the way down his back.

3 Place the tip of the brush at the tip of the papa penguin's tail, and pull the brush up to meet the line you have already painted on his back. The ink will bleed into the water and fill in a little.

4 Reload your brush with ink, and place the tip of the brush on the tip of the papa penguin's fin. Pull the brush up toward the face, along the pencil line.

5 Tidy up any lines on the edges with the very tip of your brush; you can switch to the number 6 brush if you feel you need a finer line.

6 Reload your ink brush (number 12 or number 6, whichever you prefer) with ink, and place the tip of the brush at the bottom of the papa penguin's belly outline. Pull the brush up lightly, painting a fine line that meets his upper chest.

7 Using your water brush, paint the baby penguin with water.

8 Dip your number 6 ink brush into the ink, and wipe away any excess on the rim of the jar. Place the tip of the brush on the tip of the baby penguin's beak. Hold it there, and allow the ink to flow down toward the baby's body.

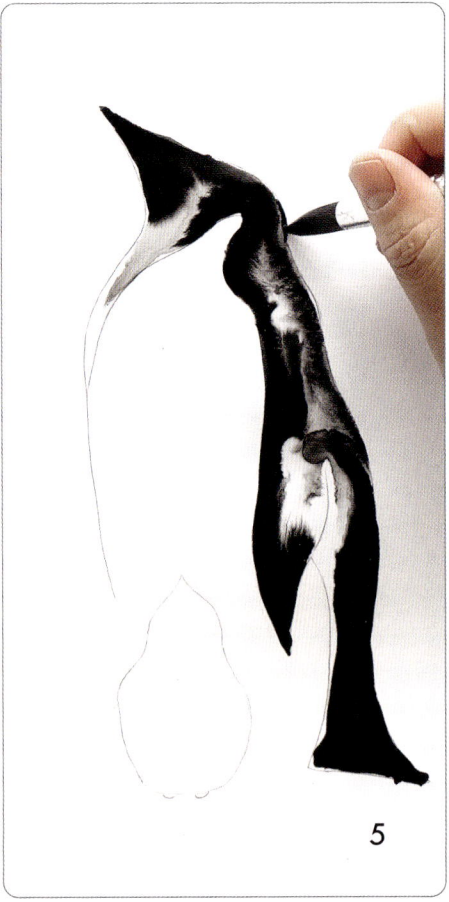

5

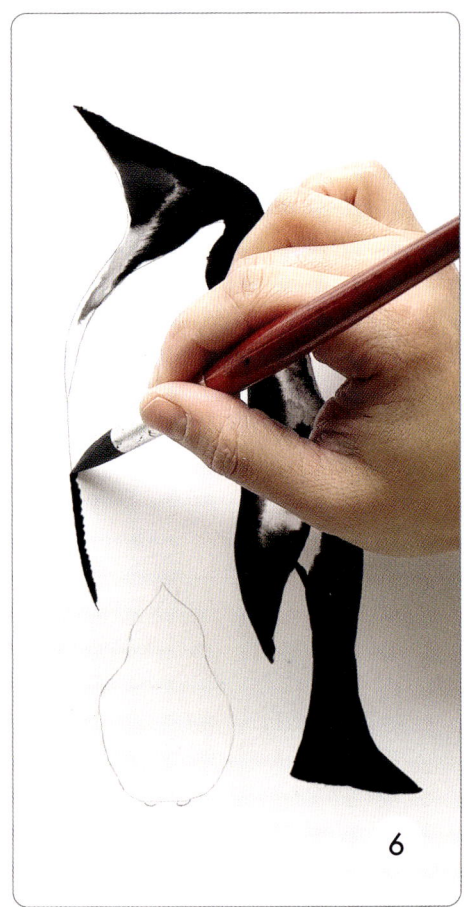

6

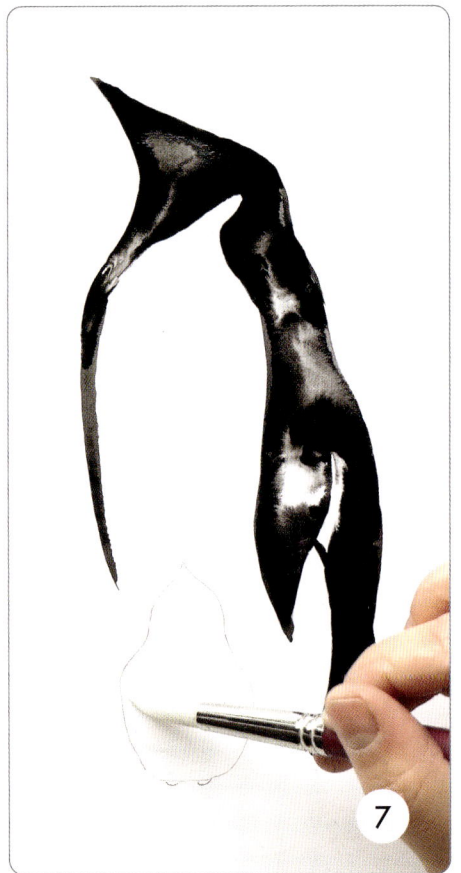

7

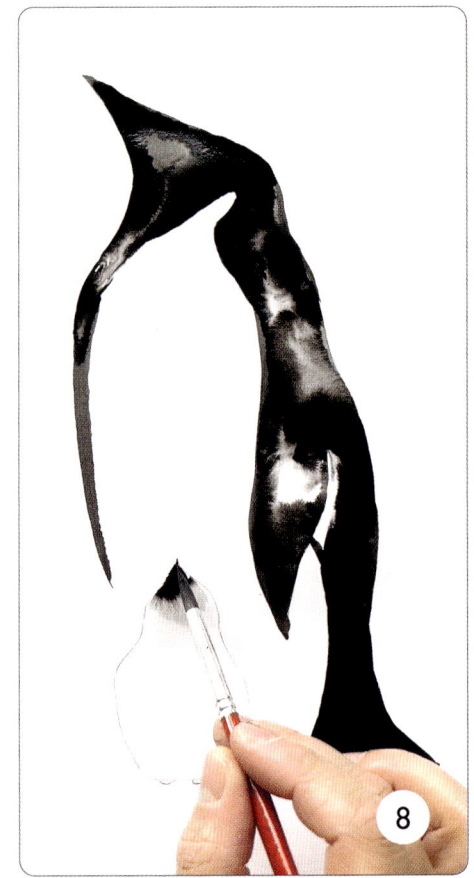

8

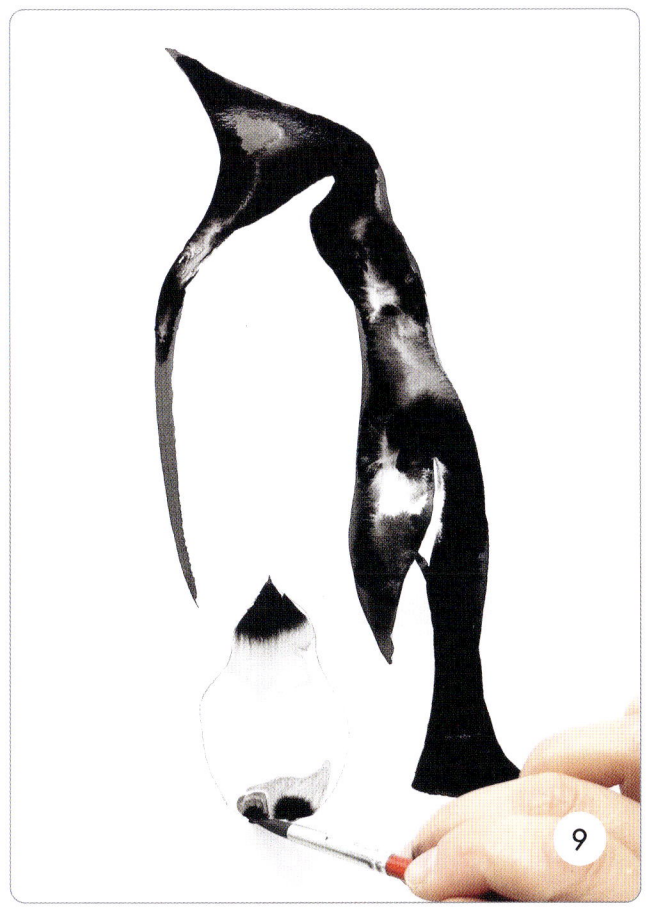

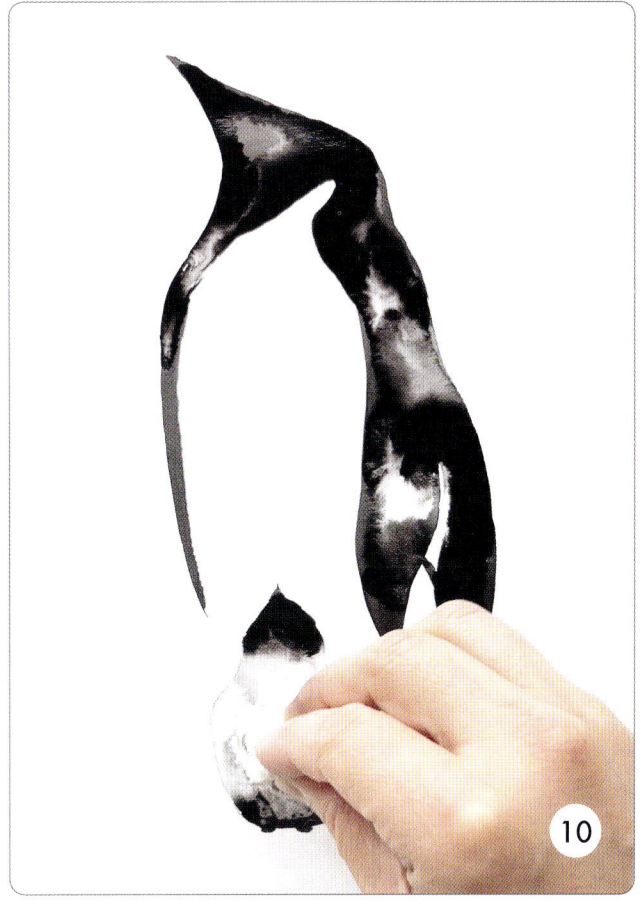

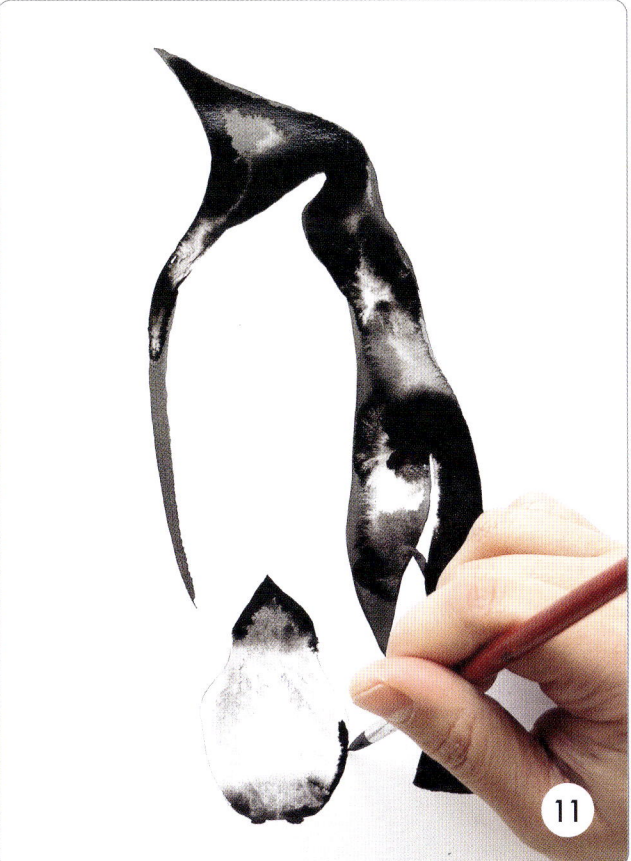

9 Lift your brush, and paint two small dots for the baby penguin's feet. The ink will bleed up into the body.

10 Scrunch up some clean paper towel, and dab it gently over baby's wet body to remove the excess water and ink. It will leave you with a textured, fluffy effect. Be careful not to wipe the paper but to just dab gently. The paper should remain damp.

11 Dip your number 6 ink brush in the ink, and remove the excess on the rim of the jar. Using the tip of the brush, carefully paint along the wing outlines of Baby Penguin.

HENNY & PENNY

I love drawing and painting chickens! They are such characters, and they always make me smile. I haven't painted faces on these little chickens. It's up to you to decide their final attitudes and see what fun expressions you can come up with! (I would recommend using your fineliner pen once they are completely dry.) Scan the QR code to watch me paint this project!

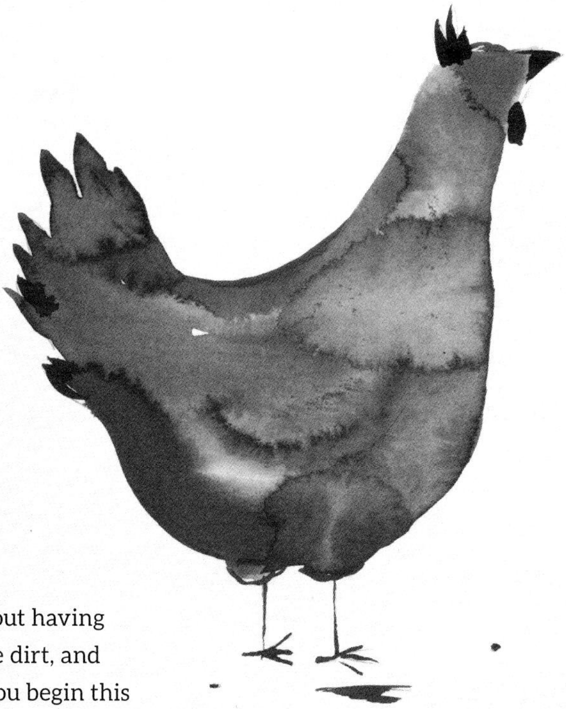

BREATH

Henny and Penny are made using a series of relatively short brushstrokes. I like to paint this one quite quickly, laying down more ink before the previous stroke has had time to settle. Because of this, I don't apply a breath to each brushstroke; I keep a steady, gentle breath going throughout.

GROUNDING

Henny and Penny are all about having fun, scratching around in the dirt, and living the good life. Before you begin this project, put on some music that you love, and have some fun—dance around, sing along, get those endorphins going. It's a great pre-painting warmup!

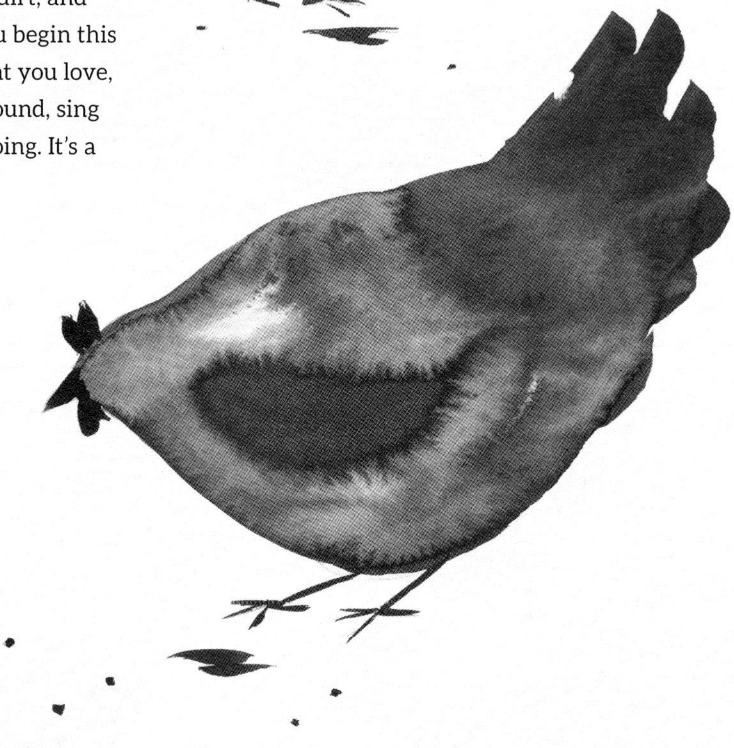

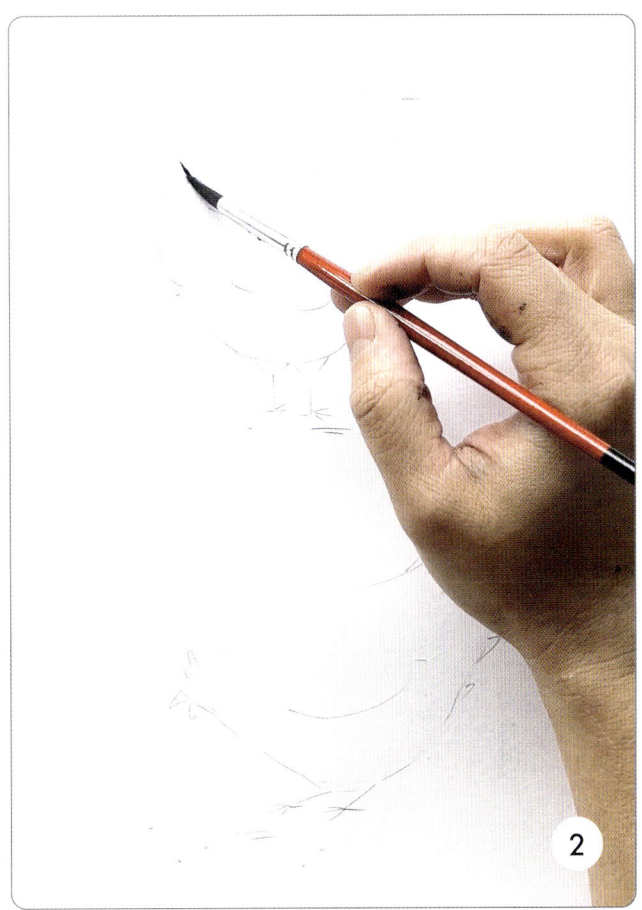

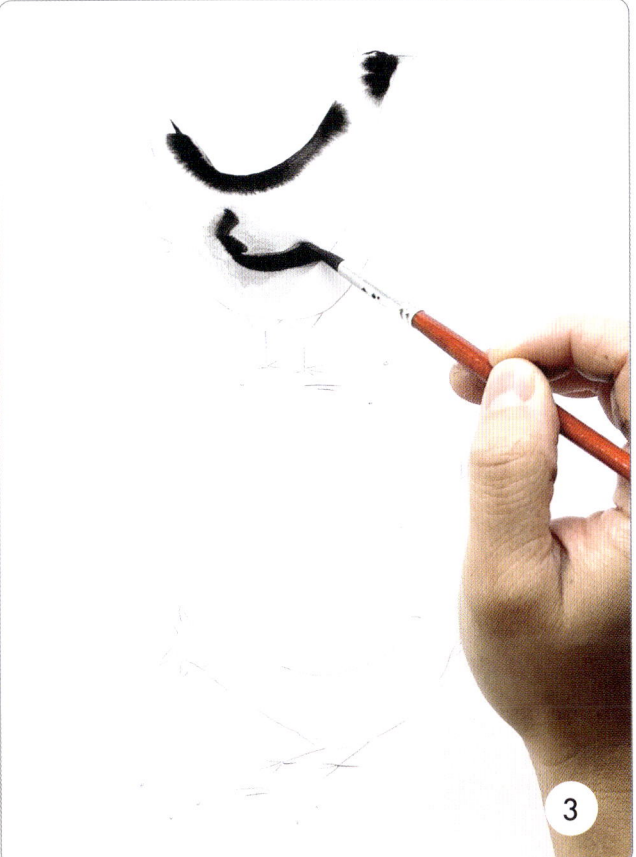

1 Trace the outline of the chickens on your page very lightly using your pencil. Dip your water brush into the water, and remove the excess by wiping it on the rim of the jar. Paint each chicken's body with water. If you don't feel confident that you will get to the second chicken before the water dries, you can paint them one at a time. Leave their beaks, combs, and feet dry.

2 Dip your number 6 ink brush into the ink, removing any excess by wiping the brush on the rim of the jar. Place the tip of the brush at the tip of the top chicken's tail. In a sweeping motion, pull the brush along the line of the chicken's back, all the way to the back of its neck. End this brushstroke by lifting the brush at the chicken's neck and placing a dot on the face.

3 Without reloading the brush with ink, pull the brush along the wing line. I work left to right because I am right-handed, but if you are left-handed, you might find it smoother and easier painting right to left.

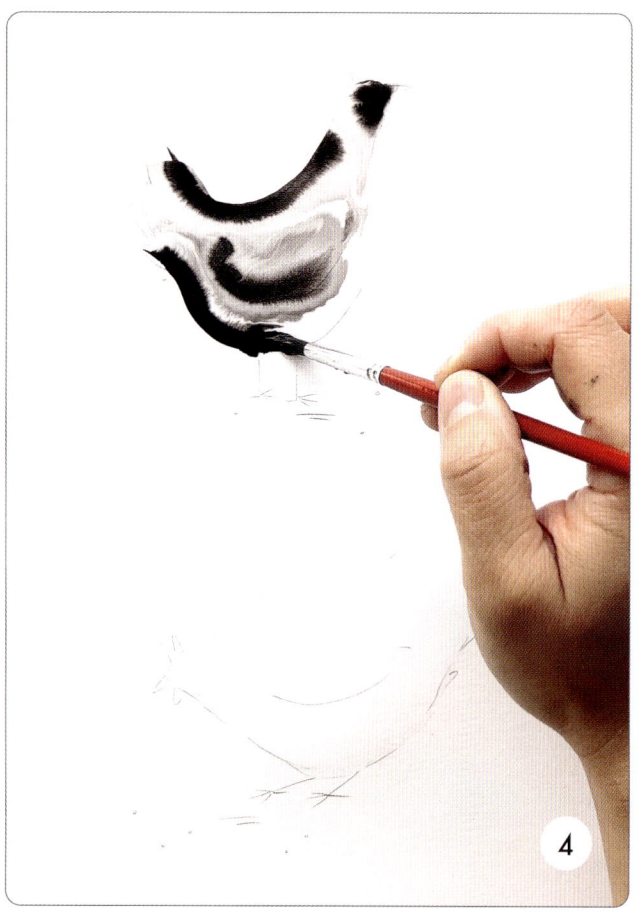

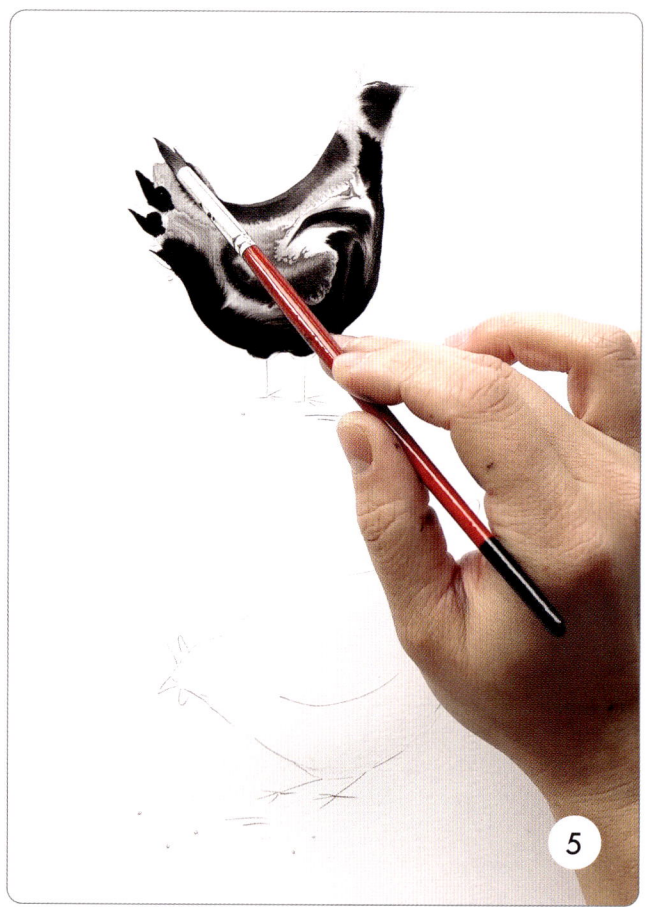

4 Once again, without reloading the brush with ink, place the tip of the brush at the base of the chicken's tail, and pull it along the chicken's underbelly, all the way up to the throat.

5 Reload the brush with ink, and use the shape of the brush to paint short feathers onto the end of the tail.

6 Place the brush at the tip of the lower chicken's head, right near the beak, and pull the brush back toward the tail. Just like with the first chicken, paint along each of the pencil lines with quick, confident strokes—the wing and the chest through to the underbelly. The ink will move about through water in the body, but don't be tempted to keep touching it with the brush. Allow the ink to dry however it decides. It may pleasantly surprise you!

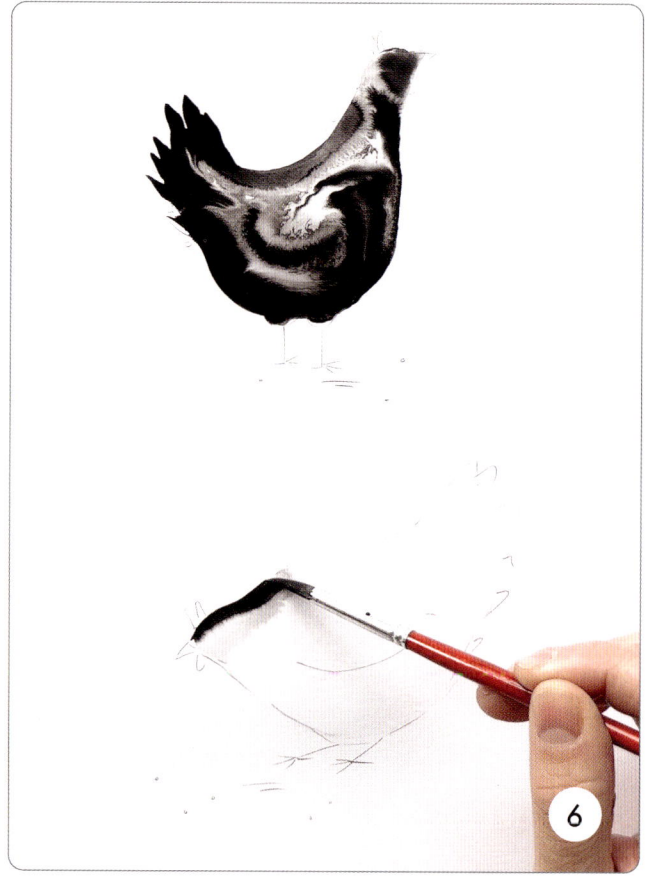

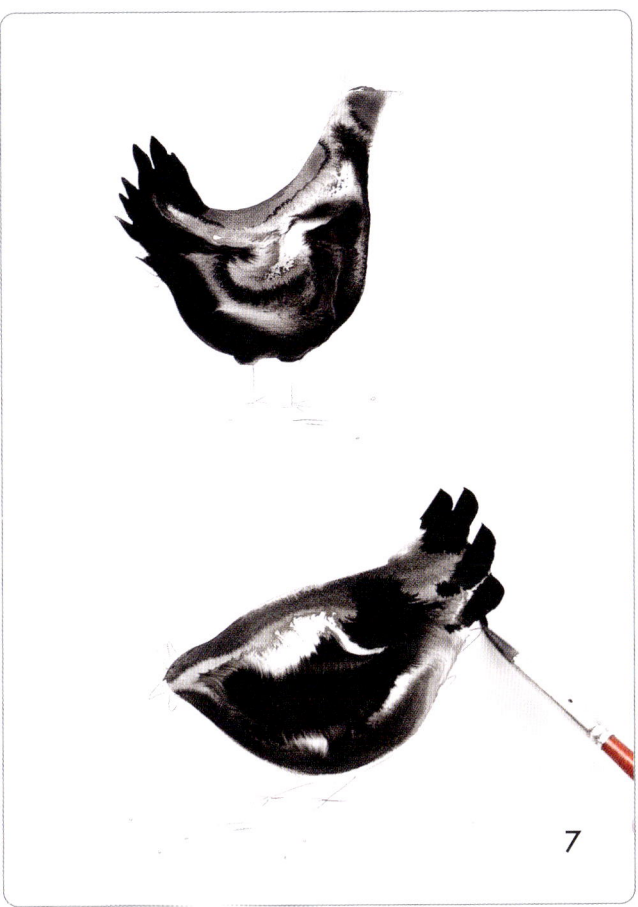

7 Add in the tail feathers on the second chicken using the tip of the brush, pulling down to the body to create a feathery shape. Leave the chickens to dry a little.

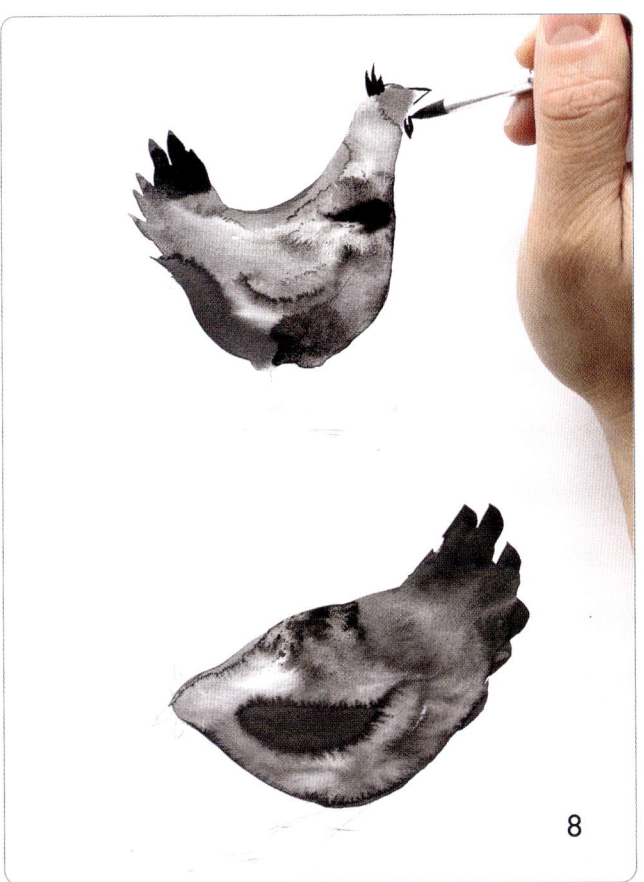

8 When they are 75 percent dry, use your number 6 ink brush to paint in the fine details of the beak, comb, and feet. Keep your hand high on the page and your touch very light. You can even add some details of what the chickens are scratching around in!

HUM

Did you know that a hummingbird's heart can beat as fast as 1,250 beats per minute? If humans could hear their heartbeats (we can't!), it would sound like a little constant hum. These busy little birds are so tiny and magical— I find them truly amazing. This is one of the few times I think about using colored ink, as their feathers are so vibrant, but nothing beats black ink.

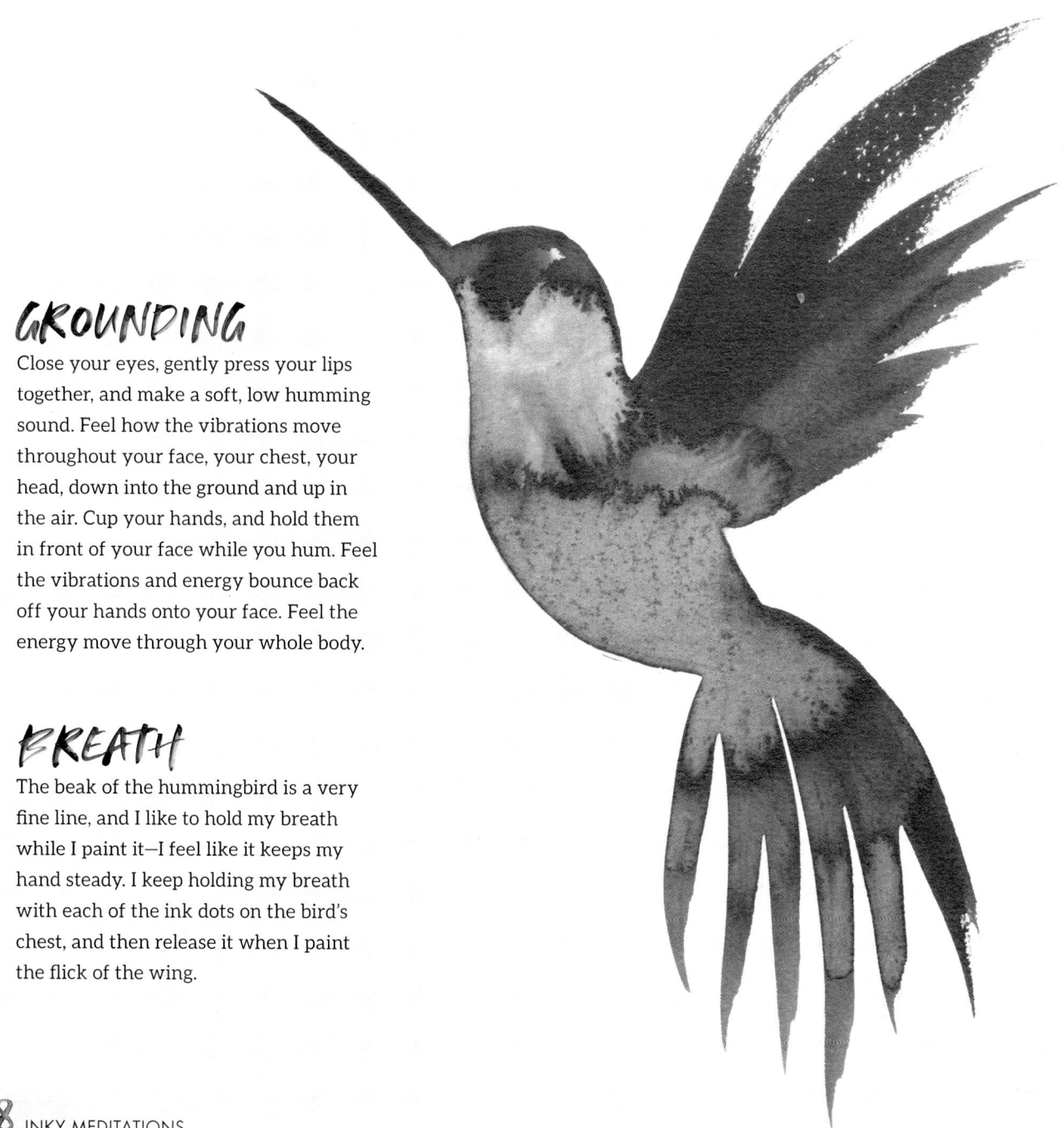

GROUNDING

Close your eyes, gently press your lips together, and make a soft, low humming sound. Feel how the vibrations move throughout your face, your chest, your head, down into the ground and up in the air. Cup your hands, and hold them in front of your face while you hum. Feel the vibrations and energy bounce back off your hands onto your face. Feel the energy move through your whole body.

BREATH

The beak of the hummingbird is a very fine line, and I like to hold my breath while I paint it—I feel like it keeps my hand steady. I keep holding my breath with each of the ink dots on the bird's chest, and then release it when I paint the flick of the wing.

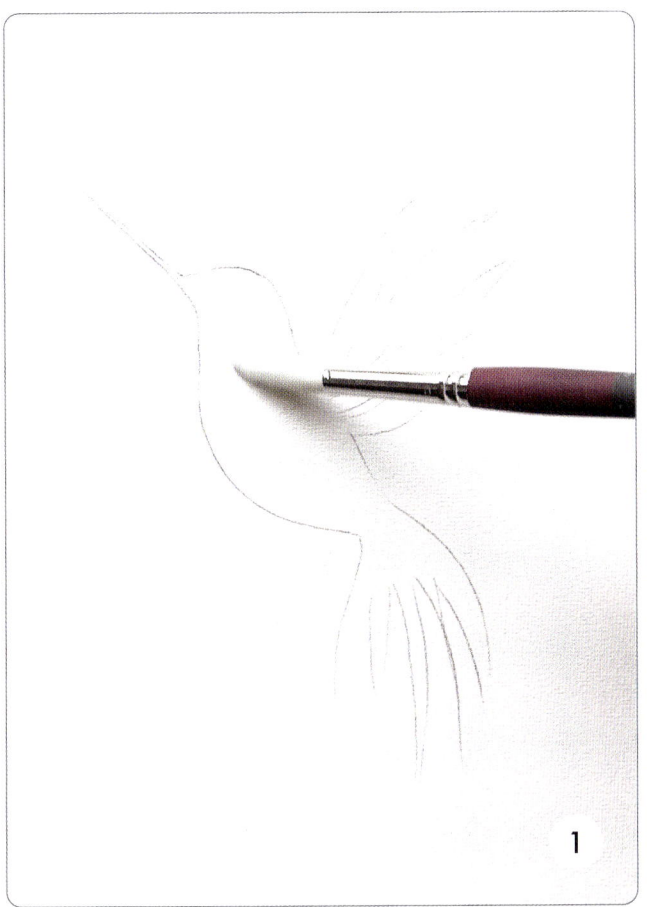

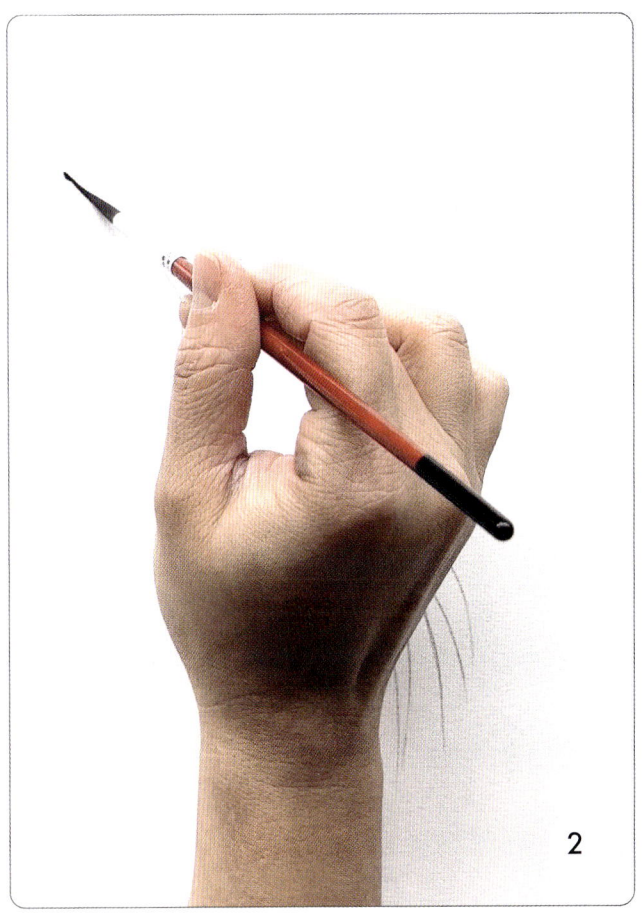

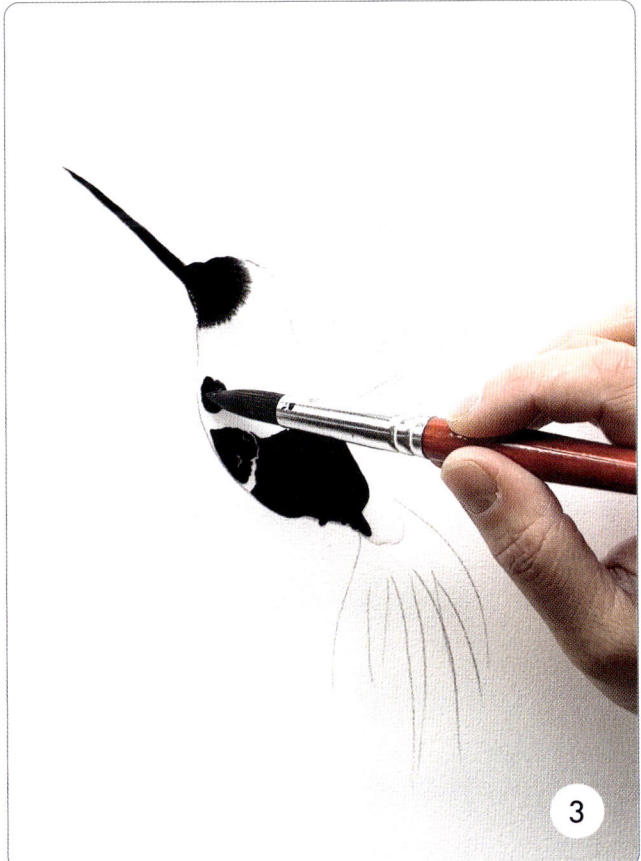

1 Trace the outline of the hummingbird on your page very lightly using your pencil. Dip your water brush into the water, and remove the excess by wiping it on the rim of the jar. Paint the body of the hummingbird with water, leaving the wings, beak, and tail dry.

2 Dip the number 6 ink brush in the ink, and remove any excess by wiping it on the rim of the jar. Be sure to really remove any excess ink, as you want to paint a very fine line. Place the tip of the brush at the tip of the hummingbird's beak. Keeping your hand light and high above the page, pull the brush down along the pencil line of the beak until you reach the water on the bird's face. The ink will bleed into the bird's face as you touch the water.

3 Dip your number 12 ink brush into the ink, and remove the excess by wiping it on the rim of the jar. Lightly touch three ink dots along the bird's chest. These will bleed into the bird's body.

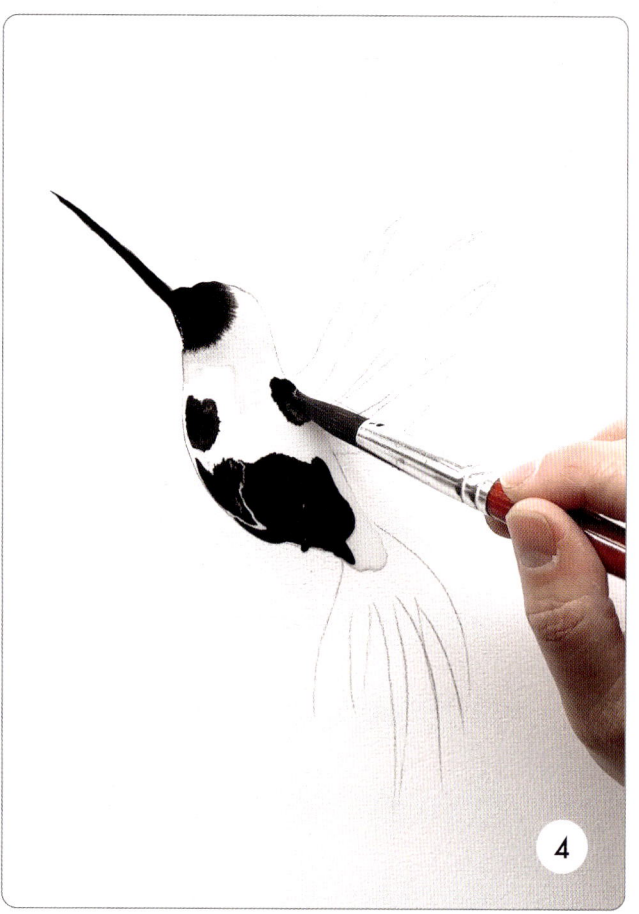

4 Push the brush down into the wet area on the bird's back so that you have the brush flat against the paper. Using a sweeping motion, flick the brush up along the page, lifting your hand as you follow the pencil line of the wing. The flick motion will give you a feathery finer point at the end of the wing.

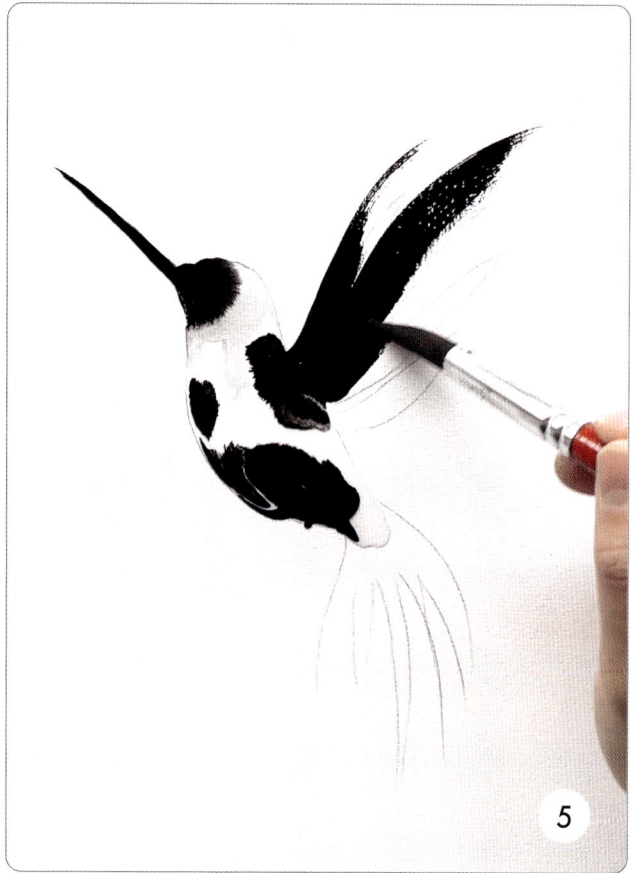

5 Repeat this stroke along each of the wing guidelines until you have covered all the pencil marks.

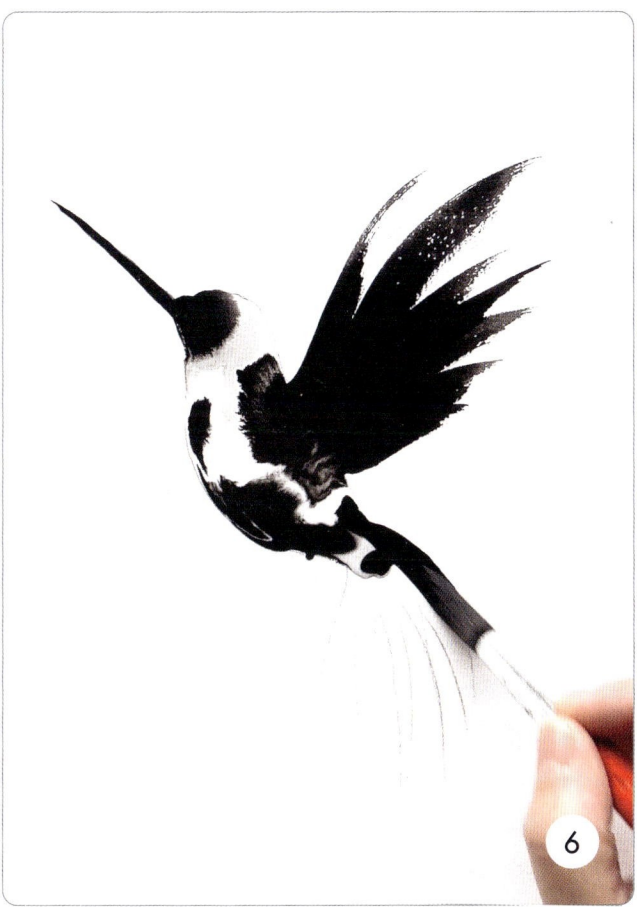

6 Using the same action, push the brush gently onto the paper where the tail meets the bird's body. Pull the brush down, flicking your hand up off the page when you reach the end of the tail. Repeat this stroke until you have enough tail feathers.

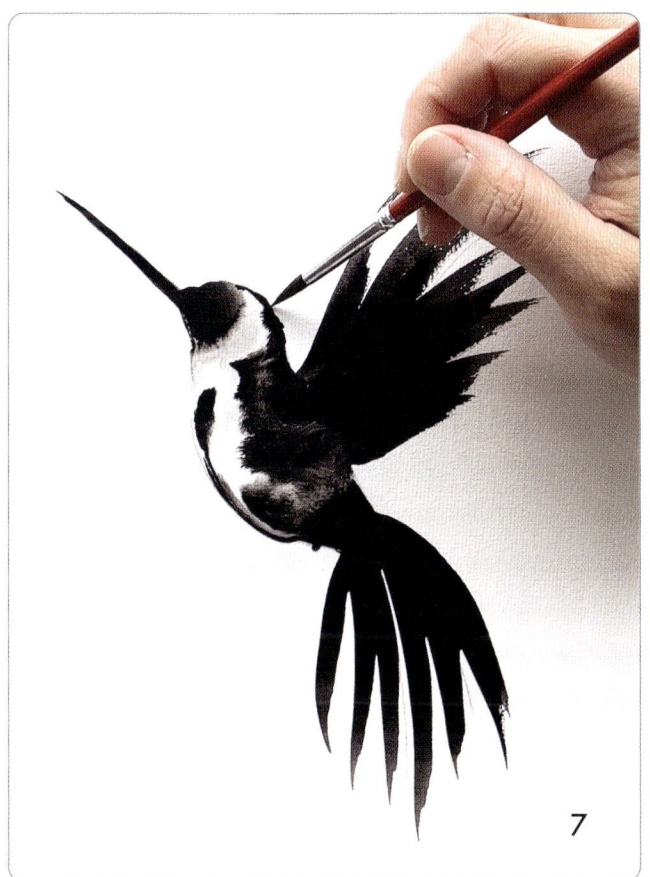

7 Use the number 6 ink brush to clean up any edges around the bird's body and beak. Cover any pencil lines that might still be showing. Hold your hand high above the page to achieve a very fine line.

MISS BLACKBIRD'S GARDEN

Miss Blackbird is one of the most detailed projects in this book, so she is the grand finale. Birds are one of my favorite things to paint, and I could spend hours watching them in my garden. In fact, I could probably do a whole book on bird paintings, but for now we have Miss Blackbird, surrounded by flowers, celebrating spring, life, and sunshine. If you find it challenging to paint both the bird and the flowers, you can start with the bird on her own as I have below. As you become more confident, you can add the floral frame to any of the creatures you've painted.

GROUNDING

Before you begin this project, try to spend a few minutes outside if you can. This could be in your garden, on a balcony, or on your front doorstep. Stand with your feet firmly but comfortably planted. Feel the earth beneath you, pressing firmly back. Take five deep breaths, in through your nose, out through your mouth. With each breath, listen for a new sound you can hear (sometimes it can help to close your eyes). Once you have noted at least five sounds, you are ready to paint.

BREATH

As always, remember to inhale when your brush is poised, ready to paint, and exhale slowly as you place the brush on the paper and paint your line. By this stage in the book, you may have found your own breathing and brushwork pattern that works for you, in which case you should continue on with it. Painting and grounding yourself in any creative practice is about finding what is best for you—there are no rules, only suggestions!

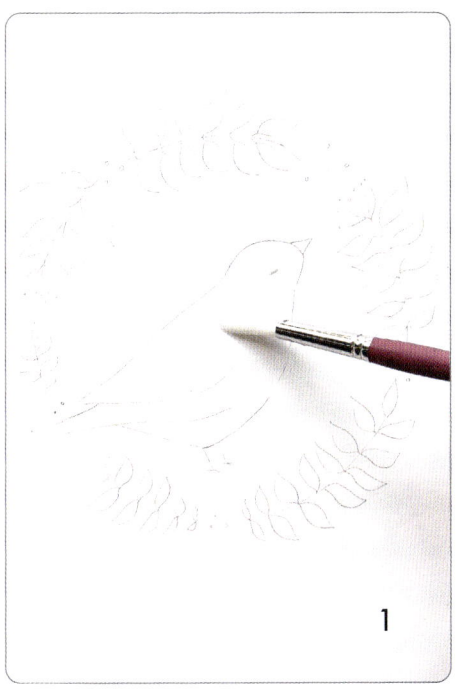

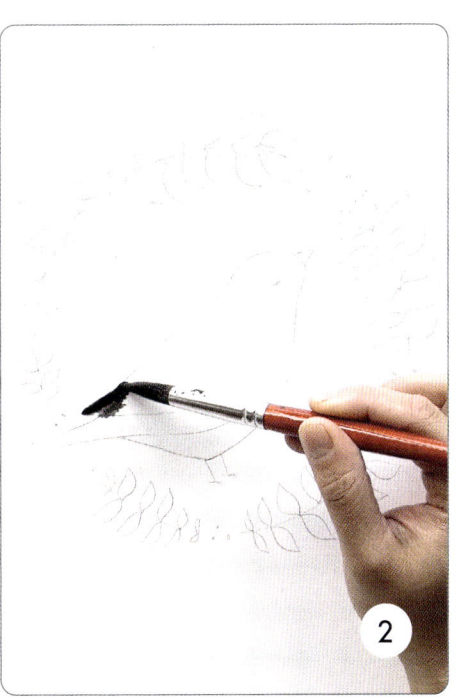

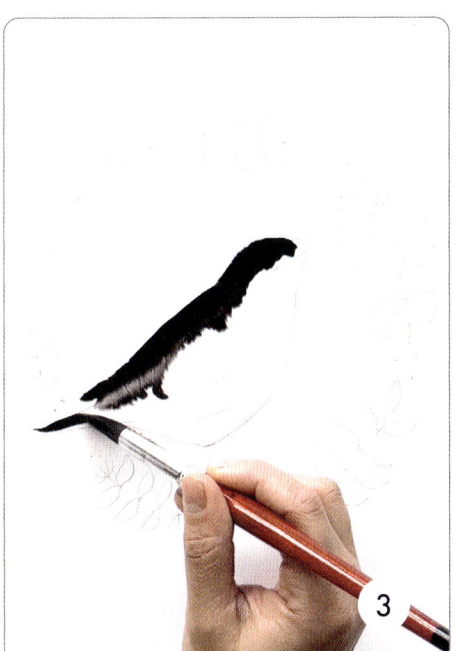

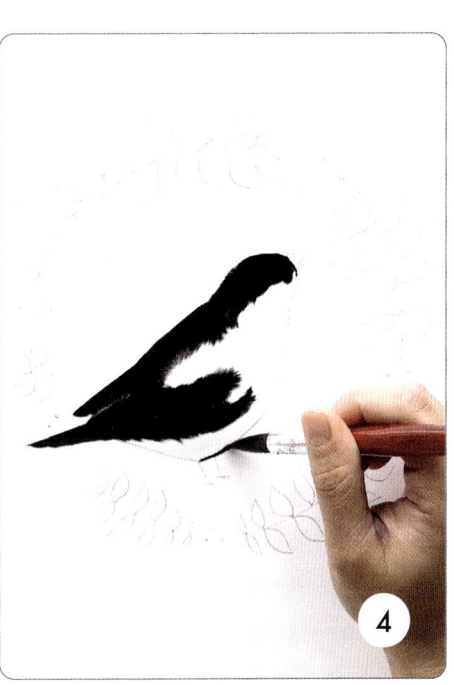

1 Trace the outline of the bird and flowers on your page very lightly using your pencil. Dip the water brush into your clean water so it is well soaked. Remove excess water by wiping the brush along the rim of your water jar. Paint water inside the body of the bird. Do not add water to the beak.

2 Dip the number 12 ink brush into your ink, and remove excess ink by wiping the brush on the rim of the jar. Place the tip of the brush on the tip of the bird's wing. Pull the brush up along the back of the bird all the way to where the head meets the beak, and then lift your brush from the page.

3 Place the tip of your brush on the tip of the bird's tail, and pull it through the water following the tail's lower pencil line. Lift the brush when you reach the end of this pencil line.

4 Reload your brush with ink if it seems a little dry. Then place the tip of your brush midway along the bird's belly, just where the legs meet the body. Pull the brush along the edge of the water, following the belly line up to the beak.

5 Place the tip of your brush under the bird's tail. Pull the brush along the edge of the water, following the underbelly, until it gets to the legs.

6 Have a look at how the ink has moved through the body of the bird. You may want to add a couple more ink blots to fill in the body, or you may want to leave it as is.

7 Using your water brush, paint clean water into the leaves of the floral frame. I think it is easier to do one branch at a time. You will also see that I have rotated my page around so my hand can flow more freely across the paper, particularly when I'm trying to avoid touching a wet area like the bird in the middle.

8 Dip the number 6 ink brush into the ink, and remove excess ink on the rim of the jar. Place the brush at the tip of the branch, and pull it along to the other end. This is just like when you painted your eucalyptus branches for the wreath. Some of the ink will spill into the wet leaves.

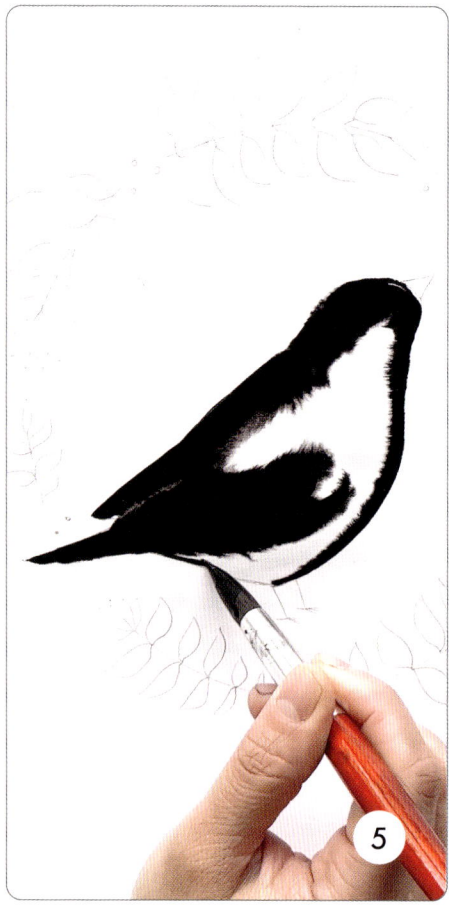

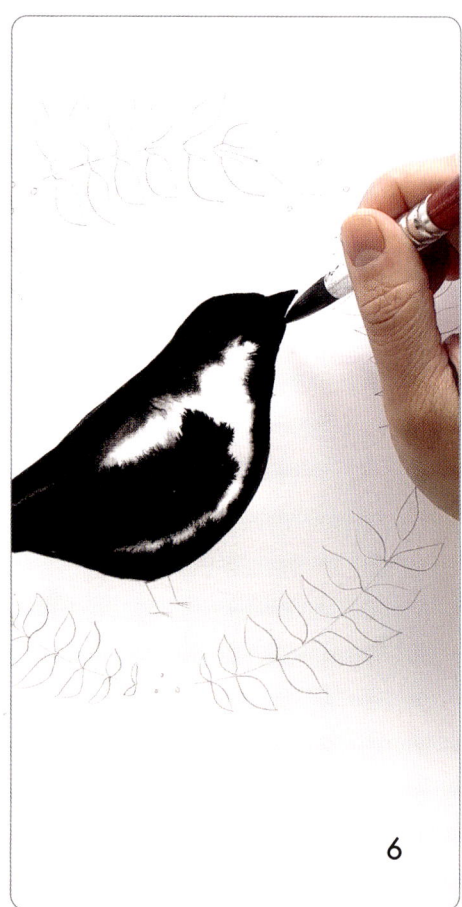

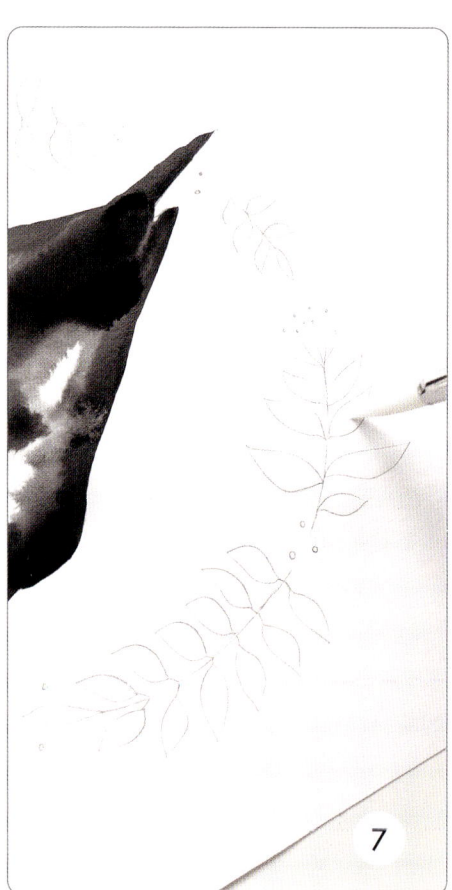

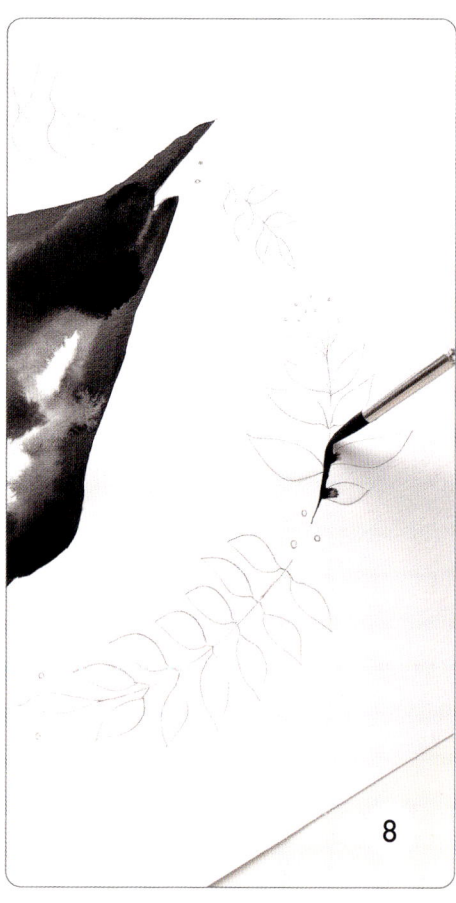

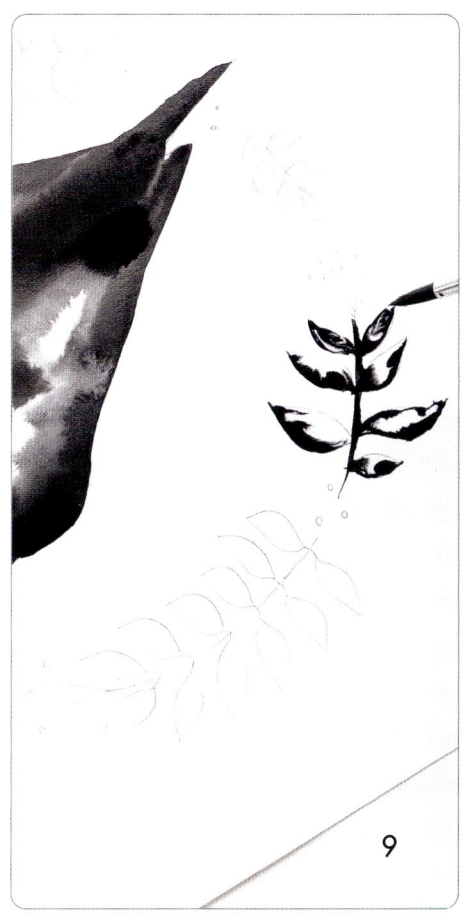

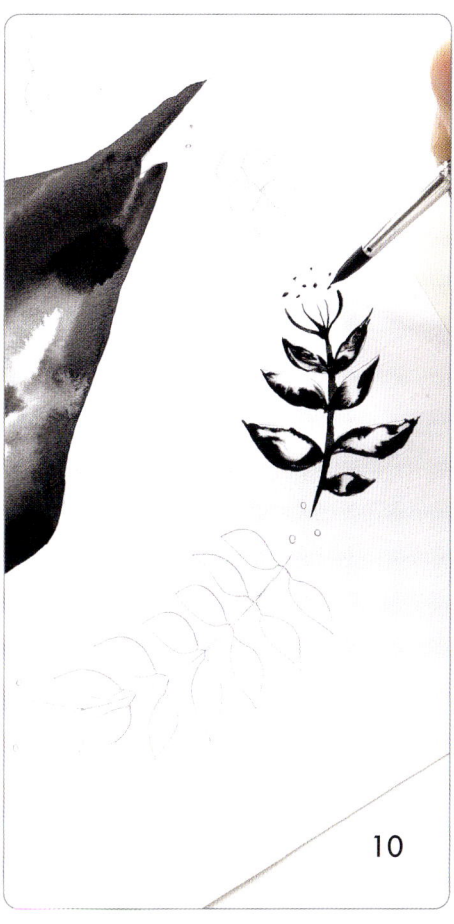

9 Still using the number 6 ink brush, gently touch the brush on any of the leaves that you feel need more ink. You might like to go over some of the pencil edges, but be sure watch what the ink is doing and not overpaint.

10 Making sure there is very little ink on your brush, and holding your hand high above the page, paint the fine lines of the flower using the tip of the brush. Repeat steps 8 through 10 until you finish painting the floral frame.

11 Dip your number 6 ink brush in the ink, and then wipe most of the ink off the brush (paper towel is useful for this). Placing the tip of the brush at the top of the leg, lightly paint very fine lines for the legs and feet. If you don't feel confident doing this with a brush, you can use a fineliner pen.

12 Once the bird is completely dry, use the number 6 ink brush or your fineliner pen to add the finishing touch of the blackbird's eye.

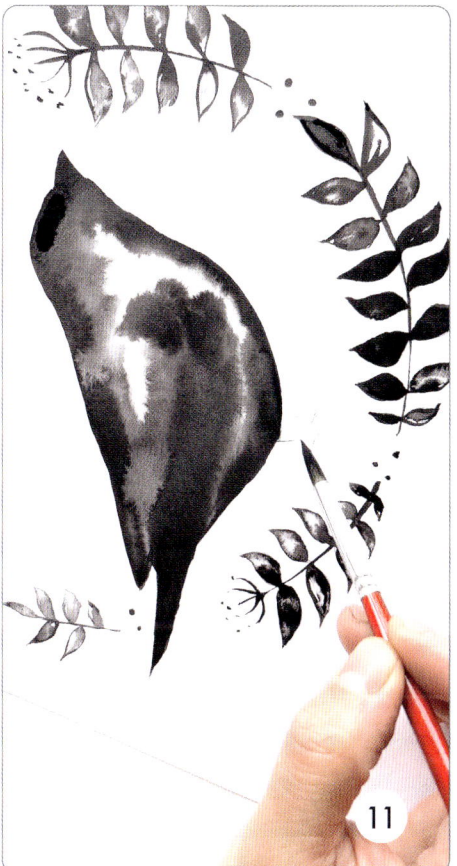

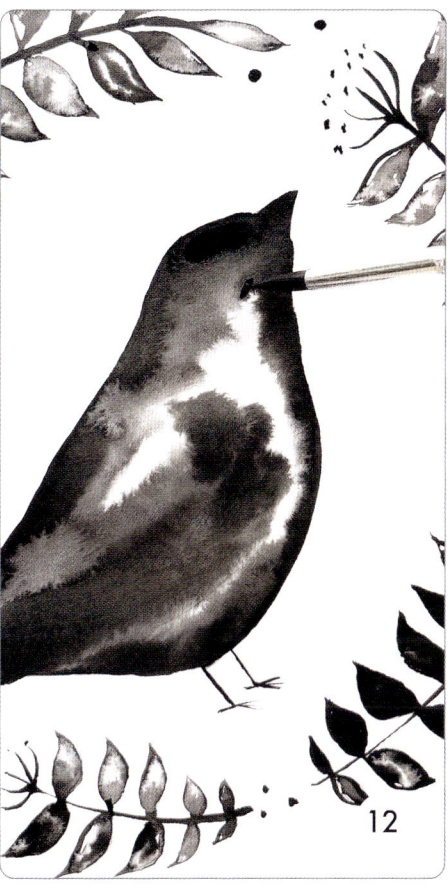

INSPIRATION & Gift Guide

If you are like me, you will suddenly find yourself with lots of ink artwork, so many that you can't store them all! Remember that your art isn't meant to be shoved in a box or live in a desk drawer. They are made to be enjoyed, either on your walls and around your house or as gifts! Here are a couple of ideas that might inspire you.

SMALL FRAMED WORKS

Framing up your works and putting them on display is a perfect way to showcase the works that you are most proud of, enjoy your progress, and decorate your home with beautiful, meaningful art! If you are working with standard size paper (A4 or A5 [8" × 11" or 5" × 9"]), it is relatively easy to buy affordable, ready-to-use frames. One of my favorite activities is to go to thrift shops and look for secondhand frames that can be upcycled to display my artwork.

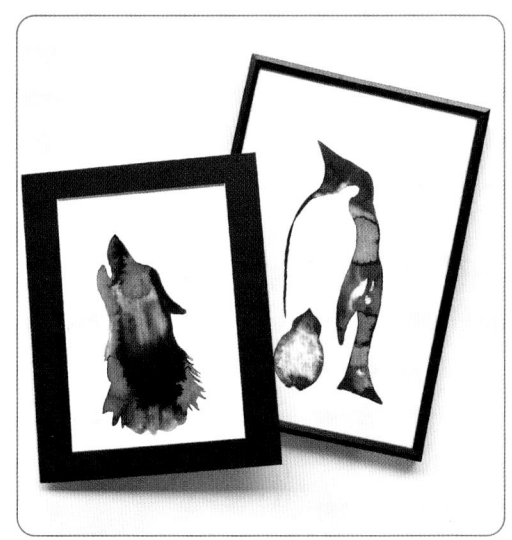

BOUND OR PASTED INTO A BOOK

If you want to have a little collection of your works, why not sew them into a book? You can easily bind pages of the same size together with a simple stitch, or alternatively paste them into a scrapbook or photo album.

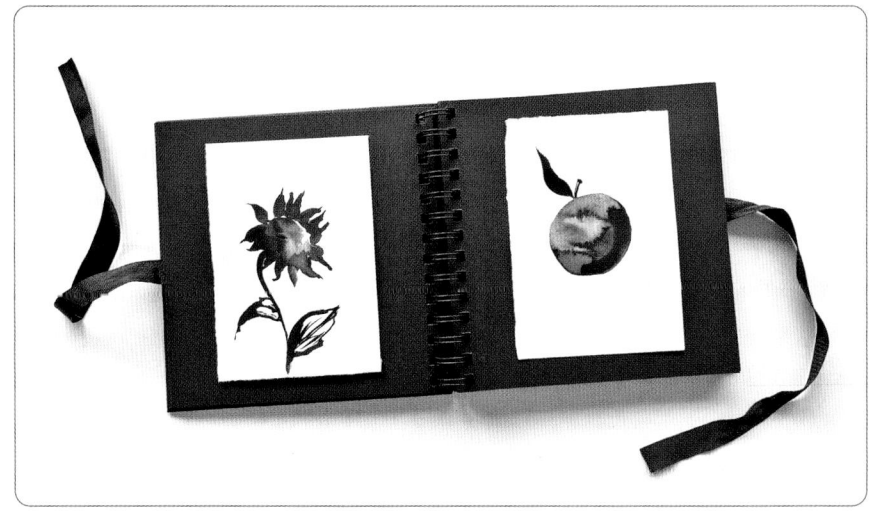

CARDS

If you prefer not to gift framed artworks, you can make beautiful, personal greeting cards. All you need is some folded heavy cardstock to stick your artwork on, and you're ready to go!

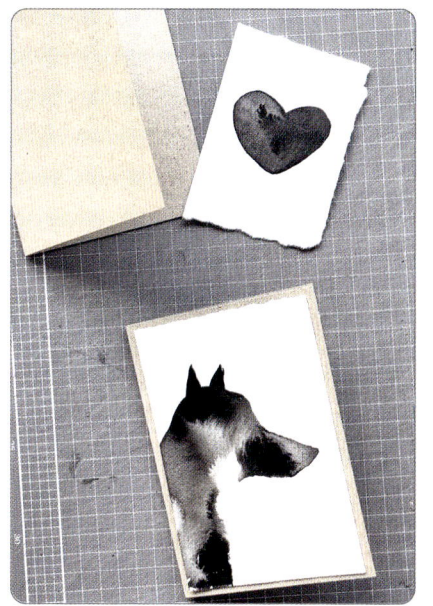
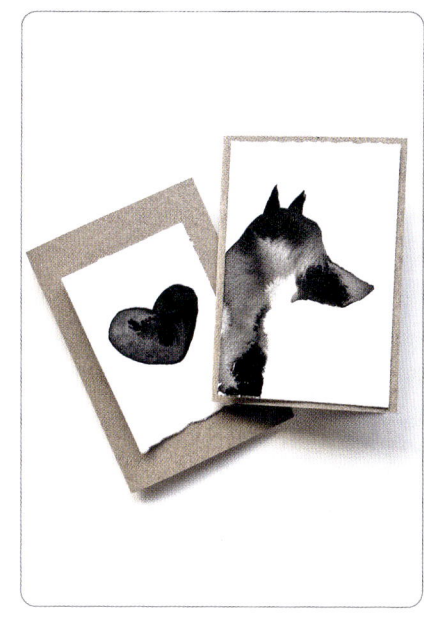

COLLAGED OR CUT UP

You won't be in love with every single inky work you paint, and this is totally normal! If you have works that you can't imagine putting on the wall or giving as a gift, tear or cut them up! This is a great practice in letting go. Cut out your favorite bits from them, and give them new life by creating collages, drawing over the top of them, or turning them into gift tags or labels for homemade presents.

Whatever you do with your inky meditations, I hope you enjoyed the process and that making these artworks brought you a sense of peace, grounding, and playful creativity.

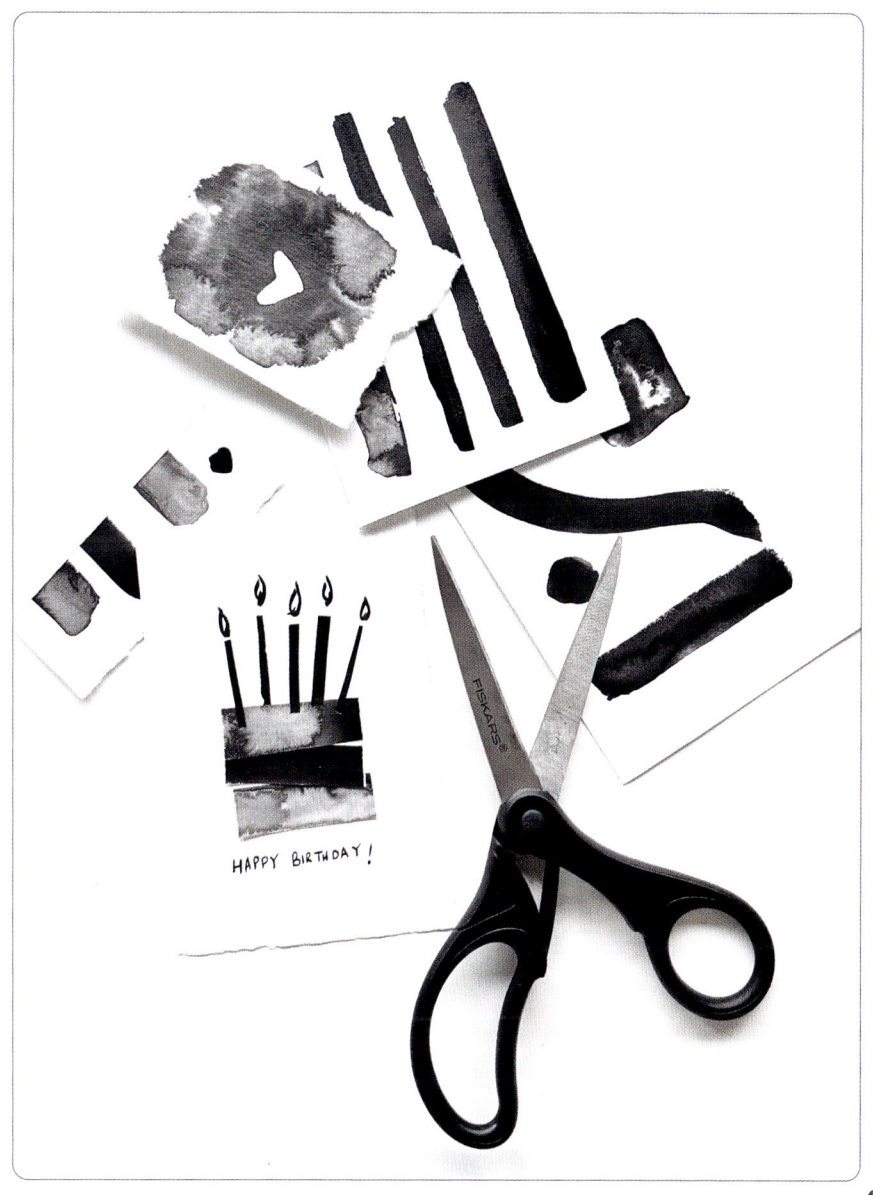

About the Artist

Inky shares hugely popular meditative painting videos with sumi ink and water on social media channels @inky_meditations. Begun in 2021 by an Australian experimental artist with a bachelor of fine arts in printmaking, Inky's work explores the spontaneous, organic, and imaginative movement of ink over water and the importance of uninhibited creativity. Inky Meditations offers a new video each week and now boasts hundreds of ink painting videos. See more at inkymeditations.com.

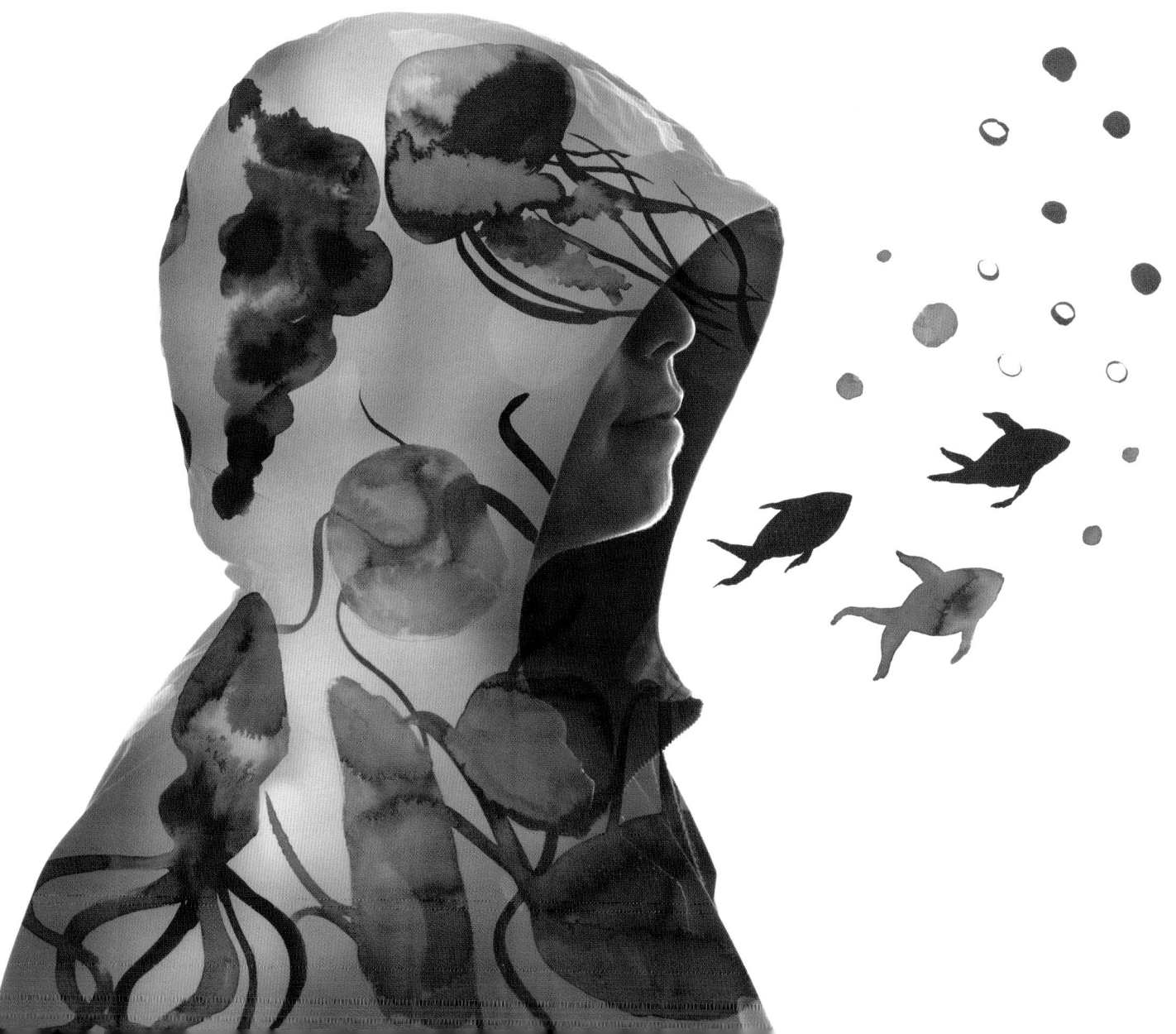